MW01486897

THE ROYAL INSIDER

THE ROYAL INSIDER

My Life with the Queen,
the King and Princess Diana

PAUL BURRELL

SPHERE

SPHERE

First published in Great Britain in 2025 by Sphere

1 3 5 7 9 10 8 6 4 2

A CIP catalogue record for this book
is available from the British Library.

Hardback ISBN 978-1-4087-3421-6
Trade paperback ISBN 978-1-4087-3420-9

Typeset in Caslon by M Rules
Printed and bound in Great Britain by Clays Ltd, Elcograf S.p.A.

Papers used by Sphere are from well-managed forests
and other responsible sources.

MIX
Paper | Supporting
responsible forestry
FSC
www.fsc.org
FSC® C104740

Sphere
An imprint of
Little, Brown Book Group
Carmelite House
50 Victoria Embankment
London EC4Y 0DZ

The authorised representative
in the EEA is
Hachette Ireland
8 Castlecourt Centre
Dublin 15, D15 XTP3, Ireland
(email: info@hbgi.ie)

An Hachette UK Company
www.hachette.co.uk

www.littlebrown.co.uk

I dedicate this book to the men in my life.

My sons, Alexander and Nicholas, who are my
greatest gifts in life. They are my touchstones to this world.

My grandson, Lucca, who is my greatest treasure.

My husband, Coop, who keeps me safe and was sent
by powers greater than we know to guide me through life.

Contents

PREFACE:
A Nation Mourns

Life is simply a string of memories and precious moments sewn into your individual tapestry. This is mine.

O n 8 September 2022, the world we knew changed for ever as the longest-serving British monarch in history, Queen Elizabeth II, died at the age of ninety-six.

I was granted one final meeting with my beloved queen in St George's Chapel at Windsor Castle and given the opportunity to thank her for all her service and for saving my life ...

September 2022

My dear friend Paul Whybrew, known affectionately as Tall Paul because of his imposing stature, said to me 'I think you need to come and pay your respects to the Queen.'

The funeral of Queen Elizabeth II had taken place at Westminster Abbey in London. Afterwards the coffin was taken to Windsor Castle for a committal service at St George's Chapel.

So I drove down with my husband, Graham Cooper, who I

call Coop, to Shaw Farm Gate on the Home Park at Windsor Castle, a place I knew very well. I didn't need to go via the front gates; instead I headed for the back entrance – the same one the Queen always used when arriving at or leaving Windsor Castle privately.

A policeman in armoured attire stood there, manning the barrier with a machine-gun.

Although I was heading back into familiar territory, I had not been there for years and I was nervous that I would be stopped from entering.

He signalled to me to wind down my window. He poked his head in and said, 'Hello, Mr Burrell. We have been expecting you. How are you?'

I replied, 'I'm very well, thank you, officer. It's strange being back here again.'

He nodded. 'I think you know your way, don't you?'

The barrier lifted and I drove into the Home Park, past Adelaide Cottage where the Waleses were in residence. I could see the lights on in the house, which indicated that Prince William, Catherine, Princess of Wales and the children, George, Charlotte and Louis, were home.

I called in to see Tall Paul, who lives opposite them in grace and favour accommodation. He had been the Queen's loyal right-hand man for more than forty years. The long-time Page of the Backstairs (the Queen's page) had a prominent role beside her coffin during the procession for her state funeral.

We headed to Town Gate and memories came flooding back to me. It felt like I'd travelled back to the 1980s. I was enveloped in a warm feeling. Happy days of walking the corgis around Adelaide Cottage. I thought, I could knock on the door and say hello to William.

I hadn't been there since I left the Queen's service in 1987. It was nice to show Coop that part of my life. And nothing had changed.

We walked up the hill to St George's Chapel. It was just before the public were allowed in.

The warden took me to the King George VI Memorial Chapel where the Queen was and she said, 'I'm going to leave you here for a while. Normally people just walk past this gate, look in and keep going, but you can stay for as long as you like. I'm sure you've got a lot to say.'

I stood there with Coop in the quietness of St George's Chapel. There is a slab on the floor that reads, 'George VI, Elizabeth, Elizabeth II, Philip'. It is hand-carved from black Belgian marble with brass inlays. And I thought, That's what she'd want. It was something so simple. No fuss. No ornament. No gilding. Just a plain piece of marble.

And then I looked across and on one side there was a slab for Princess Margaret, who was cremated when she died in 2002. Choosing to be cremated was a selfless act by Margaret so her big sister, the Queen, could be laid to rest beside Prince Philip inside the crypt. It had been made for four people: King George VI, the Queen Mother and their two daughters. But Margot sacrificed her place for Philip. So her little urn of ashes is nestled between the King and the Queen. The King always referred to his family as 'we four' – they now rest in peace, together, for ever.

Light was shining through the windows. It was a sunny day and it was quiet. I stood there holding Coop's hand. I could feel the tears running down my face as I said to the Queen, 'Thank you for everything you did for me. Thank you for saving me so many times. You saved me from myself. And you looked after me and protected me. When I was too young to protect myself, you did it. Your shadow was cast over me all my working life with you. And you showed me much about life. You educated me. I went to a great university – yours. You taught me about people. You taught me about countries. You taught me everything. Etiquette, manners. You taught me the English language. I remember feeding the dogs and you would say, "Oh, Paul, those dogs are so recalcitrant". Bewildered, I'd look up at you and say, "I don't know what that means Your Majesty". And you would reply, "Well, Paul, it's stubborn. They've got a will of their own." You would sometimes come and find me when I was walking the dogs. I always felt so proud to be walking beside you as we chatted away. On those occasions, you were all mine.

'For the eleven years I was in your service, you watched me grow from a young boy, barely eighteen, into a man as I became a husband and father. You counselled me when I was in trouble. I remember that horrible time when I was just nineteen and I didn't know the ways of the world. I didn't understand my sexuality but you knew me inside out. You knew me better than anyone. Thank you for the wedding present you sent me and my husband in 2017. Thank you for all the love and support you have given me throughout my life. Thank you for everything.'

Her love never left me until she died. And then I felt the cord cut. It was truly the end of an era. All I do now is to help to preserve her legacy and tell her story. I was reminded of a saying that someone dear to me once told me: 'Some people pass through our lives momentarily but others stay for a while and leave footprints on our hearts and we are never the same'.

This is what you should know. While much has been said of Her Majesty during her life and in her death, this account is from someone who was actually there. I walked the corridors of Buckingham Palace and saw history in the making. I had a front-row seat.

Before going to bed each night, the Queen kept a diary, written in pencil. Her entries started with the weather and noted down both the incredible and mundane events of each day and the people who came into her life. For many years I did the same. I kept a daily record of contemporaneous notes because I realised that I was living through a special part of our history and that detail would be important in the future.

I never thought that I would contemplate writing another book. *A Royal Duty* in 2003 was born out of me not having my day in court. Being able to answer my prosecution was denied to me when the Queen intervened and saved me from that indignity.

That was more than twenty years ago, and so much has happened since then.

I have already lived two lifetimes and I am onto my third and final one. Aged sixty-seven and in the autumn of my life, I would like the rest of my time to be happy and content with no serious worries but I can't guarantee that. Cancer came to visit me. It knows no boundaries. It doesn't discriminate.

In addition, false allegations against me were recently resurrected by Prince Harry in his battle with the newspapers, so I feel compelled to respond.

Many of the people whose stories I am about to share are no longer with us to give their version of events. I feel a responsibility as a loyal subject, in a time when the monarchy is going through great upheaval, to give my account of events.

There will be things in this book about which people will say, 'Well, Paul, you weren't there when this happened.' And that's true, but I have never lost contact with the world in which I once lived and worked.

This is the story of a young lad from a mining village who ended up rubbing shoulders with and being befriended by kings and queens, princes and princesses. This is the rich tapestry of my life.

1

Humble Beginnings –
From the Coal Mine to the Palace

The view from my childhood bedroom window in our two-up two-down terraced house at 47 Chapel Road in Grassmoor near Chesterfield was black and white. My earliest memories are of staring out from the back of the house where a huge sycamore tree cast its shadow and blocked the sunlight from shining into my room. I can still put myself back there, more than sixty years on, listening to the birds' tweets and thinking, I want to be free like them, while looking out at our mudslide of a garden where nothing grew and the path to the coal house. Sandwiched between it and the slag heap was a sliver of green grass where the pit ponies went for respite. That was the only colour.

From my window I would watch for my father, Graham, returning from the mines, dirty and black. He worked at the National Coal Board and drove a little shunting train. We lived in a coal mining community so it was all coal and darkness. The men would appear over the hill as an army of black-faced, hobnailed-booted miners, the sound of their boots scraping along the cobbled streets.

We could not escape from coal. It was everywhere. And all I wanted was colour. I wanted to escape.

But I couldn't – well, not yet. I lived in a Victorian world which might seem strange as I was born in 1958 but I am from a part of Britain that still lived in an era of days gone by with Dickensian streets and lamp posts with lanterns on the top. I remember the lamplighter coming round to light the mantles with his long pole.

And we were in poverty. We always knew how poor we were, but so was everyone else in the village.

The back-to-back houses were carbon copies of each other with red brick that had faded over time and grey-slated roofs with chimney-pots pumping out smoke from the roaring fires below. Inside there was wall-to-wall linoleum with no carpet, although we had rag rugs that my gran made for us using a pattern and a hook. I'd help her sometimes by sorting the colours into neat piles. The process would take hours but we had no money to buy rugs so it was our only option. I'd sometimes think of how the linoleum used to feel on my cold feet when I was walking along the plush red carpets at Buckingham Palace.

Our house was always cold. We didn't get washed in a warm bathroom but in a ribbed tin bath which was dragged in from the wash-house and filled with tepid water in front of the roaring coal fire. I'd be soaking while Mum would warm a towel in the heat from the fire. Sometimes if we were short of time, Mum would stand me in the white Belfast sink in the corner of the back room and scrub me with the freezing water from the tap. It was not a pleasant experience.

Our toilet was at the bottom of the backyard – a perilous journey, especially in the winter. As children, my brothers, Anthony and Graham, and I often relied at night on a potty under the bed. The toilet was an arachnophobe's hell as there would be spiders as big as my hand spinning their webs next to the cut-up squares of the *News of the World* which hung on a rusty nail on the wooden door to be used as toilet paper. There was no such thing as Andrex in the Burrell household!

*

My mother, Beryl, worked hard all her life. She was in the staff canteen at the pit and sometimes my grandad would take me for a walk through the hazardous pit yard to meet her. I can still remember the smell of sulphur and tar and walking past the aviary where they kept canaries in cages. Every miner took a canary down with him into the pit as the birds would collapse if there was carbon monoxide in the mine, warning the men of the danger.

There used to be much excitement when the gas or electric man came to the house as they would empty the padlocked meter. It would be full of shillings which he would organise into little piles until there was a mountain on the table. It looked like we had robbed a bank. He would put them into pound columns then tot up the bill. My mother would keep a watchful eye to oversee this process. Then he would say 'Beryl, your electric bill is eight shillings and six pence but in your meter, you have ten shillings, so you have got some back.' He would divide one of the piles and push some of it in her direction; it was like being at a casino and she had just won on roulette. She would scrape the coins off the table into the pocket of her wrap-around pinny and say, 'Don't tell your dad.' That was her little pocket money. That and the dividend or as my mum called it, 'the divvy'. A dividend was popular in the 1960s. You would join a local co-operative society and as members, you would receive a dividend every time you shopped there. This dividend was paid out several times a year. It was a little like a modern-day loyalty card. My mum used to cash in the divvy when we were going on holiday and it would usually be about five pounds and ten shillings. We thought we were so rich then, but really we were scraping an existence together.

When mum was pregnant with me, my parents had been convinced that they were having a girl. The name was chosen – Pamela Jane. My mother got a surprise when the news was broken to her by a midwife that I was in fact a boy when they welcomed me into the world on 6 June 1958 in the Queen Elizabeth ward at Scarsdale Maternity Hospital, Chesterfield.

But as the eldest child, I often assumed the role of 'mother' anyway. My mother had taken me as a young child to the cinema to see *The Sound of Music* and *Mary Poppins*. I was mesmerised by the films' make-believe worlds: it was pure escapism. By the age of eleven, I would be in charge of taking my brothers, who were seven and four at the time, to the cinema, either the Odeon or the Regal in Chesterfield. I would have the bus fare in one pocket and the money for the tickets and a treat in the other. My brother Graham still reminds me of how I was an extremely bossy 'parent', only allowing them an ice cream *or* a hot dog – never both.

The soundtrack of my childhood was not music but movies; the technicolour I saw there symbolised the exciting life for which I yearned.

We used to spend all day, from 10 a.m. to 10 p.m., watching the continuous feature – *Chitty Chitty Bang Bang* or *Captain Nemo and the Underwater City* for example. I would bundle my brothers into the gentlemen's toilets and keep them quiet while they cleared the cinema after the first presentation ended. Then when the second screening started, we would sneak back out and watch the film again. I was mesmerised. We loved it and getting back in to see the film again without being caught added a frisson of excitement. Our mother would never ask where we had been when we came home from our grand day out. The world was different back then; you would never get away with that today.

And at home I often escaped by watching the black and white television which sat on the sideboard. I'm not sure we ever had a licence for it. It was a miracle that we got a signal as our aerial was a frying pan which hung precariously on the wall with a wire coat hanger.

But it allowed me as a young boy to enter the world of the Woodentops, Bill and Ben or Andy Pandy, and later, the exciting lives of Valerie Singleton, Peter Purves and John Noakes on *Blue Peter*. The strains of the *Coronation Street* theme tune ran through my childhood and as a family we watched Ena Sharples and Minnie Caldwell sipping stout in the Rover's Return. It was a reflection of the world in which I lived. There was much excitement when the old black-and-white set was replaced with a colour one in 1973 so we could watch Princess Anne's wedding to Captain Mark Phillips in Westminster Abbey. I was mesmerised by the grandeur of the wedding. I was fifteen years old. The world was changing and so was I. Like Dorothy in *The Wizard of Oz*, I'd opened a door from my black and white world into a technicolour one.

Of course, you had to put money in the meter on the back of the television. Sometimes you would be enjoying your favourite show, the money would run out and the television would switch off. There would be a mad scramble down the back of the settee in the hope of finding shillings. Who could have imagined in years to come that I would live at Buckingham Palace and not have to worry about the television switching off unexpectedly or running out of electricity – or that Princess Anne would be on first name terms with me ...

I would often be sent out to the street to play and I would sit cross-legged underneath that gaslight on the corner of our street, Chapel Road, dipping my stick of peeled rhubarb into the corner of a paper bag of sugar. I was dreaming of what adventures I would have. My world was a small, inconsequential one. My friends – Stephen Kellett, Alan Rogers, Christopher Hardy and Michael Bennett – and I were black-faced, scabby-kneed boys. All destined to work in coal, the lifeblood of our generation. All we had to look forward to were those long summer holidays that seemed to last for ever and those glorious charabanc day trips organised by the Grassmoor Working Men's Club Committee to Skegness (Skeggy), Cleethorpes or Mablethorpe. That was our childhood and our futures felt laid out for us, just as they had been for our fathers and grandfathers before us.

My middle brother, Anthony, was a coal miner all his working life until Margaret Thatcher decimated the industry – and he retired with ill health.

Having seen my Grandad Kirk dying gasping for breath with his lungs filled with coal dust, I realised from a very young age that going down the mines wasn't the life for me.

But I wasn't sure what I could do. I wished I was more practical like my younger brother, Graham, who was always making a sixpence here and there.

'Our Paul is a dreamer,' my mum would say.

And she was right, but how could either of us ever have known that my dreams would come true one day?

Back then it was fantasy and in the corner of my bedroom, which I shared with Anthony and Graham, I was king of all that I surveyed. My brothers slept in bunk beds; I slept in a single bed squashed beside the chimney breast. The coal fire raged below in the living room and kept me warm. It was definitely a fire hazard, but it was so comfy in the winter. Graham would often leave the cold bottom bunk and crawl in with me. The faded 1950s flowery wallpaper, which was bought cheaply off the market and which I hated, was covered with images from *Photoplay* magazine which my cousin had given to me. I would lie in bed looking up at the pictures on my wall of Hollywood icons like Elizabeth Taylor, Rock Hudson, Montgomery Clift, Kirk Douglas and Bette Davis, as well as a picture of Queen Elizabeth on her coronation day. It is worth remembering that I was born only five years after the Queen's coronation and that spectacular event was still fresh in people's memories. Everyone was enamoured with this beautiful young couple, Elizabeth and

Philip. They were *our* Hollywood couple. The Burrell household was no exception. We were all royalists, and I didn't know anyone who wasn't. Like most homes in the country (including Sandringham House in Norfolk, as I would learn later), we gathered as a family around the television in our front room at 3 p.m. on Christmas Day to watch the Queen's speech; she was always part of our celebrations.

We were taught to say our prayers by kneeling beside our beds – I could see the potty under the bed and the face of Bette Davis as I recited the Lord's Prayer.

Years later, I learned that our Queen did just the same – making us all equal in God's eyes. Although I doubt she had the luxury of staring at the face of a Hollywood idol . . . and I know that she never had a potty under the bed!

But at that time I had no idea that my childhood wall was a map of what was to come. All I wanted was to live anywhere other than this coal mining village. I used to spend hours letting my imagination run away to Hollywood or other faraway places that I longed to visit. But this world felt incredibly out of reach.

I even hoped for some divine intervention. I wanted to go to the grammar school in Chesterfield but I didn't know if I was bright enough, and I was painfully shy.

I loved my mum – and she loved me; I was her first born. In her eyes, I was the achiever and she was so proud of me. She desperately wanted me to pass the eleven plus exam and elevate myself from the mines and the ordinary life she had lived. To get into the grammar school, we had to write a letter about what we wanted to be when we grew up. My teacher, Mr Thomas, who had a booming Welsh voice, chose certain people to stand up and talk about their dream career path. So he picked on me. Others wanted to follow their fathers down the mines or be policemen or truck drivers. But not me. I stood up and said: 'Mr Thomas, when I grow up, I want to be a priest.'

And the classroom fell about laughing. They thought it was the most hilarious thing. Nobody in that classroom would have said a priest. Nobody. Mr Thomas asked me, 'Why do you want to be a priest?' I said, 'Because I want to help people.'

I had witnessed my mother, who was the salt of the earth, give her last penny to someone who needed it. She used to make dinners for six even though we were only a family of five so she could give a dinner to an old age pensioner down the street who had nothing. My mother was a saint. She was the kindest, most generous woman on the planet. I wanted to follow in her footsteps in some way and I thought being a priest was a way in which I could do that. I could help people. And although I did not end up going into the church, I did dedicate my working life to helping people ... including the most famous family in the world.

But I didn't know where my future lay then. I didn't pass my eleven plus for a place at Chesterfield Boys Grammar School. Thankfully, Mr Thomas stepped in and told my parents that he thought I would be wasted at Deincourt Secondary School, where boys became men and then headed to the mines. He lobbied for me to gain a place at William Rhodes Secondary School for Boys in Chesterfield. It might not have been a grammar school but it was the next best thing. My parents were delighted.

However, it was an engineering school with lathes for metalwork and woodwork and laboratories filled with Bunsen burners and glass test tubes which could not have been further from what I was interested in. I realised I was different from the other boys and thought that I would have been better at a cookery school studying home economics. But when you are eleven you just want to fit in. And fit in I did.

I was to have a new school uniform, not second hand. My mother proudly took me on my first ever train journey from Chesterfield to Sheffield to buy it at C&A. I can still smell the sulphurous smoke of the steam engine and see the black specks of soot which came into the railway carriage when the window was open. I returned home with the smartest school uniform, a cap with the yellow and black school badge on it and a new leather satchel. I thought I was the bee's knees.

My mother proudly walked me to the school bus stop to wave me off on that first morning at William Rhodes in September 1969. I boarded the double-decker bus packed with children and I thought, I'm a big boy, I'll go upstairs. That was a mistake. As I got to the top of the bus I realised that all the rough boys go on the upper deck and sit at the back. So as I dared to walk towards them I got knocked to one side into another seat by a boy in the same school uniform. He clipped me around the ear and said, 'Take off the cap – you look like a twat.' He ruffled my hair and said, 'You're one of us now.' His name was Kim Walters. He was harder than me, bigger than me and he became my school friend. We are still in touch even now, despite living very different lives. He was good at sport and became a professional footballer for Blackburn Rovers. But for five years he looked after me while we were at William Rhodes; he was my knight in shining armour who came to my rescue so many times and always kept an eye out.

My mum always wanted so much more for me. It may not be surprising to you that my life has been shaped by strong, powerful women. After I left William Rhodes Secondary School aged sixteen with six O levels – English language, English literature, history, geography, art and woodwork – she took on two jobs so that I could attend High Peak College in Buxton to study hotel catering. It was expensive as I had to live in rented accommodation. I lodged with a married couple who let out a room in their house.

So as well as working at the mine canteen, she took a night job in Robinson's factory in Chesterfield making name tags. She worked on a machine which pressed out the name tags that you wear when you go to hospital. She did that for five days a week until 10 p.m.

every night. She thought it was worth it so that I could go to college.

To her, catering college was as good as a university. Only my cousin Michael had been to university in the family but my grades and subjects (with no science or maths) were nowhere near university standard. I wasn't bright but I studied hard. I might have been painfully shy and quiet but I watched and listened to everyone and everything around me and absorbed it all like a sponge. To this day, my husband calls me SpongeBob.

For two years I learned every aspect of hotel management, from catering to making beds. I was soon clued up on how to serve the finest food and make the neatest bed with hospital corners. I didn't think about it at the time, but this was setting me on a path; when you think of Buckingham Palace, it is run like a rather large hotel – just with some well-known guests and an even more famous owner.

One of my best friends at college was a girl called Rose. She was a farmer's daughter from my home county of Derbyshire and we got on like a house on fire. She is still a good friend all these years later. There was never a hint of anything romantic. One day she told me that Buckingham Palace was looking for girls to train in the housekeeping department. And she got the job. I sat there with my mouth open, thinking, Oh, my goodness, she's just got the best job in the world. And it inspired me to think, Well if she can do it, so can I.

So I said to the principal of the college who had put her forward for the job, 'Are they looking for boys too?' And he said, 'Not at the moment but we will let you know if they do.'

Then in the ridiculously hot summer of 1976, he came to me and said, 'They are looking for boys to train as footmen.'

Despite having no idea what a footman was, I told him, 'I'd love to go for an interview.'

I was so excited – particularly because, in those days, Buckingham Palace was not open to the general public unless you were invited.

My father drove me to London and, dressed in a dark suit, I entered the side door of the building in awe.

I was a seventeen-year-old northern lad with a northern accent, a little wet behind the ears, and I didn't have a clue what I was heading into. My mum had told me, 'Just be yourself and you'll be fine' – which in hindsight wasn't the greatest advice.

I stood in front of Michael Tims, the Master of the Household's assistant, and I sat down. This was my first mistake.

Mr Tims looked over the top of his glasses and across the huge desk that separated us and said, 'Do you always sit down before you're asked?'

I thought, Oh no. I've just lost the biggest opportunity in my life. That's it. I've failed this interview.

I kept going hoping for redemption but then at the end of our chat he said, 'Paul, do you respect your elders?'

And I said that of course I did.

'Then Paul, during this interview you were telling me all about your life and what you were doing at college, but not once did you refer to me as "sir".'

I didn't know. I had no idea. So I said, 'Thank you very much for giving me this opportunity' and left the room thinking, Oh, take it all in, Paul, because you'll never see this again. Say goodbye to those plush carpets and that view of the red-gravelled quadrangle.

Of course, two weeks later, as expected, a letter arrived informing me that I had been rejected 'on this occasion' but that my details would be kept on file.

I was so disappointed when I came home. I said to my mother, 'It's not going to happen. I'm sorry. I've let you down. I'll continue to apply for jobs in places like Cunard or P&O

and hotels like the Ritz or the Savoy. I'll do my best to make you proud, Mum, but I don't think I will do it at Buckingham Palace.'

So I wrote letters all summer to all of these companies, expressing my eagerness to work and offering my services. I finally got a job as an assistant manager in a three-star hotel called the Lincombe Hall Hotel on Meadfoot Road in Torquay. I was eighteen years old and this job would take me away from my home and my family for months. But I had my freedom and I could do whatever I wanted to do. I grew in the role, going from a quiet boy to a more outgoing member of hotel management. At the end of the summer, the hotel was closing down for the season, but senior management recognised that I had potential and transferred me to Lincombe Hall's sister hotel, the Wessex Hotel, on West Cliff Road in Bournemouth. It's still there to this day.

It was a totally different experience for me. My room was like a shoebox compared to that at Lincombe Hall which was light and airy. It had no telephone, no amenities, nothing. And I thought, Oh, my goodness, this is what my life's going to be from now on. It was a cold, miserable autumn.

Homesickness crept in. My parents were so worried about me that they wanted to take me home but I knew I had to stick it out. I didn't have a clear role. One day I would be working in the kitchen if the chef was off, then I was shunted into being a waiter. At one point I was even relegated to the basement as a storeman, counting tins of beans. I was unhappy and alone. It was the lowest point of my eighteen years on this planet, but then I was thrown a lifeline from a most unexpected place.

A call came through to the hotel unexpectedly one cold November morning; I will never forget it. It was a conversation that changed my life. I was sat in my underground storeroom among the lentils and split peas when it happened.

It was my mother. It was unusual as we only ever spoke on a Friday evening. She said, 'I had to come across to Eldred's Bakery to ring you [we didn't have a phone at home]. But I had to ring you immediately as you've had a letter from Buckingham Palace. I've opened it. I'm going to read it to you. It says that a vacancy has appeared as a footman in the Royal Household and would you like to accept it.'

It was too good to be true. Of course I was going to accept it. So I handed in my notice and left Bournemouth to start a new life.

But there was more to this story, which I didn't discover until many years later. I adored my mother. She never asked for anything and always gave to others. It was perhaps only when I left home and, more so, when I became a father myself that I understood the sacrifice she had made for me.

Everything she did was for us, her three boys. She was taken from us far too soon. She was just fifty-nine when she died. She had a hard life and worked two jobs as well as being a mother and a housewife in difficult circumstances and difficult times.

She died in 1996, the year before Princess Diana. She was on the trip of a lifetime with my dad. They were going to see Niagara Falls and Las Vegas. They had stayed with my then wife Maria and me in Kensington Palace before I took them to Heathrow to catch their British Airways flight.

I whispered in the ear of the check-in crew, 'Is there any possibility of an upgrade?' It was to be my mum's first and only business-class flight. She was over the moon. But after an exhausting day visiting Niagara Falls in Canada, she dropped dead on the street after suffering a massive heart attack. She couldn't be saved. A light in all our lives went out.

Of course, my dad, my brothers and I were all distraught. Princess Diana helped me through that bereavement. She counselled all of us and invested effort and time in helping to bring my mother's body home from Canada. We did it in a week thanks to the princess intervening and putting in a personal call to the High Commissioner.

I discovered after her death that I owed my mother more than I had ever realised. Standing beside her grave in Hasland cemetery as the coffin was being lowered into the grave, my little brother Graham turned to me and said, 'I've got something to tell you.'

I replied, 'Can it wait?'

He shook his head. 'No. Now is the time. Do you remember all those years ago when Mum rang you from the bakery and told you about the job at Buckingham Palace?'

I nodded. 'I'll never forget it. It changed my life. Look at me now. I'm working with the most famous woman in the world.'

I was a butler to Princess Diana by then.

He replied, 'Yes. And you owe it all to Mum. On that morning when that letter arrived, I remember the postman coming as two letters dropped onto the mat. Mum went to pick up the letters and stuffed them into her pinny. She later put them onto the breakfast table and saw that one had the royal crest on it. Thinking it was important or a tax bill, she took a knife, opened it and read it. She told me, "You'll never believe it. Paul's been offered a job as a footman in the Royal Household."'

Graham then said to Mum, 'Wow, that's incredible. But what's the other letter?'

She said, 'I don't really know' and she opened that one too. It was a letter from Cunard, the cruise line, offering me a job as a steward on board the *QE2*, the world's most famous ocean liner.

My brother said she studied both letters, thought carefully, then said, 'Graham, you must promise me as long as I live, never to tell Paul what I'm about to do. This is our pact.'

She took the letter from Cunard and threw it on the coal fire. They watched it go up in smoke. She took the letter from

Buckingham Palace and put it on the mantelpiece. She told him, 'The trouble with Paul is he's a dreamer. He'll chuff off on that boat and we'll never see him again. So if we give him the choice, he'll mess it up. He'll choose the *QE2* when I want him to choose ER2, which is very different.'

So she chose my path for me. She chose my destiny.

As my brother told me this beside my mother's grave, the tears were rolling down my cheeks. 'I've been dying to ask you all these years,' he said. 'What would you have chosen if you'd been given the choice?'

I replied without hesitation: 'I would have chosen a life at sea. She knew me well, didn't she? I wanted adventure. I wanted to travel. I wanted to see amazing countries and things that I'd only dreamed of.'

But she wanted me to go to Buckingham Palace. Mothers know best. You might not think it at the time. She was wise and she did it for the right reason. What my mother did for me was because she loved me and she wanted me to make the best I could of the life I had.

Years later, I met John Prescott, the deputy prime minister, and his wife, Pauline, when they came to my flower shop in Farndon, Cheshire. I was telling John about what my mother had done for me and he said, 'Well I started my life out as a steward aboard the *Queen Mary*. You should have chosen a life at sea and then you could have been deputy prime minister by now!'

But I got the best deal really.

So, unbeknown to me, my mother had made this decision for me. On 20 December 1976, my life changed for ever. I was only eighteen years old – young, naive, immature, inexperienced in life – when I walked into the tradesman's entrance of Buckingham Palace on Buckingham Palace Road and announced myself to the policeman on duty.

I had stood in front of that impressive building in the spring of 1970 when I was nearly twelve years old and my family had gone to London for the first time. My dad was visiting the International Car Show at Earl's Court and we were staying with a maiden aunt in Leyton. We travelled on the underground to Charing Cross and walked down the Mall towards Buckingham Palace with my dad belting out, 'Want to see where the Queen lives?' and 'Do you think she's in, lads?'

I was mesmerised by this huge building that stood before me. It was a world away from Grassmoor, coal and the colourless life I lived. My face pressed against the black railings, I watched the changing of the guard in awe. Then I looked at my mum and said, 'One day I want to work there.' It's the sort of comment that children make and is instantly dismissed. My dad replied, 'Sure you do, me duck.'

Just six years later I would arrive with a ridiculously large suitcase, filled with clothes and belongings from my home in Grassmoor – nothing of any value. My mother had bought me an alarm clock so that I would never be late and had splashed out on a pair of cufflinks from H. Samuel in Chesterfield, underwear from Marks & Spencer and a couple of towels from the market. Things she thought were essential for her son's new life at Buckingham Palace.

I will never forget excitedly running home from Grassmoor Junior School knowing that my mother would have bought a new quarter-pound packet of loose-leaf PG Tips tea as part of the weekly shop. In between the carton and the paper package would be a collectable picture card: trees, ships, movie stars or kings and queens of England. I had no idea that my complete collection of kings and queens would one day hang mounted in my bedroom at Buckingham Palace. I went from collecting the cards in packets of tea to living in a palace and working for a queen. The coal mines had been left behind and a new adventure was beginning. This was my fairy tale and I was determined to live it.

2

Death – End of an Era

The Queen died at approximately 3.10 p.m. on 8 September 2022 at Balmoral Castle, Scotland. She had been very poorly during her last days and was mainly bedridden. She was ninety-six and had refused any more treatment. She must have thought 'How much longer can you extend my life?' She knew that the end was imminent but she had no fear. She believed that she would soon meet God, her maker.

It wasn't long after Prince Philip had died that she was diagnosed with cancer, in the summer of 2021. It was devastating for the Queen to receive this diagnosis in the same year as her husband's death, but true to form, she carried on with grace and pragmatism. She swore everyone to secrecy. The family didn't know; only her immediate staff were informed of her diagnosis – her pages, her footmen and her dressers were included in the circle of trust and they did not tell a soul. As far as the family was concerned everything was fine, but the doctors' prognosis gave her only until Christmas.

The Queen's response to the diagnosis was, 'Well, that's a shame because next year is my Platinum Jubilee year and I'd quite like to have seen that. Can you keep me alive for that?'

They told her they couldn't make any promises, but they managed it.

Her Platinum Jubilee was a great success and she was pleased and moved by the affection afforded to her by her people. It was a celebration of her, her seventy-year reign and her selfless duty to the country and the Commonwealth.

On the way to Craigowan Lodge on the Balmoral estate in May 2022, Tall Paul broke his journey to Scotland by staying overnight with my husband and me at our home in Cheshire. At my request, he planted an English oak tree in our garden to commemorate the Queen's Platinum Jubilee. He told the Queen and she thought it was a 'wonderful idea'. It was planted on her behalf to celebrate her reaching the milestone on the throne. Of course knowing now that the Queen would die a few months later it feels even more poignant.

The Queen endured blood transfusions and scrupulously followed doctors' orders, giving up her much-loved gin and tonics, gin and Dubonnets and martinis, and instead having apple juice (and tomato juice on a Sunday as a treat) to assist in extending her life to the Jubilee. They kept her alive to witness this landmark in her reign, but she knew through it all that she was dying. Her family were told in the final few months. She intentionally kept them out of the loop as she didn't want to give them any worry. She never liked a fuss. She was also concerned that her illness might debilitate her and open the door to a regency.

This was abhorrent to her. She wanted to rule to the end and definitely did not want to be a sick queen with a regent ruling. She knew that there had been meetings with Prince Charles's household, which they called 'the bridge meetings', to discuss what would happen between her monarchy and the next but she stayed out of that. She never attended any of those meetings as they did not concern her.

As far as she was concerned, she had made a pact with God to serve her country for as long as there was breath in her body. She was never going to abdicate.

But sadly, she did deteriorate, and she had good and bad days. There were some days when she couldn't get out of bed. But right to the end, she always made an effort. She didn't cancel engagements unless it was absolutely necessary.

Even in her last days when she was quite unwell, she never neglected her duties. She carried them out conscientiously just as she had done for the previous seven decades.

Her last official duty as queen was conducted standing in the green-carpeted drawing room at Balmoral Castle that I knew so well. In front of a roaring log fire with her wheelchair nowhere in sight, just two days before her death, she bade farewell to former prime minister Boris Johnson and welcomed the new prime minister, Liz Truss, who was her fifteenth and final head of government. They were both ushered in and out very quickly and she returned to her bed to rest after the meetings.

Throughout her life she wrote her diary fastidiously every evening after prayers. The Queen would never fail to record her memories of the day in her small, hard-backed diary always beginning with the weather. Every day of her life, wherever she was, she wrote in pencil about whomever she met and what she did.

She also completed her government boxes every day at her desk or in bed. When they retrieved her final red box, embossed with her E II R cypher which was sacrosanct to the Queen, her private secretary found that she had been diligent to the end.

She completed every duty as that was her role and part of her pact with God. She once said to me, 'When I was anointed underneath the canopy at Westminster Abbey by the Archbishop of Canterbury with the holy oil, I felt the presence of God. He was with me.'

Throughout her life, she felt God's presence in everything she did. I don't think we will ever see the likes of her again.

In her final months, her beloved team of staff knew that the Queen was very ill. She had been using a wheelchair but was insistent that she must never be photographed in it. She remembered when her younger sister, Princess Margaret, who was recovering from a series of strokes, was seen in a wheelchair at the celebrations for the one hundred and first birthday of Queen Elizabeth the Queen Mother in August 2001. The Queen always regretted that her sister had been seen to be so weak and frail. Princess Margaret's dignity had been compromised by William Tallon, the Queen Mother's page, who had taken it upon himself to wheel her out for all to see. The Queen was furious and, behind closed doors, reprimanded him severely.

When she had the energy to get up, the Queen would get dressed and was often driven to the log cabin at Balmoral for a picnic lunch. The Queen was determined to carry on regardless. She had done this the day before she died.

Throughout her life, lunch was at 1 p.m., tea at 5 p.m. and dinner at 8.15 p.m. whenever possible. But towards the end, she did not attend all meals in the dining room. Instead she was having trays of food delivered to her room and she was eating very little.

The monarch was fading away in front of the nation's eyes. Her dresses weren't fitting properly and she was looking paler and thinner. I think we all knew it was inevitable; it was going to happen soon.

I think it was poignant for the Queen to pass at Balmoral as it was her favourite home – and she was Queen of Scotland too, after all. Charles had wanted to open it to the public for some time to assist with finances, but she had always said, 'No. Whilst I'm alive, this is the only home that I have that isn't open to the public and I want to keep it that way. This is the only private world I have left.' And that's the way she kept it until she died. Now, of course, King

Charles has opened it to the public, but thankfully you cannot see the room where the Queen passed.

When the Queen did die, most of the household at Balmoral had no idea. The prime minister, then Liz Truss, as well as the Queen's private secretary, Sir Edward Young, were informed immediately. Her closest staff knew and were sworn to secrecy.

The rest of the household and the estate workers were going about their business as normal. They didn't know. It was a closely guarded secret within the Royal Household because they did not want the news to leak out before it was announced officially.

Richard Sharp, the chairman of the BBC, and other media heads had been 'put on notice' and told in confidence by the prime minister. That is why presenters suddenly started appearing in black on the news despite nothing being said formally. They wanted to gather the family together before any official announcement was made.

Getting any large family together is not easy but when it comes to the Royal Family it is even harder. Princess Anne was staying nearby and so was the first of the Queen's children to be there. Prince Charles was at Birkhall on the Balmoral estate, so he just had to cross the valley to be with his mother.

But the rest of the family were elsewhere so they had to arrange a flight from London to Scotland. Of course, there has been much discussion about this flight as it was the aeroplane that famously took off without Prince Harry.

Prince William, Prince Edward and his wife, Sophie, and Prince Andrew were seen arriving together on a private plane. Harry has since claimed that he was not included in their travel plans despite the fact that there was room for him on the plane. So he did not get there until later, by which time unfortunately the Queen had passed. Despite the initial plan to wait until everyone was there before the public were informed, they announced her death without him at Balmoral.

An issue arose over Harry's wife of four years, Meghan Markle, the Duchess of Sussex attending Balmoral. This was a sacred family moment where they wanted to be one and grieve as one and they did not see Meghan as one of them. She was not welcome.

Over the previous two years since January 2020, when Harry and Meghan initiated 'Megxit' and stepped away as working Royals, they had blasted the family on many occasions, most notably with their allegations of racism and lack of support from the family around Meghan's mental health struggles during their controversial interview with Oprah Winfrey in March 2021.

It led to the Queen releasing an unprecedented statement: 'The issues raised, particularly that of race, are concerning. While some recollections may vary, they are taken very seriously and will be addressed by the family privately.'

They also upset the Queen by claiming they had been granted permission to use Lilibet, her father's family name for her, when naming their daughter in June 2021.

So when the plane was being organised they were afraid Prince Harry would want to bring Meghan with him. They did not consider her to be part of their family or want her to witness their private grief. Even William's wife, Catherine, stayed in Windsor and was spotted picking up her children from school later that day – thereby sending a message that this was a moment for blood family only.

The family all arrived and went in one by one to see the Queen in her room in bed.

Of course, as well as being head of state, the Queen was also the matriarch of the Windsor family. Her death hit them all hard but none more so than her eldest son, Prince Charles. He sat in prayer for a few minutes with his mother and his wife, Camilla, and left a changed person. He arrived at Balmoral a prince and departed a king.

It is strange that Charles had been expecting his mother's death and what would follow but now it had actually happened, he was left shaken and in tears. He finally realised the enormity and responsibility of what he was about to take on as king.

Deep down he loved his mother, but it was more acute for him. He was the son and heir and had to step into the shoes of Queen Elizabeth, who had been a constant for the public for most of their lives.

There is a bittersweet price to pay for being monarch; you have to lose your parent to succeed to that position and wear the crown.

The Queen told me long ago, 'Paul, for as long as there's breath in my body, I shall serve my country as Queen.'

So Charles had had to wait for her death to come. He must have known that she would never abdicate and move to one side. I think for a short time he may have wished that he could have been regent, but the Queen was never going to let go of the crown. No. Never. She was determined to reign as queen for her entire life.

Once the family (well all except Harry) had all paid their respects to the Queen in her bedroom, the staff were told by the Master of the Household that the Queen had passed.

With the family arriving at Balmoral and the turmoil it would cause, the staff must have realised that something was afoot. The housekeeper would have been notified because people would have needed bedrooms. So they all knew that something was happening but they did not know what exactly it was until that evening when the announcement was made. They were told just before the public announcement and then the house went into mourning and complete lockdown. While the Queen was lying upstairs, staff went about their business as usual and meals were still served. Charles was now king and he sat in the Queen's chair in the dining room, the seat she had sat in his whole life, with his back to the window. In that moment he assumed the role of king in private before he became king in public. This was a momentous change within the Royal Family but also in our country. Balmoral Castle was at the heart of the tectonic shifting of plates. And the King assumed his duties there and then. All the staff showed their respect by calling him 'Your Majesty' rather than 'Your Royal Highness'. It was automatic. No one told them there had been a passing of power; they all knew what to do. They went into mourning and everyone wore black. So there was a very dour atmosphere within Balmoral Castle, but it was sombre and fitting.

The household took the role of mourning their beloved Queen very seriously. They did not appreciate the interruption of Prince Harry, whom many thought was petulant. His mother, Diana, had always reminded him of his responsibility and duty, the price he had to pay for such a privileged life. She had sacrificed her precious time with her boys in order that they could be part of the Royal Family. He came through the doors of Balmoral as though he was expecting to be embraced and welcomed back into the fold. And he was sadly disappointed. He arrived late that night and was met by a total glacial front from his family. Balmoral was an iceberg. He was no longer a working Royal and he was not trusted by the family.

Cold and calculating this might appear, but this is the way the Windsors work. They freeze people out – even their own – to preserve the continuity of the family. They will turn against you if you do not follow the party line and do not accept the rules and regulations of the system.

Prince Harry knew those rules well. He had been taught them. He was born into the institution. He knew the routine when something like this happened because he had lived through it before.

He spent his summers at Balmoral. This was the place where Harry heard the news that his mother had died in 1997.

Walking into Balmoral, Harry must have remembered that fateful day and now he was back in the castle surrounded by death again. It must have brought back all those memories and all that pain. So Balmoral means a lot to William and Harry. Among other things, it is a place of death for them.

That night in September, Harry joined his family for a sombre dinner and must have realised that the power of the throne had shifted. The atmosphere was arctic. He went to bed early and got up the next morning before anybody else was awake. But when he went down to breakfast, nothing was ready. Mealtimes are run to a strict timetable and Harry wanted breakfast too early; it just wasn't ready. So he left with his tail between his legs in the early hours of the morning. He didn't speak to a soul and went back south. Harry had every right to be there but the circumstances should have been so different.

Sadly I believe that if the Queen had died before Harry had met Meghan it would have been different. He would have still been in the inner circle and enveloped into the family. But Harry had changed and had moved on to a different world. The family remains in their own particular orbit whereas Harry was now in the orbit of celebrity, which the Royals don't understand and do not particularly like.

But regardless of what I think of Prince Harry, you cannot help but feel sorry for him. He had come to pay his respects to his grandmother who adored him and whom he loved. His grandmother had desperately wanted him to be happy and to stay within the Royal Family but now she was no longer there to protect him and guide him. All those thoughts must have crossed his mind. He was lost at sea without the support of his wife.

It was much the same for me when Princess Diana died and she was no longer there to protect me. Once that protection has gone, it won't come back.

You might think that Harry could have turned to his father. But no: Charles was hurt by his younger son's behaviour and he was preoccupied with grieving the loss of his mother and assuming the responsibility of becoming king.

And then you think, Well what about William? The brothers were always close? No. Harry had upset that apple cart a long time ago. Plus, like his father, William was contemplating his future too. He was now heir to the throne. They were all too busy to think about Harry's pain. There was no one there for him. No one to embrace him or understand how he was feeling. It must have been a strange and difficult time for him.

The fact is that the moment the Queen took her last breath, there was a seismic shift within the family as the principals moved up a rung on the ladder. William more than most would have felt that. But everyone had to own the responsibility that came with the shift.

Charles, now king, would no longer be the Duke of Cornwall and no longer receive income from the Duchy of Cornwall. In place of this, he would now receive income from the Duchy of Lancaster, the monarch being Duke of Lancaster. He would also inherit his mother's personal wealth and the private collections of jewellery and property, including the substantial estates of Balmoral and Sandringham, acquired by the family over the centuries.

William had inherited his father's titles as Prince of Wales and Duke of Cornwall, bringing with it the income from the Duchy of Cornwall.

But where was Harry? He may have received a bequest from the Queen, and he had recently received an inheritance from his great-grandmother, Queen Elizabeth the Queen Mother, but he does not have the significant wealth of his father or brother.

And so suddenly, Harry is not only separated by blood, he is separated by wealth and title. He's falling down the ladder as others are climbing up it and you have to feel for him in that respect, particularly as both boys were equal in Diana's eyes. But he ignited this firework. Perhaps he didn't consider what he might miss out on in the long term. I think he's still reeling from what he's lost. And he's lost so much.

*

It might be a morbid thought, but royal bodies are always em-balmed. The Royals who do not have a chapel dedicated to them in St George's Chapel or Westminster Abbey are entombed in cat-acomb-like settings in the crypt of St George's Chapel. The coffins are transported on a 'lift' device which sinks from the floor of the nave to the underground labyrinth below. An ancient machine of cogs and wheels springs into action at the allocated time and as if by magic, the coffin disappears from view, having been denuded of its decorations and ornaments from the world above.

So according to tradition, the Queen was embalmed, mum-mified for eternity. It is always done at the place of death and everything is kept very secret.

It would have been a difficult procedure to administer in the Queen's bedroom at Balmoral, the room in which Queen Victoria had slept. After being embalmed, she would have been placed in a lead-lined English-oak coffin which was carried down the wide staircase from the first floor, overlooked by the marble statue of Prince Albert.

The coffin was then driven in a hearse from the front door of Balmoral Castle to the Pend Yard at the back of the castle where there is a back door into the ballroom. The wooden Victorian staircase from the house to the ballroom is very narrow and non-negotiable. The Queen was laid to rest in the ballroom where the household and estate workers could pay their respects to their employer.

On 11 September, the Queen left her beloved Balmoral for the final time and travelled to Edinburgh as Queen of Scotland in a hearse, her coffin draped in the Scottish version of the Royal Standard with a wreath of white flowers placed on top. Accompanied by her daughter, Princess Anne, she made a three-day journey back to London and her final resting place.

3

It's a Jungle Out There

But where was I when all this furore was going on in Scotland? Well, while my former colleagues were in mourning at Balmoral, I was in the Kruger National Park in South Africa about to go into the jungle to compete in *I'm a Celebrity . . . Get Me Out of Here! South Africa*. I had first appeared on the British version of the show filmed in Australia in 2004 but it felt like such a long time ago. Now in 2022, I was a different person. I had changed so much: I had divorced, I had come out, I had remarried and, encouraged by my husband, Coop, I wanted to let people see the real me. What better show to do so on than arguably the biggest one on British television?

This time around, I thought, I can actually be myself. I won't have to feel like I'm looking over my shoulder the whole time.

But I had had some distressing news when I had undergone a medical examination for the programme in the summer. Out of that came a surprisingly high result from a PSA (prostate-specific antigen) test (a test for the level of a chemical released by the prostate gland). I had no idea what a PSA test was. I was worried but my GP had told me to carry on with the show and that we would investigate the issue when I got home.

I was sitting in my isolation tent waiting to go into the jungle camp when I had a call from Tall Paul, who had, like me, joined

Royal service in 1976. We were the Queen's two Pauls. The Queen had encouraged our friendship to grow and to reconnect after the Diana years.

I thought it was strange for him to be calling me on my mobile phone, particularly as he had no idea where I was. As I answered, he said, 'London Bridge has fallen,' which was the code for the Queen's death.

My heart sank. 'Oh no, no,' I said. 'Are you OK?'

He was rushing to get a train to be with the Queen in Balmoral as he had been on leave.

He added, 'I just wanted to share this with you because I know how much you care for the Queen.'

Paul had last seen the Queen before his break and had taken care of her at Craigowan Lodge, less than half a mile from Balmoral Castle, before she had taken up official residence with her family at the castle.

The Queen had taken great pleasure in that house, which was small, comfortable and modern, having had a lift installed in recent years for Her Majesty's convenience. With only seven bedrooms, it was far more intimate than the fifty-two-bedroomed Balmoral Castle. The castle had barely changed since Queen Victoria had lived there over a century ago. It still has flocked wallpaper embossed with Victoria's initials, endless tartan-carpeted corridors lined with mounted deer heads, trophies from stalking parties past, and rooms filled with antiques and gold-framed paintings from Victoria and Albert's world.

As Paul placed her in her car on that final morning of his duty, he had no idea that that would be the last time he saw her alive.

So, duty bound, he was heading to Balmoral while I was heading into the jungle. I sat there on my bunk in my tent in the safari holding camp absorbing the news. And in that moment a giraffe walked past my window and looked in. It was so surreal.

I phoned Coop to tell him the sad news. He said, 'I know how much this is going to affect you. Are you sure you want to go into the show?'

I said, 'Yes, I'm prepared for it. I think this is right.'

The PSA test was weighing on my mind. The result was through the ceiling. The Queen's death had overshadowed my fear that I might be dying too, but I honestly thought that I might be.

I contacted Micky Van Praag, the show's executive producer. She was already aware of the news and told me that if I wanted to go home I could.

I thought about it. What good would it do if I left?

I would become part of the media circus. I found comfort in the idea of just going into the jungle with fourteen celebrities, sitting around a campfire and being able to grieve more privately. That probably doesn't make sense, as I would be surrounded by cameras, but the idea of being able to contemplate my thoughts of not just the Queen but also of my own mortality seemed like the right choice.

As well as that, I thought I could share my experiences and my journey with my campmates; she was their Queen too.

The production team allowed me to keep my mobile phone until the day we went into the jungle so that I could stay in contact with Coop and my family.

So I was given three weeks of isolation in the jungle, competing in silly games and, in my quiet times, lying on my bunk in the heat, thinking about my life and how the Queen had changed it.

But I was also worrying about whether I would be joining her soon on the other side. That probably sounds dramatic, but that was how I felt.

I believe in an afterlife, as did the Queen, and I take solace in the idea of passing on to somewhere where I would see familiar faces. It was a comfort to me to think that wherever she went next, Diana would be there to greet her. I believe that we see our loved ones in whatever form, whatever spirit, after death.

I lay on my bunk underneath the canopy of the national park watching the celebrities, joining in their conversations and thinking that in that environment, we were all equal and had our own particular troubles. I watched Carol Vorderman exercising every morning on her mat, the actress Helen Flanagan dancing around the campfire in a bejewelled bikini (my very own Princess Jasmine), the former world champion boxer Amir Khan throwing logs on the fire and the loveliest man, Andy Whyment from *Coronation Street*, being constantly interrupted by the loud drawl of Janice Dickinson, the American supermodel. In addition to all of this, what my campmates didn't know was that halfway through my jungle experience, I contracted a serious foot infection which had to be dressed every day by the doctor on site. It wasn't unusual for any contestant to be called by the bush telegraph to go to the trials gate for a battery change for our lanyard microphones or to take prescription medicines. My calls were to see the doctor and to be given clean, dry socks and dry boots. Everything seemed so surreal at that time.

As the nation back home in Britain stood in silence for two minutes during Her Majesty's funeral service at Westminster Abbey, we campmates held hands and made a circle around the fire. As we stood in silence, a gentle breeze caught the canopy above us and it rippled. A sign maybe?

There was something quite poetic about sitting around a fire contemplating the Queen's mortality alongside my own. It was the circle of life and I was quite literally in the middle of the jungle, in my own recreation of *The Lion King*. It gave me a lot of time to think about it and to reflect on my memories of the Queen, who was such a kind and generous woman. She was so different away from the public eye.

I thought back to arriving at Buckingham Palace at eighteen.

I was invited into this incredible world that most people only get to peep into as her subjects.

Within a year I was elevated to the position of her personal footman, and was in her presence every day. That was when I was lucky enough to witness first-hand how special and incredible she was: unlike anybody I'd ever met in my life before. And despite her being our Queen, she embraced me, this ordinary lad from a working-class coal-mining community.

And it occurred to me, sitting in that jungle clearing, that the Queen had been a maternal figure to me for much of my life. I was a boy when I met her and I had spent as much time with her as I had with my own mother. She taught me much about life. It probably sounds ridiculous because she was the monarch, remote and so untouchable, but it was this feeling that I have always had that she really cared. So the tears I shed in the jungle were for her. I cried a lot because I really loved her. I realised what a journey I had gone on with her. I stood beside her for eleven years and I never wanted to leave her. When I moved to work with Prince Charles and Princess Diana in 1987, I sobbed because I wanted to stay by her side. I didn't want to leave her behind. I said to her when I told her I was going, 'Who's going to look after you now?' And she said, 'Oh, don't worry, Paul, there's always somebody.' So she was very stoic and I was a mess.

It was very hard to think about her no longer being here and what a gaping hole she had left. I felt an enormous grief at her death, but I knew it was being felt by millions around the world. That isolated jungle became a place of solitude for me to contemplate my life.

Looking at the light coming through the trees and the monkeys swinging from branch to branch, life seemed to make sense. Death was inevitable and would happen to us all. I was isolated from the public outpouring of grief but in a way protected as I had time to process those feelings for myself. Surrounded by my jungle family of celebrities. Although we were all from different walks of life and known publicly for different reasons, they understood the public life that we lead now and that there was still a private aspect to our lives too.

And I shared a lot of it with some of my campmates. Carol Vorderman particularly understood how I was feeling. We are of a similar age and we really connected. She took me to one side, where there were no cameras, held me to her bosom and said, 'Let it out, Paul. Just let it out.' I had a good cathartic cry. I wasn't doing it for dramatic effect or to make good television. It was just how I was feeling at the time.

I finished fifth in the competition, leaving the jungle the same day as my pal Carol. The show wasn't aired until April the following year so none of our discussions about the Queen were ever broadcast; it would have made the programme seem dated. It felt appropriate that we got to mourn her together privately.

As I was in South Africa, I didn't get to tune in like millions of others on that bank holiday Monday to watch the funeral. By the time I got back, the funeral was over. I had to catch up by watching it on television privately and reading all the newspapers, which Coop had kept for me. It was strange to see all those faces I knew so well following the coffin. It was like looking through a window into a part of my life that I had left behind. Yet here it was, displayed publicly for everyone to see.

I thought it was very dignified. It was the right measure of decorum and sadness.

As I watched I remembered the Queen calling for her private secretary one day and I told her, 'He's out somewhere, Your Majesty.'

'Out where?'

'Do you really want to know? He's at your funeral.'

She replied, 'Oh, yes, of course. It all has to be rehearsed.

Everyone has to know where to stand and what to do. The only one who isn't there is me, but I will be there one day.' Tall Paul and I never took part in any of the rehearsals as we were always on duty.

She had also told me about the former prime minister Winston Churchill's funeral in 1965. She said, 'I will never forget the silence inside St Paul's Cathedral as the coffin was carried down the nave. I could hear the click, click, click of the soldiers' boots on the marble floor. I always remember as we stood at the great west door that they were struggling with the coffin. I was thinking, Oh my goodness, don't slip on those marble floors. I was willing them to get to the top and not to fall because, Paul, that coffin weighed half a tonne. I pity the poor guardsmen who have to carry me.'

'The exterior English-oak coffin disguises an interior coffin which is lined with lead and almost vacuum sealed,' she continued. I kept thinking, I don't want to know this, Your Majesty, but she went into all the details: 'We're all embalmed so we will look the same in one hundred years' time. It's the way of life and you have to talk about it because it's the most inevitable part – your own mortality. One day you will die.'

Even then when I was only nineteen, she was teaching me about life and my own mortality. While I was watching her being carried through Westminster Abbey, I couldn't help but think about the clicking of the boots.

When Prince Philip died in April 2021, the Queen did not want him to go to St George's Chapel to lie in rest. Instead she said, 'I'd like him to stay near to me.' His coffin was placed in the private chapel inside Windsor Castle at the end of the green corridor. It was a spot that was special to the prince as he had redesigned it himself after the fire in 1992. She visited him every day while he was there. She made those little journeys herself down the corridor and into the chapel.

On the day of Philip's funeral the Queen sat in her car at the sovereign's entrance at Windsor Castle. She was trying to look over at the state entrance from where he would be leaving. But she couldn't see. She asked the chauffeur, 'Can you move the car forward a little so I know when Philip is leaving?' But he replied, 'I'm sorry, Your Majesty, I can't because the moment I move the car, everyone else will start moving.'

It struck me as odd that even the Queen cannot always have her wish. So she had to miss watching her husband leave. It was the only time in her life that she followed Prince Philip; throughout their lives, he had followed her, his Queen, two steps behind.

Although she was sitting all alone at the funeral at St George's Chapel, metaphorically speaking, Philip was sitting with her; inside her handbag, she was carrying a photograph of him and one of his handkerchiefs.

As the elevator took the coffin down into the abyss, she must have been considering her own mortality. Prince Philip's coffin stayed on the shelf in the crypt waiting for his wife, his Queen. So she knew she was saying 'goodbye for now' to Prince Philip, as he was waiting for her literally downstairs. They didn't put him in the tomb until they were both together, as lifting the slab of the tomb was not practical until the Queen died. And now they are reunited side by side.

As I had been away I was unable to join the queue to see Her Majesty lying in state at Westminster Hall, so I was grateful to be able to pay my respects at St George's Chapel. Had I been in the country, I would have stood in line with everyone else on the Embankment, queuing to get in.

As I paid my respects to the Queen, I couldn't help thinking about the last day I worked for her, in 1987. My then wife, Maria, and I had decided to move to Highgrove to work for Prince Charles and Princess Diana. Maria was miserable in her Royal mews flat having to drag a pushchair up and down the stairs for our two-year-old son, Alexander, while pregnant with our second son, Nicholas. I did not want to leave the Queen's side as it felt like a backward career move. But my wife and child deserved to be happy. The only thing for which I would give up the best job in the world was my family. So it was decided we would move to the country for a better home life. The Queen had understood and said, 'Paul, look at it this way. You are not actually leaving me. You are simply moving to one side for now. Charles and Diana need people like you. One day, when I'm gone and they are king and queen, you will be back here again. You are leaving me for the best possible reason, for your family, I understand that.'

Usually, the Queen would speak to me when she came to have her breakfast. I would stand to attention and bow and she would say to me, 'Good morning and how are you today?' But on my last morning in her service, she didn't. She avoided me. And I thought, There's no reason not to speak to me. Why have you done that? So she went through to her dining room and had breakfast and then she pressed her bell for the private secretary to come up. She avoided me all morning. Everything I did for her was for the last time, my last breakfast service, my last walk with the corgis, my last walk down the Queen's corridor at Buckingham Palace.

She was leaving that afternoon to go to Portsmouth, where she would board the Royal Yacht *Britannia* to embark on the Western Isles cruise.

I packed her bags. She had a little blue leather bag, which we called the sweet bag that always travelled with her. Inside were Elizabeth Shaw peppermint creams and Bendicks Bittermints as well as her Charbonnel et Walker Easter egg which travelled the entire world with her wherever she went. She nibbled at it throughout the year until it was gone. Tiny little corners. Sometimes I'd pop in some leftover fudge from her last trip to

Balmoral. Then I would pack her magazines in another bag: *Horse & Hound*, *Country Life*, *Tatler*, *Vogue*, *The Lady*. She finished with her private secretary and rang her bell for the dogs to be taken out for a walk in the garden.

So I took the nine corgis out to the garden. I thought, This is odd, I've not even said goodbye yet – I've not had a word with her. I brought the dogs back. I would normally put them in the car with the Queen. Each dog had its own place to sit. Chipper and Piper sat in the back window like nodding dogs. Smoky had to be placed away from Shadow because they did not like each other. The rest sat on the back seat with the Queen but on this occasion, the dogs were going to stay with the gamekeeper's wife, Mrs Fenwick, at Windsor.

I took the bags down to the car with a rug and stood there at the garden entrance at the side of Buckingham Palace. The Queen descended in the elevator from her first-floor apartment and was met by members of her household waiting to bid her farewell. She said her goodbyes to the Master of the Household, her private secretary, her press secretary and the housekeeper then walked towards the car. I thought that she would glance at me and say something as I opened the car door. She didn't even look at me.

I thought, I don't understand this. She got into the car. Now I couldn't be any closer to her than when I took the rug and placed it over her knees. I was literally almost nose to nose with her and she still didn't look at me. I closed the car door and stood there, staring at her, but she was looking straight ahead. The car started to move. I bowed. I could see my reflection in the glass. She didn't wave. She didn't smile. She didn't say, 'Have a nice holiday. I hope you're OK.' Nothing. The car left.

I stood there deflated. And I said to someone, 'She never said goodbye. She never said anything. I've been with her for eleven years and she never said a word. Not a word.'

I went upstairs and I said the same thing to the Queen's page. I wandered around her apartment putting dust sheets on furniture, tidying up her desk and taking the silver, including framed photographs of her mother and father, paper knives and four miniature models of her corgis, down to the silver pantry. I just couldn't work it out. It bothered me all day. So the next morning I rang the Queen's lady-in-waiting and said, 'All the years I've been with the Queen she's been so nice and kind. But yesterday not a word. So completely out of character. Do you know why the Queen didn't say goodbye to me?'

And she said, 'Paul, don't you understand? She was really upset to know that you wouldn't be there next time. She couldn't cry so she looked straight ahead.'

That is the Queen in a nutshell. Everyone looks up to her. She is the symbol of authority and the head of state and as such, should not display weakness or emotion.

I couldn't help but think of that day as I watched more than a million people line the streets of London for her funeral procession to say their goodbyes. I knew how much work and planning had gone into it; this event had been years in the making and was practised regularly so that no one would put a foot wrong.

Operation London Bridge was the code name for the death of Her Majesty. Everything was in place and the stage was set. The succession of Charles III had already begun.

The King's ceremonial succession was known as Operation Springtide and his coronation plans were known as Operation Golden Orb. The Royals always have a plan, and for generations, each plan has been given a different code name.

'London Bridge is falling' meant that the monarch was dying, but because the Queen died in Scotland (rather than England, as had long been anticipated), the operation was renamed Unicorn in September 2022.

Operations Unicorn, Springtide and Golden Orb all ran

concurrently, which was a nightmare for the Lord Chamberlain's Department at St James's Palace, but somehow all three plans were executed seamlessly.

4

The Queens of the Palace and Immoral Balmoral

I arrived at the doors of Buckingham Palace as a naive teenager. I didn't know much about the world and my formative years in Grassmoor had kept me sheltered and unprepared for the world outside.

I didn't realise when I joined the Royal Household in 1976 that I would be stepping back in time to witness something quite extraordinary. A pantomime world of dress-up which hadn't really changed for two hundred years, where everyone would have the most extraordinary costumes and titles and be dipped in gold, rolled in glitter and dripping in diamonds, emeralds and pearls (and that was just the men!).

Footmen, pages of the backstairs, pages of the presence, women of the bedchamber, mistresses of the robes, yeomen of the pantries and yeomen of the cellars all had a place in this make-believe world.

The royal residences became my home and my playground too.

Is it any wonder that this environment bred a homosexual culture, one which had survived, been protected and thrived for generations?

On my first day at Buckingham Palace, I remember being met

at the tradesman's entrance on Buckingham Palace Road by an elderly gentleman in uniform called Charlie Hampson. I will never forget his white hair and black-rimmed spectacles. He took me to my room on the top floor of the palace (the Pages' Lobby) via a labyrinth of underground corridors and staircases. We seemed to walk for miles before we came to a service elevator with sliding doors. At times on our journey, doors opened and closed to reveal tantalising glimpses into the world beyond of plush-red-carpeted corridors filled with gilded furniture and antiques as liveried footmen went about their duties. I thought I was in a dream. I eventually dropped off my suitcase jam-packed with all the essentials Mum had bought for me. Then I went to meet with the deputy sergeant footman, Martin Bubb, to report for duty. I would later know him by his nickname, Bubbles, and my nickname would become Buttons – everyone had a nickname at the palace.

I was led downstairs to the basement to get kitted out. The room was as big as my home in Grassmoor and lined with wardrobes containing liveries for every possible occasion.

He said, 'Let's start with the grandest, the state uniform, a gold-embroidered scarlet coat embossed with the Queen's cypher, pink velvet knee breeches, pink silk stockings and patent leather buckled shoes.'

It was like I was back in school, playing the role of Buttons in a pantomime.

'In the past, we had a cupboard full of wigs as footmen had to wear them,' he explained. 'But the Queen stopped all that.'

Pages and footmen used to powder their hair with chalk, but the Queen abolished this tradition on her succession, as she had noticed chalk dust, like dandruff, falling into food as it was being served. It was also making the servants bald, so it was a blessing for them when it was no longer required.

We went on to the day livery which consisted of a black tailcoat and a scarlet waistcoat with the Queen's ciphered buttons . . . then it was on to the livery only worn on the Royal Yacht *Britannia* consisting of a scarlet double-breasted epaulette coat and black trousers. This was followed by a livery for semi-state occasions when blue velvet trousers were worn with white stockings, then a scarlet tailcoat with white waistcoat and three stiff-fronted starched shirts with matching starched collars and a white bow tie which was worn for Royal Ascot – and of course, three hats: a blue velvet riding cap, a black silk top hat and a tricorn with tassels hanging off the corners. Finally, there was a ceremonial sword for state occasions chosen from a cupboard full of them. I was groaning under the weight of it all.

'I am going to need to write all this down,' I said in a panic. 'I'll never remember what to wear and when.'

It didn't feel like the real world. I ended up with so many clothes that I had to have help to take them back to my room. I hung them all up and lay in bed that night thinking, Pinch me – I'm going to wake up soon.

But before I went to sleep I remembered the words of warning that the deputy sergeant footman had given to me earlier that day: 'There's a key on the inside of your door. Lock your door. Remember this for me. When you go to bed, lock the door.'

And I'd thought, Why would he be so insistent that I lock my door? I'm sleeping in Buckingham Palace!

He went on: 'They will be looking for you tonight. There's been a book opened on you. The first one to get you wins.'

I was puzzled. 'What? Who will be looking for me? What do you mean "the first one"?'

He explained: 'The first one to sleep with you, Paul!'

Puzzled and dismayed, I said indignantly, 'I'm not going to be sleeping with anybody here. Anyway, my bed is only a single.'

It was a kind warning. I think that he had noticed that I was particularly vulnerable and not yet as streetwise as the other footmen who were already established in the household.

I was only eighteen. I had never had a sexual experience and here I was in the Queen's home, not knowing what would happen next. I couldn't help thinking, She's asleep downstairs in her bed, so surely I will be safe here in mine?

But that night as I lay in my bed dreaming of my new uniforms and the roles that I would play when wearing them, I was woken by footsteps and rattling at the door and I thought, It's happening. I barely slept another wink that night, not just through the excitement but also the disturbance of someone trying to get into my room. It was quite the eye-opener for me!

I heeded the deputy sergeant's warning, but of course I forgot before long. I was tired and shut the door without turning the key, and I awoke in the middle of the night to find myself in quite a compromising position, with a naked member of the Royal Household trying to get into bed with me. The room was pitch black so I scrambled for the bedside light and turned it on. It was Prince Charles's valet, Stephen Barry. He was drunk and his clothes were in a heap on the floor. I'd never slept with a man; I'd never slept with anyone. I was scared. I was frightened. I had to do something so I said, 'If you don't leave my room, I'm going to go outside to the corridor where there's a telephone and I'm going to ring the police at the side door and get them to come up and remove you.'

He quickly bundled up his clothes into a big ball and left my room, still naked. God knows where he went. It was horrible for me and he never spoke to me again.

It wasn't just bed-hopping that went on in the palaces; there was a degree of inebriation which often helped loosen people's inhibitions. Forget Buckingham Palace, it was nicknamed 'Gin Palace' after the spirit that flowed freely through the everyday workings of the building. Gin, always Gordon's, was the drink of choice – both of the queens and the staff.

Coming from a world where a pint of Mansfield Bitter pulled by my auntie Pearl in the local was the norm, with a cherry brandy or a snowball at Christmas, I wasn't used to such extravagance, but I quickly became quite familiar with the ingenious ways in which the household smuggled booze for their soirées.

I would be ordered by senior members of staff to empty a screw-topped tonic water bottle each night and fill it with gin for them to use for parties in their rooms.

These parties were for a select group of staff. There was a hierarchy downstairs as well as upstairs. Certain cliques of servants, depending on your rank and length of service, were invited to the soirées.

I would be invited only as I had been ordered to decant the Queen's gin and place it in a cupboard for collection. There would be a riot if I forgot when they came to collect it for the evening's gathering.

'Just going upstairs to wash my hands' would be the signal for the juniors to be left in charge of the household. Gallons of gin were consumed every week – some legitimately, some not.

Footmen could be seen carrying Russell Hobbs electric kettles around the palace, not full of water but full of gin! Who would suspect that more gin was smuggled through the corridors of the palace than through the streets of Chicago during prohibition?

Even the chefs, who travelled the world and cooked in every home the Queen owned, would party hard after the family had been fed.

After long, arduous days from seven in the morning until late at night, they drank into the small hours, consuming leftovers from the Royal table and sampling the finest drink from the royal cellars, such as a brandy which was laid down at the time of the Battle of Waterloo. The Yeoman of the Royal Cellars was a good friend to have on side. He could provide a very nice bottle of claret or champagne at a minute's notice, which allowed some members of staff to abuse the system.

The Royals drank gin so the staff drank gin – and in enormous quantities!

Bottles of Gordon's gin would be poured over jugs of ice at Balmoral and Sandringham for martinis for house party pre-dinner drinks in the drawing rooms.

Both the Queen and the Queen Mother would drink gin and Dubonnet for a lunchtime aperitif – half gin/half Dubonnet – with two cubes of ice and a slice of lemon. They would sometimes have two of those. I used to call them 'rocket fuel' and they certainly fuelled the queens for the rest of the day.

Then there was a glass of wine at lunch, usually a sweet German wine like a Moselle or a Riesling. The Queen preferred wine from the Rhine Valley and said her palate never developed into fine wines, unlike her mother who would prefer a full-bodied claret. We would decant a fine château wine into a crystal decanter and leave it on the hot plate to warm. Sommeliers and wine connoisseurs will be fainting at the prospect of a vintage Château Margaux being served at the temperature of mulled wine, but that's the way she liked it.

Tea would be served at 5 p.m. in the small drawing room at Balmoral or Sandringham or the Oak Room at Windsor. The Queen would have the tea in front of her in a silver tea caddy. Loose-leaf Earl Grey or Darjeeling for guests. She would make the tea in the way any mother would, but in a silver tea pot on a silver salver with regiments of teacups in front of her: large cups for men and small cups for ladies. It was always a challenge to match the right size of cups with guests when setting the table. The Queen would ask how you would like your tea, then pour it and pass it down the table. The tea was poured first into the china cup, then sweetened with sugar or honey and finally milk was added to colour. I watched a gentleman commit the cardinal sin of putting the milk in first, in response to which an elderly duchess screamed, 'Oh dear! Are you a MILF, a "milk in first"?' She was most displeased and gave him a withering look like Dame Maggie Smith in *Downton Abbey*.

After tea, the drinks trolley would appear and a couple of half-and-half gin and tonics were served before it was time to change for dinner. Once in evening attire, it was acceptable to have a couple of martinis. I saw a TV programme recently that said the Queen liked them shaken like James Bond. Rubbish! She liked martinis stirred, not shaken. Lots of ice in a jug, a bottle of gin, a tiny drop of vermouth and lots of lemon peel.

When I started making martinis I was quite nervous about getting it right. Once in the saloon drawing room at Sandringham, I was being observed by Queen Elizabeth the Queen Mother. I was about to add the dry vermouth but she stopped me.

'Just show the jug the bottle of vermouth, Paul. That's how dry a martini should be.'

The Queen would drink two or three of those before eating and then probably take the jug with her into dinner. Sometimes Prince Philip would mix a martini and take it to the Queen as she was dressing for dinner: a simple act of love between a husband and a wife. He enjoyed a glass of Glenfiddich whisky or sometimes a bottle of Double Diamond bitter. The brewer still made it especially for him. He had drunk it all his life. Princess Margaret was a serious drinker and could consume a bottle of Famous Grouse whisky in an evening. She was also the only smoker, much to her sister's displeasure. Interestingly, only Princess Diana didn't indulge and remained teetotal.

The Queen wasn't a great champagne lover but she would have a glass to toast when the occasion called for it, such as at a state banquet, but she probably just took a sip. The Queen Mother loved champagne and she had a special ivory swizzle stick made which she would put into a glass of champagne to get the bubbles out. She didn't like the bubbles. What is the point of getting the bubbles out of champagne? She liked the wine but never the bubbles.

People would ask me if I'd ever seen the Queen drunk. The answer is no, but perhaps a little tipsy on occasion.

Booze seemed to run through the veins of the palace in all directions; it was the lifeblood of the palace. It did sometimes go too far and the staff became so inebriated it was impossible for them to serve dinner, especially on board the royal yacht. The chefs would be slaving away in the galley to provide food for every meal and reception but the rest of the staff would have a more leisurely time and could often be found on the funnel deck sunbathing. Cries of 'tickets please' could be heard from the galley as the staff climbed the ladders wearing swimwear and carrying towels and suntan lotion.

Drinks in the Royal Household mess were so cheap in foreign waters that a round for everyone would cost no more than two pounds. On some occasions I have to admit to feeling very queasy serving food around the dining room table on board, and I don't think I could always attribute that to the swell of the sea; it was probably more due to too many 'dark and stormys' (ginger beer and rum), a favourite of sailors on board.

Is it any wonder that sometimes the dining room was so depleted of royal staff that we had to rely on Royal Naval stewards to supplement us? The sea wasn't always as choppy as the staff's footsteps!

I didn't realise it at the time, but I was witnessing the end of a golden era: a world that was changing, even though some of the stars in it never did.

All of the Queen's personal staff loved a drink. Some drank more than others, but we covered for each other and made sure that the Queen received the best possible service.

The Royals were aware that the staff drank alcohol on duty but they accepted it and never complained. The Queen was very understanding and never made a fuss.

One member of staff of whom the Queen was very fond was

caught on CCTV helping himself to a supply of gin. Even the Queen couldn't stop him losing his job.

'If only he had been in livery ... I could have saved him,' she said.

Gin, known as mother's ruin, caused the downfall of many and ruined many a footman or page's career.

I often saw senior members of staff bouncing off the walls of the Royal apartments as they tried to negotiate a straight line down a red-carpeted corridor. Once a senior member of staff appeared as if by magic through a doorway while the Queen and I were feeding the dogs. He lumbered from one wall to the next, totally drunk, weaving his way through nine corgis and past a bemused Queen whom he didn't even notice. The Queen smiled at me and said, 'How extraordinary!'

Back in the day, every royal residence had a bar, a NAAFI canteen where members of the household staff could drink alcohol in between duties. This led to unparalleled alcoholism in the lower ranks. Prices were subsidised, which made alcohol easily accessible. Today, the practice has been abolished in most residences.

I had my twenty-first birthday celebrations at the canteen inside Buckingham Palace to which the staff were invited, including Her Majesty's closest attendants.

The Queen had greeted me with a warm smile that morning, 'Happy Birthday, Paul. I hear it's a special one.'

While some subjects receive cards for their one hundredth birthday, there are not many who have had personal greetings from the monarch.

Later that day, I would find myself working in the Royal Box at Epsom for the Derby, sipping champagne, a gift from Her Majesty. Caring, considerate and generous as she always was, it was such an honour to be in her presence.

Although I do remember occasions when we found ourselves on the wrong side of her temper. One evening, I was helping to clear the saloon drawing room at Sandringham of pre-dinner drinks. It is a cavernous room with a huge baronial fireplace complete with a minstrel's gallery. My friend Roger Gleed and I would 'finish off' any drinks that had been left behind. It would have been a shame to rinse them down the sink. Roger was knocking back a martini in one when his eyes lifted and he saw his monarch's face watching him from the window above. He almost choked but the Queen said nothing and he was saved by her silence.

On another occasion, I noticed a large G and T with ice and a slice that had not been touched. It was much too good to waste. It was delicious and much needed after a busy day of working and dog walking.

Then I heard the Queen's high-pitched voice screaming down the corridor and through the burgundy baize door which sep-arated and soundproofed the Royal side of the house from the servants' side.

'The beast! He's stolen my drink!'

Apparently she had intended to take her G and T upstairs with her to dress for dinner; she had forgotten and now I had downed it.

'I had a brand-new drink and it's gorn,' she continued.

I quickly made another G and T with correct measures and rushed it upstairs on a silver salver to the disappointed Queen to quench her thirst. She was soon revived and I was cleared of any guilty charges.

I was known for months afterwards as 'the Beast'. My favourite Disney movie is *Beauty and the Beast* . . . I never saw myself in the role of the beast, but clearly the Queen did!

But it wasn't just the servants who overindulged; the Royals did too.

One day the Queen told me, 'I'm going to leave Princess Margaret in charge of the house.' I heard myself thinking, Do you think that is wise? but I said nothing.

Her Majesty was heading south to open Parliament and would be gone from Balmoral for a couple of days so her sister was left as the senior royal lady in the house.

'Don't put the drinks trolley into the drawing room too early,' she said with a knowing tone. 'And keep an eye on the whisky bottle.'

So I did as Her Majesty had asked. The Queen even took a pencil from her desk and drew a line on the label of the Famous Grouse bottle just to check how much was being consumed.

Princess Margaret hardly touched a drop of whisky while the Queen was away; the line on that bottle did not move – but I did notice that the vodka was disappearing rather quickly. She'd learned to disguise her drink with Robinsons barley water.

One evening they were having a dinner party so I went with Cyril Dickman, the elderly palace steward (think Carson in *Downton Abbey*), to see Princess Margaret in her sitting room to make arrangements. She had to decide the menu to be served and the seating plan.

And she was rather spaced out. She had a long cigarette holder in one hand and a drink in the other. The steward was desperately trying to ascertain the names of the guests so that they could be put on the dinner board.

She recalled, 'Mrs Wills and Mrs Rhodes and ... some gal.'

The palace steward was flabbergasted. 'I'm sorry, Your Royal Highness, but some gal? What's her name?'

Margot said, 'I don't know ... some gal.'

The steward said, 'I can hardly put "some gal" on a card and put it in front of the place setting.'

Margot simply took a long drag of her cigarette and blew the smoke into the face of the steward, reminding him of her position and of his.

*

As a servant, assuming the station of your master (or mistress) isn't unusual. It has happened for centuries below stairs. Visiting maids and valets would be afforded the role and title of their employers and would be called by their names. For instance, if the Earl and Countess of Halifax were visiting with their valet and lady's maid (dresser) they would be known as Master Halifax and Miss Halifax and were given precedence in the servants' hall according to their employers' station.

With this in mind, my dear late friend Mark Simpson, the nursery footman, who was nicknamed Wallis because he had the same surname as King Edward VIII's American wife, would drop the largest curtsey to me early in the morning with a shriek. 'Good morning, ma'am!' was his greeting – the height of campery.

On one occasion, poor Wallis found himself in hot water. He was to attend Royal Ascot (well, ride a carriage to Ascot) and he decided to go full hog for the occasion and have a perm. His normally straight hair turned into a tight bob of Shirley Temple curls which completely altered his appearance.

Being seen in a corridor at Buckingham Palace was one thing; being seen in public with the Royal Family was too much for the Master of the Household.

Poor Wallis was suspended from public duties until his hair returned to normal and he never made Ascot that year. Petty in today's world but back then the household was run with an iron fist of discipline.

Hierarchy was everything.

On special occasions, I would greet Queen Elizabeth the Queen Mother at the garden entrance of Buckingham Palace as she was coming from Clarence House to see her daughter. Sometimes dressed in a marshmallow-tulle Norman Hartnell creation dipped in glitter and dripping in jewels, she would look like a fairy that had fallen off the Christmas tree, a style that she had adopted in the 1940s and never changed. She was always late. She would be last to arrive and first to leave despite having the shortest distance to travel. The Queen Mum would often raise her hand, as if clutching her pearls, and whisper 'Isn't it gay?' I think she meant it as it was intended in the 1950s but it's undeniable that there was a degree of campness amongst the household staff.

The more gay the servants acted, the more natural it seemed. The stiff upper lip of the Elizabethan court approved.

The Queen Mother would leave her 'palace' across the road in the capable hands of William Tallon (Backstairs Billy) and his partner Reg Wilcock. Their household was run hilariously. Any new staff recruits would have to undergo an initiation ceremony. At midnight on a given date with Her Majesty in residence, they would have to run naked around the formal apartments and back to the safety of their own rooms. I don't think that anyone other than the staff ever witnessed one of these streaks, but it must have been very embarrassing for a new recruit, and not quite what he expected when working for royalty I'm sure.

Buckingham Palace didn't have a similar initiation ceremony. Instead, as I've mentioned, the older gay members of staff would run bets on who would 'get him first' when any new male member of staff joined.

The gay mafia were very present and they needed to be handled carefully because if you incurred their wrath, you would suffer the consequences.

Prince Charles's valet, Stephen Barry, was openly gay, very grand and very extravagant.

He hosted parties in the Prince of Wales's apartments where the Queen's chefs cooked the food and her footmen and butlers served the meal. Wines came from the royal cellars, and guests arrived at the front gates and were escorted to the second floor.

I have no idea how he got away with it, but he was never chastised or reprimanded. He was entertaining on behalf of the prince. He was untouchable. He was non-negotiable as far as Charles was concerned – well until Diana came along. Then he had to go. He moved to New York, wrote a book and died an untimely death.

Of course it wasn't just Buckingham Palace that was jam packed with 'queens'. The Queen's Scottish residence was nicknamed 'Immoral Balmoral' because of the goings on there. The estate in Aberdeenshire was bought by Queen Victoria and her husband Prince Albert in 1852 but the original castle was found to be too small, so the current building was commissioned.

It was a hedonistic place where time seemed to stand still. The Queen usually moved to Balmoral for twelve weeks in the summer, beginning with the ten-day Western Isles cruise, which transported the family to Aberdeen. From there they travelled to Balmoral by car. Balmoral was always considered Her Majesty's summer break – she loved the Scottish retreat. Of course, work continued, with daily red boxes, government agendas to be signed off and meetings with prime ministers – but there were also endless house parties.

This is where she died: surrounded by happy memories with a view from her bedroom window of the Scottish Highlands.

It was also a happy place for generations of long-serving staff. We divided the twelve weeks into two halves and worked every day for six weeks, then took our annual leave in the other half. So each year, I would be at Balmoral from July to August, then take my holidays with my family.

The changeover usually coincided with the Ghillies Ball, a grand affair in the castle ballroom attended by the Royal Family, their guests and the household staff. The staff would also have a fancy dress party in the staff recreation hall.

While the Queen and her guests swished around in diamonds and finery, the staff made their fancy dress outfits from crepe paper and papier mâché. There was a parade before a prize was bestowed on the best costume. Tall Paul and I gained a reputation for often winning the competition with our respective outfits. My creations included Noddy (complete with his yellow car), Andy Pandy, Florence from *The Magic Roundabout* and a huge Pete's Dragon.

One year Paul was so successful that the Queen decided he should wear his costume when he announced dinner and then lead the guests to their table.

Imagine the hilarity as the Queen, Prince Philip and the Royal Household as well as the prime minister, Margaret Thatcher, were led into dinner by the Queen's footman dressed as Liberace wielding a candelabra.

It was very easy to relax and have fun at Balmoral, with bonfires, barbecues, singalongs, picnics and regular gatherings in the staff canteen at both lunch and dinner time. These events were never drunken but rarely sober. Those summers taught the Royal servants how to hide their inebriation well.

Balmoral entailed long hours: from 7 a.m. until well after dinner – sometimes until 11 p.m. at night. It meant the Queen allowed staff extra privileges and allowances. She was understanding and tolerant.

Affairs, romances, parties and fun and games were the order of the day downstairs. The Royals were known to have fun too but a little more discreetly. This was a castle where everyone let their hair down.

Once, the morning after the Ghillies Ball I was asked to make sure that a member of the household, who lived next to me on my corridor, was awake. I was always up early as I had to take the corgi puppies for their early morning walk. They slept in my room with me. The Queen approved of this so they weren't alone. I would take them out first before the older dogs.

I knocked on my neighbour's door but there was no answer. I tried the handle and the door was unlocked. I crept in slowly to find a littered path of a Scottish Highlander's uniform between the bed and the door – a kilt here, a sporran there, socks and a jacket. I didn't realise that I would be waking two people up in a single bed that morning.

It was customary for people to fall in love at Balmoral. Holiday romances rarely lasted more than the summer break but at least the household staff bonded and had a great deal of fun.

Even I, in my single days when I was first enchanted by Balmoral's Brigadoon-like charm, once returned to my room to find a (naked) royal chauffeur hiding behind the curtains.

Downstairs, life was a hedonistic mix of homosexual and heterosexual activity very much in the vein of *Downton Abbey*. Although I didn't see any of this even mentioned in *The Crown* ...

Even royal affairs blossomed within the castle walls and suitors were brought to see if they could survive the family. It was the monarch's most informal and relaxed residence – somewhere private, away from public and press scrutiny.

This is where I first met a young Lady Diana. Her romance with Charles flourished there. Although she confessed to me during that first meeting that she was lost in the corridor and looking for her room; it was clear she felt out of her depth.

The 'Balmoral test' was cruel. Outsiders, most importantly potential brides, were brought there like specimens to be inspected by the family to see if they came up to scratch and if they were suitable.

Lady Jane Wellesley, the daughter of the Duke of Wellington, Lady Jane Kerr, Amanda Knatchbull and several other suitors to Prince Charles had trodden the same path of suitability. Diana wasn't the first subject to be scrutinised. Even Princess Anne brought a cavalry officer called Mark Phillips here to meet the family.

It had been this way since Queen Victoria's day which is no surprise as the castle hasn't changed much either. But hedonistic activity wasn't confined to Balmoral. During my service, I heard a legendary tale of Queen Elizabeth the Queen Mother's former footman being caught in a gentlemen's lavatory in St James's Park with his pants down – quite literally. He was arrested and taken to Canon Row Police Station, but fearing a scandal might break in the newspapers, someone rushed to forewarn the Queen Mother. She was informed by her private secretary, Sir Ralph Anstruther, who was an elderly stiff-upper-lipped Etonian. He told her in a blunt, matter-of-fact manner.

She didn't flinch and replied, 'Oh dear, how unfortunate. Would you please send a car to pick him up.'

He was told later that he had been a 'naughty boy' and reinstated into his position.

Like her mother, Queen Elizabeth II was very tolerant, understanding and forgiving. Her own favourite personal protection officer, Mike Trestrail, who was then a commander in the Metropolitan Police, was compromised by his homosexuality and forced to resign. It really was a different time then.

The Queen was adamant that he should stay as she liked him. In fact the entire household liked him but he 'fell on his sword' and insisted he went, citing the fact that his homosexuality could lead to a weakness in the Queen's protection.

I remember the Queen being so sad on the day he left – she liked continuity, familiarity and the security of knowing everyone around her.

She loathed change. 'Nothing is ever quite the same,' she would say.

Gay men had fewer distractions, were dedicated to their role of serving their Queen and were devoted to her.

When Stephen Barry had appeared naked in my bedroom, I confided in an elderly 'uncle' who was good and kind about my concerns.

He sagely told me, 'Take no notice of them. Be yourself. Hold your head high, and even when they jeer at you and probe, just whistle and carry on! They will hate that but just carry on being you. You are stronger and bigger than them! You will win in the end. They are sad, lonely and stuck in the past, you have a life ahead of you.'

While there was debauchery and risqué behaviour going on within the palace walls with the various queens, there was of course one who was never improper – Her Majesty the Queen.

5

Duty Calls

There is no doubt that the Queen took her duty as monarch very seriously. On her Coronation Day, 2 June 1953, she said, 'I have in sincerity pledged myself to your service, as so many of you are pledged to mine. Throughout all my life and with all my heart I shall strive to be worthy of your trust.'

She did not let that oath or her duty falter, right up to her death. Most people have an idea of what she was like through seeing her on state occasions and family weddings, at events such as Royal Ascot and the Royal Variety Performance or from her speeches viewed with the family on Christmas Day. But I was one of the lucky few who got to really know what the Queen was like up close and it was because of one absent-minded smile that I managed to penetrate all those layers and rise to have the Queen's ear.

The letter that Mum opened only offered me the role of under-butler, a job cleaning silver, but a last-minute vacancy as a footman on an annual salary of £1,200 came up and I was given it. Even so I was number fourteen out of fourteen, and getting the top job as one of the Queen's personal footmen seemed unachievable.

The first time that I ever saw Her Majesty in real life was in December 1976, when all her staff were sent to Windsor Castle for Christmas; in those days she went there for the festive season rather than Sandringham.

The palace steward, Cyril Dickman, would waddle around with his hands on his hips. He was like mother hen pecking at all his little chicks and he would say, 'Come on, come on, line up, boys. I want a straight line into the dining room. Chop, chop! Hurry up.'

As the newest and one of the youngest, I was at the back of the queue and my simple task was to 'back up' with the coffee cups. It felt like a huge task.

Waiting in the Octagon Room adjacent to the state dining room I was staring up at the high Pugin-style ceiling and oak-panelled walls. I got more and more nervous as the line shortened and I got closer to entering the room. I had been waiting for two hours watching an endless stream of uniformed footmen, under-butlers, pages and wine waiters come and go like a human conveyor belt serving Christmas dinner. Everything was operating like clockwork. Then I was able to peek through a crack in the door and I gasped when I saw the Queen sitting just yards away from me, looking relaxed but so regal.

She was wearing diamonds that were sparkling in the light. It was like an animated Madame Tussauds. Someone I had seen so many times throughout my life in pictures, and who had adorned my childhood bedroom wall, was now sitting just in front of me talking.

It made me even more nervous. I was carrying a solid silver tray and on it were twenty fine Royal Worcester monogrammed demi-tasse coffee cups, saucers and gilt spoons. As I walked into the dining room, I spotted the Queen again. She was relaxed and smiling with her family. The Queen Mother was engrossed in a chat with Prince Charles. There were around thirty members of the Royal Family present, all in evening dress. Then my nerves got the better of me and the cups and saucers all started to rattle. I will never forget the noise. All I had to do was stand behind the Queen and the pages would come to me and collect the cups. The rattling continued so loudly that the Queen turned around to look at what the commotion was. And she just smiled. That was my first introduction to her.

She got to know my face along with those of the other footmen when we would wait on her for the 'meet the people' lunches in the 1844 room at Buckingham Palace.

I had progressed beyond empty cups to serving potatoes and gravy. We were always told never to look at the Queen or stare at her: never look her in the eye, always look down. One day she caught me unawares. I was serving someone else but I couldn't take my eyes off her. Suddenly she was looking straight at me. I had committed the cardinal sin.

After lunch, the Queen enquired of the palace steward who I was and said that I had 'smiled' at her.

He panicked. 'Oh he's our newest recruit, Paul. I'm terribly sorry, Your Majesty.'

She replied, 'Oh that's quite all right. It's just no one ever smiles at me.'

In April 1978, the Queen's footman was hospitalised after a suicide attempt and was retired on ill health. Then her page, Ernest Bennet, retired too leading to a restructure of the Queen's immediate household.

She was looking for a replacement and that young boy who had dared to smile at her came to mind. It seemed like such a minor incident, but I had made my mark. She asked for me to be sent upstairs to spend the day with her to 'see if I like him' but in reality, it was more important that the corgis liked me.

The first thing she said to me was 'Do you like dogs?' to which I replied, 'I love dogs, Your Majesty.' In a flash she said, 'Well, let's see if they like you.'

She then introduced me one by one to her beloved pets: Brush, Jolly, Socks, Smoky, Piper, Fable, Chipper, Myth and Shadow.

Nine in total. She walked over to a sideboard where a glass bowl of doggy treats sat topped with a silver model of a corgi on its lid and gathered a handful of dog leads. She clipped the leads onto each of them and told me to take them for a short walk to see how we got on with each other.

Now I knew ahead of time that I was to be formally introduced to the Queen and I would have to impress her dogs, so at breakfast I had wrapped a couple of sausages in a napkin and put them in the pocket of my tailcoat, thinking that they might come in handy later.

I took the dogs out into the garden beneath the Queen's rooms and I could see her net curtain twitching as she watched me. I took them off their leads and I began to run across the lawn. Lo and behold, all the dogs followed me. I stopped behind the summer house out of sight and rewarded my charges with a treat of sausages.

When I returned she said, 'I was watching you and they do like you. I think I'll keep you.'

She kept me for ten happy years working alongside Tall Paul. She had two Pauls.

Having two Pauls made the Queen's life easier, but it used to exasperate Princess Margaret when she rang to speak with her sister. She would say, 'Oh, Lilibet, it is so confusing to have two Pauls! Why don't you change one of their names?' To which the Queen replied, 'Oh no, Margot. It's perfect. When I shout "Paul", one of them appears.' It was Princess Margaret who decided otherwise. She nicknamed Paul Whybrew, who is six feet four inches, 'Tall Paul' and at five feet ten inches, I was to be forever known as 'Small Paul'.

If I had stayed with the Queen, my life would have been straightforward. She would have had two Pauls for the rest of her life and I would have grown old with her. I probably would have been with her when she died, but my path was to be a different one.

My duty was to stay with her and not to jump ship to the Waleses but I did it for my family. It was not a selfish act and the Queen understood that. I kept in contact with her for the rest of her life. She always remembered me and remained fond of me.

And when I became known in the public eye, she watched out for me. When I appeared on *I'm a Celebrity . . . Get Me Out of Here!* in 2004, finishing runner up to the comedian Joe Pasquale, I was told by Tall Paul that she thought it was hilarious. She enjoyed that she actually knew someone who was in the jungle.

She would open the *Radio Times* and say, 'When is Paul going to be on?' It seems bonkers to me that the Queen was watching me on television pulling faces and screaming while doing the 'Hell Holes' trial. I'll never get my head around it.

Mike Tindall followed in my wake and went into the jungle too, sharing stories of what the Queen is really like. He was brilliant on the programme.

I think the world believes that she thought ill of me for taking part. She didn't.

Even when my book *A Royal Duty* came out in 2003, she understood why I had written it, even though she did not read it. She knew where I was coming from and the situation I was in. Neither she nor Prince Philip had a bad word to say about me as they knew it was the truth. Prince Philip read the manuscript before the book was printed and no objection was raised by the Palace. I didn't have to justify myself because I really didn't talk about the Queen very much when she was still alive.

Now that she has gone I've decided to speak about her more so that I can pay my respects to a wonderful lady.

So who was she? She was the beating heart of our nation. A familiar face in an ever-changing world. Apart from Diana, probably the most photographed woman in the world. Our Queen for most of our lives. She had a divine presence and I witnessed famous, intelligent, important people moved by being in her company.

Men would forget themselves and curtsy instead of bowing. They would be dumbstruck and muddle their words.

A remote figure to many but for those who came into her orbit, she was kind, generous and humble. While she was a woman of regal majesty, she had no airs or graces. I don't think she ever realised how famous, important or wealthy she was. If you could ask her what her greatest achievement was, she would say that it was her Commonwealth of countries. She loved the fact that her influence could hold together almost a third of the world's land mass.

I was once asked by a celebrity if she was a 'shapeshifter'. They added, 'Does she ever unzip her skin at night? Are there bright lights under her door?'

Of course I never saw the Queen transform into a reptilian alien. She was human like you and me.

I witnessed first-hand her getting bitten trying to separate her corgis when they fought. She would bleed – red blood not blue – and need to be stitched up like anyone else. Then she would take a couple of arnica pills and offer some to me, insisting that they helped with the healing.

She was humble and frugal in so many ways. At Balmoral, Peggy, her dresser, would often find snow on the green tartan carpet in the Queen's bedroom as the windows had been left open all night. Looking at her old-fashioned three-bar electric fire, she would say, 'Put a bar on for the corgis, Peggy. They might be cold.' She never spoiled herself but loved giving to others. She was incredibly thoughtful, for example, at Christmas when she took great pleasure in organising the Christmas crackers. She would choose all the contents that went inside each cracker and how they were decorated. When they were pulled, many guests would leave the contents behind so she would go around collecting whistles, powder compacts, dice and magnifying glasses as well as all the jokes and paper hats. She had a drawer full of them. She never liked to throw anything away.

She would save a piece of wrapping paper that came with a beautiful present. She would smooth it out, fold it up neatly and then say to me, 'Keep that somewhere safe. It will come in handy.' She was a woman of her generation; she was not wasteful.

In some ways, she was just a typical grandmother, which is partly why so many people could relate to her. As a young boy growing up in Grassmoor, my last job of the day was to put a tea towel over the cage containing Peter, our budgerigar. I had no idea that the Queen kept more than twenty breeding pairs of green and blue budgerigars in an aviary underneath her sitting-room window at Windsor Castle.

When I saw her with Paddington Bear in that heartfelt television clip as part of her Platinum Jubilee celebrations where she jokingly put her marmalade sandwich in her handbag saying, 'I keep mine in here for later.' I thought, That is my Queen.

The public got a glimpse of the woman I stood behind for more than a decade.

Her son Charles is very different. He is extravagant and flamboyant in many ways. And yet the Queen wasn't.

The Queen didn't like to be ostentatious. She would, for example, wear the garter star for formal occasions when it was required but she never tried to be over the top. In contrast, the King would wear every diamond and decoration he possibly could.

The Queen always tried to do what she thought was right but she did not like confrontation. She avoided it as she liked a steady ship and she had Prince Philip at the helm to steer it. He kept her shielded from conflict.

Hers was a life ruled by duty, service and discipline. Her path never meandered, always straight ahead, no nonsense, truthful and sound. In all that she did, she tried to please everyone.

Perhaps the biggest struggle for the Queen was her duty as a mother because as far as she was concerned being the monarch came first, being a parent came second. We joked at Buckingham

Palace that after being the Queen, her priorities were horses, dogs, husband and children in that order. She had sworn an oath before God in Westminster Abbey as to her role as monarch.

Being Queen was paramount to her which is why she said that she would serve her country for as long as there was breath in her body. That is what she did to the very end. She was devoted and dedicated to this country and everything else had to take second place.

The family knew it. Her children, Charles, Anne, Andrew and Edward all knew it. I think that is why Anne didn't want her husband or her children to have royal titles. She knew the restrictions that came with being a prince or a princess. She wanted them to have as normal a life as possible. She didn't want them to have the life that she had had as a daughter of the Queen. She is her father's daughter and she has a more common-sense approach. She knew what the pitfalls were to being royal and she just didn't want that for her children.

Prince Philip knew it too and he accepted that he would always walk two paces behind his wife in public. Interestingly, not in private, because his role as patriarch of the family was very important behind closed doors. That is when the Queen submitted. She left her crown at the door of all her private homes and deferred all family matters to Prince Philip. She became a wife and a mother.

But even with family it was difficult for her to truly take off her crown. She couldn't, for example, put her role to one side and allow her sister Princess Margaret to marry Group Captain Peter Townsend when she was twenty-two. He was a divorcee and under the 1772 Royal Marriages Act, Margaret needed the Queen's permission to marry. She did not grant her request. It was something Margot still lamented on her death bed in 2002. It was a real struggle for her to put state before her beloved sister's happiness.

It was the same in her relationship with Princess Diana; she could not simply be her mother-in-law, she had to be queen first.

The greatest mistake the public makes is that they assume

the Royals are just like us, when they rarely behave as a man in the street would. Their family dynamics are also very different. Parental duties and responsibilities are fractured and in the past were primarily carried out by other people: nannies, members of staff or tutors. Diana did break the mould in that respect and wanted to be as 'hands on' as possible, much to the confusion of Prince Charles who had a more traditional and Victorian approach.

After all, he grew up having to make a telephone call to the Queen's page to make an appointment to see his mother, especially if he wished to join her at lunch, tea or dinner. When I joined service in 1976, Prince Andrew and Prince Edward were still in the Royal nursery with Mabel Anderson, their nanny. They took all of their meals there until they were sixteen, when they were deemed able to hold conversation and behave appropriately and allowed to eat in the dining room with their family.

I am pleased to note that William has taken his mother's approach to parenting. At six-monthly diary meetings with their team, he and Catherine make it quite clear what they can and cannot do. They build their royal life around their children's world and ensure that they are at home as much as possible, especially after school, at weekends and during school holidays. They are not fond of attending Royal Ascot, for example, or the dressing up in tiaras and robes that is expected of them and this pomp is sure to decline when William becomes king. He intends to be royal with a small 'r'.

In the next few years, William and Catherine will deputise more and more for the eldest Royals, especially on longer trips. But where the young Prince Charles was left at home when his mother travelled overseas, William will want his children with him just like Diana did – bringing her 'Wombat', her nickname for William, on a charm-offensive tour of Australia.

This parenting approach can sometimes cause friction with the King, who grew up – like all the Queen's children – knowing that he was secondary to her kingdom.

While the parenting style may differ, it is always advantageous to be related to the monarch particularly if you are having financial issues. Margaret and the Queen Mother were both often overdrawn and the Queen would sort it. She fixed everyone's problems. She became a cash cow for them and most of the family has benefited from the Queen's financial kindness over the years. The King doesn't want to continue with this approach. He is more careful about where money goes within the family.

While the Queen might have always put her family after her role as monarch, she did realise that being a parent was paramount for me and recognised that fact on the night my eldest son, Alexander, was born. It was a stormy night in London and the Queen was dining alone. The phone kept ringing in the pantry and she asked, 'Who keeps calling? Can someone answer it?'

It was the police informing me that Maria, who was two weeks overdue and in Westminster Hospital, was finally delivering our first child.

The Queen exclaimed, 'What? Why are you standing there! Go! And when the baby arrives please let me know.'

So, along with my friend Roger Gleed, I dashed from the palace in the pouring rain. I was by Maria's side all night and at 6.45 a.m. on 22 May 1985, my son, Alexander Paul Burrell, was born with a piercing scream. On her instruction, I rang the Queen's page to let Her Majesty know. The Queen, not my mum or dad, was the first to hear our lovely news. Frances Simpson and Harold Brown, housekeeper and butler to the Prince and Princess of Wales at Kensington Palace arrived bearing gifts of flowers and bubble bath with a note reading, 'What a clever lady you are! With love from Diana, William and Harry.'

The Queen was keen to meet our new bundle of joy, whom the *Sunday Mirror* had hilariously described as 'Maria's Royal Baby' referring to Alexander as 'a new royal child'. This amused the Queen, who met us casually dressed in her black riding boots, breeches and long-sleeved shirt as she had been riding her horse Burmese in her garden in rehearsal for Trooping the Colour.

She said, 'What tiny fingers and tiny toes. I had quite forgotten.' For a few seconds I could see that she was transported back to those heady days when she was a young mother. She placed her forefinger into our son's clenched fist and was mesmerised by him. 'I want you to have a little something from me,' she said.

And she presented us with two knitted cardigans. Both parents were proud as punch with our audience with the Queen; our son Alexander was less impressed and remained fast asleep throughout.

The following year she announced, 'I'm going to film my Christmas broadcast from the stables in the Royal Mews this year. Would Maria and Alexander like to take part?'

Of course they would. Imagine your son and wife being filmed standing beside the Queen on such an important occasion!

Years later, she would ask Tall Paul to be beside her and Daniel Craig, as they filmed a piece for the opening ceremony of the Olympic Games.

Another time the Queen displayed her kindness to my family was during Alexander's first year of life. We were living in the Royal Mews above the stables and she asked, 'Where does Maria take the baby in the pram?'

I told her how she would walk around Green Park with him and the Queen said, 'I shall have a key made for you for the private gardens at Buckingham Palace. We've got a sandpit for William and Harry so when he's older he will be able to play in it. Maria can walk around in peace and no one will mind.'

Of course everyone minded, from the gardeners to the footmen, because she was breaking precedence and showing me favouritism that she had never shown anyone else. Jealousy was rife. These were the days when Buckingham Palace wasn't open to the public. Nobody saw the gardens unless you were invited to a garden party but the Queen always considered other people's feelings and her kindness extended to my family on many occasions.

She was always looking out for me from then on – through my awful trial and right until her final days. And in return it was my duty to take care of her and preserve her memory as I am trying to do now.

Princess Diana also took her duty very seriously.

Her wedding day at St Paul's Cathedral on 29 July 1981 launched her into public duty. At the time it was the most-watched non-sport event in history, with 750 million people across 74 countries tuning in to see Lady Diana Spencer tie the knot with the future king of the United Kingdom. It would be surpassed by the screening of her funeral in 1997.

After that beautiful wedding, there was only a short time for respite with a honeymoon cruise on board the Queen's ship, the Royal Yacht *Britannia*, sailing through the Mediterranean around the Greek islands. Life was blissful. A double bed had been installed on board (all beds were traditionally single – even the Queen's). Diana wrote to her mother, sisters and mother-in-law, expressing her happiness.

'Charles is so attentive towards me. We are constantly mobbing each other up.'

Diana was in love.

Then a bombshell hit the newlywed bride. She found a pair of cufflinks decorated with intertwined 'C's. At first, she thought that they were Chanel, but then the penny dropped. Of course, they were for Charles and Camilla – a wedding present for the groom from a previous girlfriend.

It didn't go down well at all and the couple had their first marital spat – sadly it wasn't to be their last.

Despite the sour taste of this 'inappropriate gift', Diana soldiered on and each time the ship dropped anchor, the Royal couple had to meet with local VIPs and attend formal dinners. Diana complained, 'This is more like a state visit than a honeymoon.'

Sometimes duty came before pleasure when you were a princess. It was the beginning of a sharp learning curve for the new Princess of Wales. It wasn't quite the fairy tale she had expected.

Years later she said to me, 'I kissed a lot of frogs and all I ended up with was toads.' She even kept a collection of stone frogs in her sitting room at Kensington Palace to remind her of this.

To put some things right, there have been certain misconceptions reported *incorrectly* over the years, including that Diana was afraid of the Queen. Nonsense! She admired the monarch and sympathised with her. Diana was no anarchist. She was proud to be a member of the Royal Family and supported it wholeheartedly. The only time that she was upset was when it was time to say goodbye to her extended family after the separation.

Diana taught her boys from the beginning that their privileged lifestyle comes from being royal and that the payback for that privilege was a duty to the nation.

William understands that to this day. It seems that Prince Harry has forgotten it. He was trained to be beside William and to support him on the way to being king; he always knew that.

Diana fell in love with Charles. She adored him and wanted to make him happy and thought that she could beguile him with her beauty and her work ethic. She wanted Charles to be proud of her and how seriously she took her duty to the Royal Family, and to say 'Well done' from time to time. He never did. As the years rolled by, he became jealous of her popularity and of the affection showered on her by the public worldwide. It was a bit like the film *A Star Is Born* as her star began to rise and eclipse Charles's.

However, she gave him her greatest gifts – his two sons; they were the most important people in her life. He loves them.

Devotion and dedication to duty comes at a price.

From 1976 to 1987, my duty to our dear late Queen and to my family, Maria, Alexander and Nicholas, was straightforward. It was always easy for me to draw a line between the Royal world and mine. One I was privileged to witness and the other I lived in. Some royal servants got lost along the way but I never did.

With Her Majesty, I was able to put my duty to my family ahead of that to the Royal Family. That was all about to change after my move to the Waleses' household, when I discovered that my time wasn't always my own. It was a huge risk leaving a secure job where I could be happy for the rest of my days to work with the Wales family. I was called to have tea with the Queen's lady-in-waiting, of whom I had grown fond over the years.

'Are you sure that you're doing the right thing, Paul?' she said to me, while pouring me a cup of Darjeeling tea. 'The Queen told me that you were leaving for honourable reasons. And that one day, when Charles and Diana are king and queen, you'll be back here doing the same for them that you're doing for her. But Paul, all isn't as it seems. There are cracks and divisions in the Wales household and Diana could be gone and forgotten in a couple of years.'

I was astounded that she was being so indiscreet. Obviously, it was known within the household that by 1987 there were problems. But surely this was something about nothing. Surely it could be fixed. I had no idea of the storm into which my little ship, with all I treasured most in the world, was heading.

Diana often confided in me too, over many things – including her conflict over duty . . . perhaps that's why I earned the nickname of her 'rock'. She never expressed this to me directly but it was a label attached to me by her friends. Diana did describe me as her 'third eye' and 'Magic Merlin' and Susie Kassem, a close friend of the princess, still calls me Merlin to this day.

I was grounded and happy with my family life, something which always eluded Diana. Once, sitting in my kitchen at Highgrove in the early 1990s, she was searching for a biscuit to go with the black coffee I'd just made her.

'All I've ever wanted is a happy home and a happy family who can put their arms around me and tell me "I love you" and mean it.'

While at Highgrove I was often compromised as the Waleses' marriage disintegrated.

My duty to the prince was total during the week and split between him and the princess at weekends. The prince's valet often reminded me, 'Remember which side your bread is buttered on, Paul. He has the money and he pays the wages.'

But it wasn't as simple as that. I wanted to please both of them, but I was conflicted. Would I go with my head or my heart?

You probably already know the answer to that – my loyalty lay with Princess Diana – it still does.

But my duty to the princess meant that I often neglected my family. The more she needed me, the happier I was. This came at a personal cost as I began to neglect my responsibilities as a husband and a father.

I now realise that I was selfish in life, yet selfless in duty. I missed my boys' formative years – parents' evenings, sports days and bedtime stories. I was missing while their mother carried on, holding everything together. For years after her death, I have carried the baton and flown the flag for Diana.

Even William has said to me, 'You can let go now, Harry and I can take over.'

But still, I can't let go . . . I never grieved her passing. I carried on . . . never sought counselling but now I am reminded, by my sons and my ex-wife, of how they suffered in silence.

. My boys have witnessed far too much. I wish that I could have protected them more. The adult life of their father has been laid bare for all to see. They have defended me to their peers, to teachers and friends and lost friendships because of it. They stood by frightened as their home was raided by the Metropolitan Police. They saw their father recorded by hidden cameras in hotel rooms, duped by a fake sheikh and read my love letters in newspapers. They were bullied and beaten up in the playground. And yet they have accepted my new world with my husband; they have always stood in my corner and supported me. When they needed me to listen to them, I wasn't there. I am so sorry for that. I want to be there for them, their partners and my grandchildren. Going forward, my duty is always to them now. I need to act on this before it is too late.

6

Life at the Palace

While I always felt like I was living the dream being one of the Queen's footmen, it was not an easy job by any means.

Every morning the alarm would ring at 6 a.m. and I would get out of my single bed and draw the curtains in my small room on the top floor of the most famous building in London – Buckingham Palace. I would stare out of the window as dawn broke over the trees in St James's Park, the light catching the gold leaf on Victory raising her laurel high above the Queen Victoria Memorial. I would watch the taxis and cars speeding around its roundabout and hear the guardsmen marching up and down beneath my window four floors below.

I never tired of that view, and neither did my mother; she would sit in the window seat and stare out from this privileged vantage point at the tourists beyond the railings. She often said how lucky she was to have her son 'live' there. I'm sure that she never really understood what I did inside that building. My bedroom was a simple room with just a bed (which doubled as a settee during the day), a wardrobe, a chest of drawers, a television and a sink. I had framed a photo of the Queen and Duke in the Grand Corridor at Windsor Castle from the Silver Jubilee by Peter Grugeon, which hung above my bed. We all shared two bathrooms at the end of the corridor and there was a kitchen in Pages' Lobby where we each had a lockable cupboard to keep food and could prepare light meals instead of going down to the staff canteen, especially when we were off duty. We had the luxury of maids to make and change our beds and clean the rooms.

I lived there for eight years until I married and moved to the Royal Mews next door.

All the footmen had similar rooms. There were twelve household footmen and two Queen's footmen. Some lived on Pages' Lobby with me with similar views on the front of the palace, others looked inward into the red-gravelled courtyard with views of the glass canopy of the state entrance and the adjacent King's door which the Prince of Wales and the Duke of Edinburgh used regularly. The Queen would leave from this door for Trooping the Colour and Prince Philip's converted electric Hackney carriage cab (London taxi) would often be parked there as he used it to slip out into the London traffic unnoticed.

By 6.30 a.m. I would be dressed in my day livery, a black tail-coat, black trousers and shoes, white shirt, black tie and scarlet waistcoat edged with gold braid and emblazoned with gold buttons bearing the E II R cypher.

My first duty of the day was to walk the corgis at 7 a.m. I knew all the shortcuts in the palace such as down the back staircase onto the Prince of Wales's corridor then past Princess Anne's suite down to the Queen's floor, walking very quietly to avoid waking Her Majesty.

I would leash the dogs, take them down the minister's stairs past the giant marble statue of Venus and Mars by Canova and go onto the terrace and the main lawn.

I always felt guilty for not picking up 'corgi mess' – there was too much of it and I didn't have time. The gardeners must have cursed me as I left their immaculate lawn littered with dog poo. Then I would put the dogs back into their room ready for the dresser to take them into the Queen's bedroom at calling time.

Like many animal lovers, the Queen liked having her dogs in the bedroom – even in bed with her. Prince Philip, who did share a bed with his wife, was not so keen and would mumble about 'those bloody dogs', adding 'I don't know why you have to have so many' to which the Queen would respond, 'But darling they are so collectable.'

The Queen had an 8.15 a.m. wake-up call when the maid would bring a calling tray for the Duke of Edinburgh with Darjeeling tea with milk and a rich tea biscuit. The Queen often took the biscuit for the dogs. The Queen only had a cup of Earl Grey tea with milk in bed on Easter morning and Christmas Day – anything more was spoiling, she thought.

She would then go to her dressing room to get ready for breakfast at 9 a.m. when her pipe major played her favourite tunes underneath her window. Have you ever heard 'Happy Birthday' played on the bagpipes? We did every year, on 21 April.

The Queen would never eat a cooked breakfast but only a slice of toast, carefully measured three inches by two inches with the crusts cut off, served hot in a silver toast rack. She would smear butter on with a spoonful of Frank Cooper's coarse-cut vintage Oxford marmalade: her favourite.

Then she would read most of the national newspapers: *The Times*, *Daily Telegraph*, *Daily Express*, *Daily Mail*, *Daily Mirror* and *Sporting Life*, always beginning with *Sporting Life*, to see what was happening in the world while listening to her Roberts Radio. In those days, she would listen to Terry Wogan on Radio 2. She liked him and would giggle at his silly sense of humour. She would then carry the radio back to her room to clean her teeth.

Every morning at 10 a.m., she would ring her mother, Queen Elizabeth, at Clarence House, up to her death in 2002. She would talk to her about the day's duties, what she was doing and where she was going and ask advice as appropriate. She often said to me, 'I'm not really Queen, my mother's still Queen.' The Queen

Mother would always express her wishes to her daughter, which were rarely ignored. The Queen once explained to me how uncomfortable it had been for her when Wallis Simpson died as she had expressed a desire to be buried with her husband, the Duke of Windsor, at the Royal Burial Ground in Frogmore, Windsor. It is well known that the Queen Mother disliked the American divorcee and refused as a senior member of the Royal Family to be at her graveside for her committal. Exasperated by this, the Queen insisted that Charles and Diana accompany her and Philip instead. Although there was nearly no burial at all. I had been walking the dogs in Frogmore Gardens that morning and had noticed that the freshly dug grave had filled with water. After I had informed the Queen of a potential catastrophe, she looked at me and said, 'We will have to do something about that otherwise we will be launching her, not burying her.' The Queen Mother was a formidable woman and she always had the last say. She did not attend the committal and refused to stand beside 'that woman's' grave. She did however attend her funeral in St George's Chapel but insisted that Wallis's name was never spoken during the service.

So Queen Elizabeth the Queen Mother was always queen in her daughter's eyes and it was only when she died that she felt that she could really make her own decisions, even though she was seventy-six years of age by then.

After her call with her mother, she would buzz on a dictograph for her private secretary, who would bring her paperwork and documents to sign and discuss invitations for future engagements.

We would place her daily engagement card on her desk in a silver gilt stand so that she could glance at it at any time to see what she would be doing during that day. She was very punctual and organised, even with everyone around her. She would say to me, 'Paul, you've got to start packing as we are leaving soon.' She would often attend an engagement in the afternoon then be home for tea and to feed her dogs.

Meals were always at the same time and the day was split into compartments around the meals. Breakfast at 9 a.m., lunch at 1 p.m., afternoon tea at 5 p.m. and dinner at 8.15 p.m. Times have changed in that regard. Although breakfast and dinner remain roughly the same for the King, he does not have a formal lunch as he prefers to work through and an extravagant tea has been replaced with a slice of fruit cake. When family or friends are in residence at Sandringham or Balmoral, the King has dispensed with the formalities of waited lunch and tea in favour of the informality of a buffet service where everyone helps themselves.

I would help the Queen feed the dogs at 4 p.m. then she would take them out for a walk. By the time she had undertaken all of her engagements, she had little time left for herself, but she tried to complete the *Telegraph* crossword every day.

The Queen had to change her clothes regularly. She would get up and put one dress on, change for an engagement, get back into her original dress on her return and into another one for the next engagement. She would always change again for dinner. She never bathed in the morning; she was of a generation who only ever bathed in the evening. And she never showered, whereas Prince Philip preferred to shower.

Every Monday afternoon on her return from Windsor to Buckingham Palace, her hairdresser, Mr Charles, would be waiting to give the Queen her weekly shampoo and set. Princess Diana said her one luxury in life was to have her hair washed and blown every morning. The Queen would maintain her hair herself during the week unless she needed to wear a tiara. The hairdresser would have to come in for that as it needed to be set in. Her Majesty slept in a snood to keep her hair in place. She didn't like fuss and bother or extravagance.

The weekly audience with the prime minister of the day to discuss government issues would usually happen on Tuesday evening when Parliament was in session.

From Winston Churchill to Liz Truss, there were fifteen Prime Ministers, some more popular than others. Harold Wilson was a particular favourite and allowed to smoke his pipe in the Queen's presence. Margaret Thatcher was the only woman among men in the early years and followed the Queen's example as a woman in a man's world.

Mrs Thatcher was a monarchist and she was hugely respectful of the Queen. I have never seen anyone curtsy so deeply in reverence to Her Majesty.

She relished her Tuesday-evening audience. She would always arrive early at the King's door inside the quadrangle of Buckingham Palace, be met by the Queen's equerry in waiting in full ceremonial uniform and taken to the private secretary's office. In my day that was Sir Martin Charteris or Sir Philip Moore. Sir William Heseltine and Sir Robert Fellowes would follow. Mrs Thatcher would be offered her favourite tipple – a whisky with a drop of water.

Five minutes later, she would be ascending the spiral staircase which connects the King's door to the Duke of Edinburgh's floor and then onto the Queen's floor where she would be met by the Queen's page. She would then be escorted into the Empire Room, a holding area, while Her Majesty was reading her brief in her sitting room.

Once I was on duty and had the honour of greeting Mrs Thatcher and informing the Queen that the Prime Minister had arrived. She was reading her notes, then she looked up at me and said, 'What colour is she wearing?'

The answer was, 'Blue, Your Majesty.'

The Queen looked down at what she was wearing. She had a blue dress on too.

'I suppose I ought to change,' and with that she disappeared into her dressing room to summon her dresser.

Five minutes later, the Queen re-appeared in red. Mrs Thatcher was being entertained by the equerry and was told that Her Majesty was ready. Mrs Thatcher always sat opposite her and would balance precariously on the edge of her chair in a rather uncomfortable way. Some of the other prime ministers would sit beside her on the settee in a more relaxed fashion.

The private audience was never recorded or witnessed once the door was closed. It was the Queen and her minister talking candidly and openly, something that the Queen rarely did.

A red flag would drop into a box in Pages' Lobby to indicate that the audience was over. The equerry would lead the prime minister back out of the palace and the Queen would return to her sitting room, to her dogs and her world, and move on to her next task.

She never spoke of what happened during those meetings. She knew that it was to be kept private and her ministers knew that too.

I met Mrs Thatcher on many occasions. She was always polite and courteous but there were times when I saw conflict between my working life and duty and my family life, especially during the miners' strike. I didn't always agree with her policies but I had to be impartial and get on with my job. She would always ask after my health and my family; many others didn't. She bobbed down the corridor in an almost reticent way to her weekly encounters, proud to be prime minister. The last time I saw her was aboard the *QE2* for a lunch to commemorate the Falklands War in 2002 where she and her daughter, Carol, were guests of honour. Sadly, by this time, she was suffering from dementia and throughout the lunch would stand up to say, 'We fought them on land, on sea, and in the air!'

'Not now, Mummy,' Carol would say. She was her steadfast support and always beside her in her later years. Much the same as Mary Wilson, who never left Harold Wilson's side at the Garter lunch in the Waterloo Chamber in Windsor Castle. I saw him in his dark blue Garter robes and he said in a loud voice, 'Is the Queen coming to lunch?'

She was sat halfway down the table; he was oblivious to her presence.

Away from the Royals, downstairs routines in the palace were not dissimilar to those on the *Titanic* – this was a world where time stood still: a bubble where everyone knew their place, unaffected by the outside world. The attitude was very much 'carry on' and 'if it isn't broken then it doesn't need fixing'.

We would eat our meals at odd times to avoid clashing with serving the Royals upstairs. Food sometimes came from the Royal estates. The Queen only ate something light for her lunch. Her favourite was lamb chops or calf liver and onions. She also enjoyed venison from Balmoral and salmon from the River Dee for dinner. She loved home-grown produce. You have no idea how many jars of jam and honey she was sent by people. She was often gifted the first prizes at the Royal agricultural shows. All were incorporated into the meals that she had.

Each year on her annual visit to Helmingham Hall, the moated manor house in Suffolk and home of the Tollemache family, Lady Tollemache would give the Queen a jar of quince jelly made from fruit grown in her garden. This jar appeared on the table every teatime, whichever residence Her Majesty was in. This meant carrying the jar around the world at times until it was finished.

Twice a week, the burgundy leather-bound menu book would arrive on the Queen's desk containing choices, written in French by the head chef, for lunch and dinner menus for the next few days. A choice of three starters, three main courses and three puddings for each meal. The Queen would scratch out the things that she didn't want, leaving behind the things that she did. This tradition was carried out in all royal households, including that of Princess Diana.

The head chef had a good idea of what the Queen liked – simple, traditional food.

Her favourite pudding (the Queen would always say 'pudding' and not 'dessert' or 'sweet') was a crème de menthe bombe: mint flavoured ice cream filled with grated chocolate and decorated with Bendicks Bittermints. She used to say that her downfall was cheese, which was only ever served at lunchtime. She always gave it up for Lent as one of her favourite things.

All dairy products like milk and butter came from the Royal Dairy within the Home Park at Windsor. Every day dozens of bottles of milk, emblazoned with the Queen's cypher, and wax cartons of double cream would be driven up the motorway from Windsor to London so that the Queen could have a drop of milk in her tea from her own herd.

The Queen did not like garlic or heavily spiced food although she would have a curry as long as it was not too hot. I don't think she ever had a McDonald's or a pizza! On foreign visits, she would take Imodium with her . . . just in case. Her private medical officer, Surgeon Captain Norman Blacklock, would also accompany her as a member of the royal party.

On occasion, she was presented with inedible foods. I was with her on the South Pacific island of Tuvalu; we were all sat cross-legged on rush matting when she was presented with a monkey's brain. No, she did not eat it.

The Queen had the art of diplomacy down to a tee. I watched as she cut it up as if she was about to eat it and move it around her plate to give the impression that she had tried the dish. She never did. Another time she was presented with a traditional kava kava drink by a group of Maori; she tipped it towards her lips but did not drink it.

Etiquette and manners were not just the preserve of a queen. As we sailed around the South Pacific on board the Royal Yacht *Britannia*, the Queen entertained dignitaries from various islands. At a state banquet, she stared bemused at a Tongan prince who had no idea what to do with a crystal bowl of water placed in front of him on the dessert service. The bowl was intended to be used to rinse his fingers after eating the fruit, but as the fruit was passed around the table, he created a fruit soup in the bowl, topped off with cream and sugar. Only when he raised the bowl to his lips did he notice the Queen smiling at him and realised that he had made a faux pas. Instantly, the Queen lifted her bowl and took a sip from it to make him feel at ease. That is diplomacy at its finest.

Wherever the Queen went in the world, she never drank local water. She didn't even drink water from the tap in Buckingham Palace. She always drank Malvern water. I had a special case made with compartments to hold twelve bottles of Malvern water which went with her everywhere on tour. She even cleaned her teeth in bottled water as she couldn't afford to be ill.

Royals also avoid shellfish. One bad mussel or oyster could put a Royal out of action for days.

But of course, the Queen did fall ill on occasion. She would rarely cancel an engagement but would try and battle through. She had several doctors who would attend her immediately as required.

Afternoon tea was a simple affair at Buckingham Palace but always much grander at Balmoral and Sandringham where it was a social event and everyone was expected to attend. The household footmen would set the table with the Queen's favourite china – the service edged with tartan or the one decorated with wild strawberries. A silver Victorian spirit kettle would be placed at the head of the table where Her Majesty sat to enable her to make the tea. The table would be groaning with food: cucumber sandwiches on white bread, cheese sandwiches on brown bread, crumpets, potted shrimps, Langes de Chat dipped in chocolate, a large Dundee or Victoria sponge cake in the middle – although chocolate cake (Sachertorte) was the Queen's favourite. Warm scones (which she would pronounce 'scon') were nestled in a white napkin folded like a water lily and there would always be 'jam pennies' – white bread and butter smeared with strawberry jam cut into the size of an old fashioned penny. The Queen eats bread and jam? was my first thought, but they were a reminder of teatime in the nursery which she shared with her sister, Princess Margaret.

Every Sunday afternoon when William was at Eton, he would walk up to Windsor Castle and have afternoon tea with his granny. It was during those meetings that she taught him the art of kingship: Queen Elizabeth was preparing William for what is to come.

The Queen loved having guests to visit her. When Ronald and Nancy Reagan came to stay on a state visit to England, I looked after them in the 240 Lancaster Suite in Windsor Castle. Before their arrival, the Queen called me into the Oak Room where she was looking down into the quadrangle at a cavalcade of cars. 'Look at all these people,' she said. 'They are all from the president's secret service team and have come to check that the castle is safe for him. I have already told them that if it is safe enough for me, why isn't it safe enough for the president of the United States?' She was most indignant but understood the protocol that lay behind it. After the visit, the Queen asked me twenty questions.

'Well?' she said. 'Tell me what they were like in private.'

She was inquisitive.

'You will be delighted to know that they are devoted to each other and often sat on the settee holding hands.'

The Queen was surprised that her judgement had been correct.

'He even gave me a jar of his presidential jelly beans and a belt buckle!' I said.

'How very kind of him.' She chuckled.

The Queen rarely lost her temper but when she did – it was of biblical proportions. With one look over the top of her half-rimmed spectacles, everyone knew to hide! Being caught in her crossfire wasn't advisable. Unfortunately those closest to her bore the brunt and there was no way but to deal with it head on. Hurricane Elizabeth took no prisoners.

Annie Leibovitz was invited to take Her Majesty's portrait at Buckingham Palace. The picture gallery had originally been chosen as a backdrop. Annie wanted the Queen to be posed on her horse in the picture gallery as if riding out for Trooping the Colour. The Queen greeted the suggestion with one word: 'ridiculous'. That idea was scrapped in favour of the White Drawing Room, where the Queen would wear evening dress, garter robes and a diadem. 'Far more tasteful,' she said.

But the thought of asking her to pose on a horse in the picture gallery had set the hares running. It was not going to be an easy appointment for anyone.

Even on entering the photoshoot, she was in a foul mood. Then she spotted several members of Annie's family waiting in the line-up to meet her.

'No one asked or told me about this,' she whispered under her breath.

She greeted everyone civilly as she always did, but continued to mutter.

The final straw came as Annie asked the Queen, 'Can you remove your crown please?'

The dam burst.

'It is not a crown – it's a diadem. Do you know how long it takes to put it on?'

The Queen does not take off her crown or her diadem or even disrobe in front of a camera. The photoshoot was fraught with problems and the press caught wind of it.

The headlines read, 'The Queen storms out.'

The truth was that the Queen had actually stormed *in*, but the results of the photoshoot were beautiful. The images were the best in a long time.

Of course there was another portrait that was more regrettable. In 2005, to celebrate the Queen's eightieth birthday, the gregarious TV personality Rolf Harris was commissioned to paint her official painting.

He had two face-to-face sittings with her in the Yellow Drawing Room at Buckingham Palace over the summer. It was the focus of a BBC TV programme documenting its creation. The oil painting then hung in the Queen's Gallery at Buckingham Palace for six months before it was moved to Liverpool's Walker Art Gallery in 2012.

Harris had also provided BBC Radio 2 with the commentary for Charles and Diana's wedding at St Paul's Cathedral in 1981. I met him and his wife Alwen at several charity events. She was lovely, with her hair in braids. He was always charming and polite to us, but we later learned that he was a monster, hiding in plain sight.

After the Jimmy Savile sexual abuse scandal, Harris was arrested in 2013 as part of Operation Yewtree regarding historical allegations of sexual offences.

Harris was convicted the following year of the sexual assault of four underage girls, which effectively ended his career. He was released on licence in 2017 after serving nearly three years of his sentence at HM Prison Stafford. He died from neck cancer aged ninety-three in 2023.

As for the painting, it has vanished. It is not in the Royal Collection and the BBC insist that they do not have it either. To be honest, knowing what we know now about the artist, perhaps it is better that it is lost for good.

If the Queen wasn't entertaining and she and Prince Philip were alone, they would often watch the small television in the dining room surrounded by Stubbs paintings. The Queen enjoyed *Dad's Army*, *Morecambe and Wise* and crime detective shows, and the weather forecast was a must – particularly when presented by Tomasz Schafernaker. She also loved watching horse racing and races involving her horses were taped on VHS so that she could watch them back. She had copious amounts of books and charts on horses and kept a record of the lineage of every horse that she had owned. She knew the exact bloodline of each horse. She was very invested. The Queen was delighted when Will Farish, the owner of Lane's End Farm in Kentucky who had reared all her yearlings and kept her brood mares, became the American ambassador in London. She would visit Lexington, Kentucky every year to see their progress and I was once asked to go into the stables with her to watch a 'marriage' for breeding. That was the most embarrassing situation I think I've ever been in with the Queen. Once ready, the stallion climbs several steps to be presented to the mare. It is over in seconds. The Queen watched everything to see if it was done properly. She was fascinated by it! On one such visit, I was taking the Queen's breakfast tray down a large marble staircase when I lost my footing and found myself in a heap at the bottom of the stairs covered in marmalade and cold tea. Alarmed by the noise, the Queen peered over the balcony in her night dress and said, 'Are you all right?' to which I replied, 'I don't think I am. I can't feel my legs.' I had ruptured my spine and was rushed to the nearest hospital to have emergency surgery. After the operation, I awoke to find Lord Porchester, the Queen's racing manager, sat at my bedside. 'You are a very lucky man,' he said. 'The Queen intervened and insisted that you had the best surgeon operate on you immediately. Any delay and you would have been paralysed from the waist down.' The Queen returned home from Kentucky and left me to recover from my operation for the next two weeks, after which she sent her brand-new BAe 146 jet fitted out as a hospital so that I could travel home in comfort. That whole episode cost in excess of $250,000, which was paid for entirely by the Queen.

As the most travelled monarch in British history, planes, boats and trains featured heavily in the Queen's life – the Queen's Flight, the Royal Yacht *Britannia* and the Royal Train. The Queen loved visiting the far reaches of the United Kingdom and meeting her subjects. These were called 'away days', often involving the Royal Train. Imagine fourteen carriages in purple livery, each with the Royal coat of arms, weaving their way through the countryside. I loved the overnight train journeys just as much as Her Majesty did. The dresser and I would leave Buckingham Palace late on a Thursday evening bound for platform one at Euston station an hour earlier than the Queen to prepare the train for her arrival. My first task would be to unpack the pillow bag and place a clean linen pillow slip with its embroidered royal cypher on the duck feather pillow for her single bed. Then we would unpack the Queen's clothes, including the outfit she would wear for the following day's engagement and her pink mule slippers. I would then concentrate on her on-board sitting room and unpack her magazines, newspapers and crosswords, as well as a selection of sweets, before placing bottles of Malvern water in her bedroom, bathroom and sitting room. Here particularly I felt an integral and personal part of the Queen's team. Shortly after midnight, the train would depart for a corner of the Queen's realm. The dresser would run her bath and put a hot water bottle in her bed. After breakfast the following morning, the Queen would dress and appear in her sitting room shortly before alighting from the train. 'Is there anybody there?' she would say as the train pulled into the station. The train would stop with the door of the Queen's carriage exactly in the line with the red carpet and she would alight to much cheering from the large crowds.

These away days gave the Queen an insight into her country and the people in every corner of it. Fascinated by regional accents, she would absorb the various dialects like a sponge and at times during the weekend following, I would hear a Scouse, Welsh or Scottish accent coming from her direction as she regaled her household with stories of her adventures.

My interest in my former employer has led me to have my own adventure. Like many, I am fascinated by my ancestry, so remembering what my grandfather had told me about his father being a farmer in Bardney in Lincolnshire, my son Nicholas and I travelled there to find out more.

For generations – at least since 1600 – the Burrell family have been born, married and buried in this area. During the Second World War, it was the location of many air bases, which means much history and heritage was destroyed by bombing. The local parish church took a direct hit when a parachute bomb wrapped itself around the spire and detonated, causing valuable church records to be lost and turning graves to rubble.

Our search was difficult until we found a church warden who had knowledge of our family. She directed us to South Ormsby, where we found our ancestral home. Standing in the hallway of this mansion, I looked up at the family portraits and saw my great great aunt, Elizabeth, who had married into the Massingberd-Mundy family, and instantly recognised the family resemblance.

The current owners kindly showed us the estate and told us that in 1649, when a member of the family was a Member of Parliament in Lincolnshire, he refused to sign the death warrant of King Charles I. It was odd to think that those royalist genes survived through the years down to a man who served both a queen and a king. But that's not where the connection ends as it reminded me of something which happened during my service to Her Majesty Queen Elizabeth II, King Charles III's mother.

'You'll never guess what someone sent me today,' the Queen said while doling out dog biscuits at feeding time. 'Have a look. There's a letter on my desk. Come on, go and get it and read it.'

I went through the dining room into her sitting room to her desk in the middle of the bow window.

'Did you find it?' she shouted. 'Oh, Smoky, do stop doing that,' I heard her saying.

Her desk was always a mess piled high with correspondence and stacked with government boxes.

'It's got a piece of Sellotape attached to the corner,' she shouted.

I found it and brought it back to the dog feeding station in the corridor.

'Well, go on. Read it out aloud,' she said excitedly.

The letter was from a lady whose ancestor was standing in the crowd when King Charles I walked out onto the scaffolding erected outside the banqueting room in Whitehall in 1649. The letter went on to describe the scene.

'At the moment the axe lopped off his head,' the lady wrote, 'a piece of his collar bone splintered and flew out into the crowd and my ancestor caught it. It has been passed down in my family and I have no one to pass it on to. So I thought, Your Majesty, that you might like it.'

And there it was: a piece of bone sellotaped to a letter. The bone of a king more than 350 years old.

'Quite extraordinary, isn't it?' the Queen said. 'What should we do with it?'

The corgis looked up at us, wishing the bone was theirs.

'Why don't you give it back to its owner?' I suggested.

'Oh, good idea. Let's take it to Windsor with us at the weekend.' So that's exactly what we did.

'Could you ask the Dean of Windsor to come up for a cup of tea?' the Queen said that Sunday afternoon. She then, to his astonishment, tore the piece of bone from the letter and charged him with returning it to its rightful owner.

'Do tell me what you find,' she said to him.

The following weekend, he returned with a tale to tell.

'We went down into the crypt, Your Majesty, at St George's Chapel, and looked along the shelves. We passed the Georges and the Jameses and the queens and their children. Some of the coffins were so tiny. Eventually we found Charles I and Charles II. We took the coffin of Charles I down from its shelf, put it on a trestle table and carefully prised open the lid, and there he was, his face hidden underneath a muslin veil, perfectly preserved as he had been embalmed and someone had kindly sewn his head back onto his shoulders.'

'How very kind,' the Queen said solemnly.

The dean continued, 'The bone is now with its owner, Your Majesty.'

'I'm so glad,' the Queen responded before making polite small talk. The conversation switched from the surreal to the real – mission accomplished.

Away from returning ancient relics to their owners, there was always an interest in the gardens of the various palaces. Gardening was a passion of not only Prince Charles but the Queen too. Her Majesty would regularly be seen deadheading the roses in the gardens at Buckingham Palace and on the East Terrace sunken garden at Windsor Castle. She particularly loved scented roses of all colours and would instruct her head gardener, Mark Lane, to plant her favourites.

In the spring, the King's border facing her apartments at Buckingham Palace would be planted with regiments of tall multi-coloured tulips, sections of colour all labelled in their varieties, and she took pleasure in walking her dogs beside them. Her favourite was 'Queen of the Night', a tall dark purple flower which commanded attention. I now plant them in pots at my home in Cheshire. The Queen's favourite flower, though, was lily of the valley and those 'in the know' sent them for Her Majesty's birthday on 21 April. They reminded her of purity and simplicity. They were included in Catherine's bouquet when she married William in 2012.

Of course my life was very different when I went to work at Highgrove for Prince Charles and Princess Diana. Most of the time they lived quite separate lives, but the house would come alive at weekends when the Wales family was complete. The staff swelled with the addition of a chauffeur, a dresser and two back-up policemen.

Everyone preferred it when Charles wasn't around as Diana tended to be more relaxed. She would host barbecues to which all the staff would be invited and we would tuck into Magnum ice creams for pudding. The garden would be scattered with miniature tractors, cars, swings and slides, and had a purpose-built sandpit and open-air swimming pool. One of the princess's favourite games was to push everyone into the swimming pool fully clothed at the end of a barbecue. She would have her sons giggling in hysterics as they swam around with the entire household staff. She called it 'human soup'.

And my role changed again when I was the butler for Diana at Kensington Palace. I became a Jack of all trades then.

Every Monday morning would start at 4 a.m. with a visit to the flower market at Nine Elms to bring home the blooms and plants for the week. I would be back at Kensington Palace by 6.30 a.m. in time to see the boss leave, driving herself to the Harbour Club for a workout at the gym.

By the time I had arranged the flowers in her bedroom and dressing room – stargazer lilies (her favourite), scented stock, lily of the valley and freesias, but never carnations or chrysanthemums – and set the table for breakfast, she would be back and our day would begin. I would always stand to attention, bow and say,

'Good morning, Your Royal Highness.' She would giggle nervously and say, 'Please stop doing that.'

Breakfast was easy. She would usually eat half a grapefruit and drink a black coffee followed by a spoon of honey which she would pop into her mouth and suck like a lollipop.

While I served the Queen at Buckingham Palace, I always knew my territory and where the line was in the sand. With Diana it was different. She would invite me over the line and treat me – in private at least – as an equal. I always tried to remain professional and I knew my place – though others observing the scene may not have understood that.

Years later when I met with William, he said to me, 'Mummy drew you too close to her, Paul. It wasn't fair to do that. We won't do that with our household.'

It may have made some people jealous, and it certainly confused them.

But I was always there, and I experienced the highs and lows of whatever came my way.

As the years rolled by, I began travelling overseas with the princess. Sometimes she was without a dresser or a lady-in-waiting, and some people considered it most unusual for Diana to have a male companion travelling with her and in an adjoining room.

I remember stepping out of the shower once, totally naked, to find Diana in my room. She looked me up and down, giggled and asked me for a bottle of water.

I always travelled with water and a bunch of bananas – which she loved. There seemed to be no barrier between our worlds in those private moments.

7

Conflict – Diana at War

L et's make this quite clear. Diana *never* wanted a divorce.
She accepted the fact that she and Charles could no longer
live together so a separation was necessary, but not a divorce.
Despite everything that happened, I have no doubt that Diana fell
in love with Prince Charles. Unfortunately for Diana, the feeling
was not mutual. Diana once told me that Charles had told her in
the middle of one of their epic arguments, 'I never loved you. I
only married you to have children.'

Having been brought up in a divorced and dysfunctional family
in a cavernous home, Althorp (pronounced Alltrop), she didn't
want her boys to suffer the same fate.

She told me, 'It will be far better for William and Harry to have
a family – two parents.'

No one who watched the fairy-tale marriage in July 1981, when
a beautiful lady in a white dress with a huge train walked up the
aisle towards her prince, would have expected it to end this way.

In fact, many of the staff had no idea how bad relations were between the Prince and Princess of Wales. I certainly didn't. I didn't
realise that I had entered a war zone when I reached Highgrove
House in Gloucestershire in 1987. I had made the decision to leave
my happy life with the Queen at Buckingham Palace for the good
of my family.

Her Majesty had assured me that I would be back in Buckingham Palace again when Charles and Diana became king and queen, so even she could not have predicted how things would end up between them.

Just six years into Diana's marriage to the heir to the throne, the battle of the Waleses was raging in plain sight.

It made my job incredibly hard and it wasn't easy planning my daily routines between Prince Charles and his world and Princess Diana and hers, especially with the added influence of Camilla Parker-Bowles.

The princess made the journey from apartments 8 and 9 Kensington Palace every Friday after school for a family weekend at their country house, driving with her personal protection officer Ken Wharfe beside her. Diana was a city girl. She disliked country pursuits: horses, shooting, mud and particularly hunting which she thought was barbaric.

Whereas Mrs Parker-Bowles thought they were attractive parts of everyday life. She was a country girl at heart and shared Prince Charles's passions wholeheartedly; he loved that they hunted together.

But Diana tried so hard to please her husband. I remember her returning from her first stalking party on the moors at Balmoral, her face covered in blood. She hated every moment of it, from crawling around face down in the heather stalking that majestic beast to shooting it with her ghillie. Then watching its belly being slit with the entrails coming out and the blood smeared on her face – being blooded for the first time was a ritual performed on your first kill. She was disgusted by it. She did it for Charles – to fit in, to be accepted, not only by him but by the family, but she never did it again.

She thought it was her duty to Prince Charles to join in the tradition and put up with everything. But she had entered a bloodied world and she was as innocent and defenceless as the poor stag she had slain – and there were plenty in the Royal Household who would happily have put the knife in. Diana was an outsider and not to be trusted.

Members of the Royal Household had told her to 'be quiet and shut up' so it is no wonder that she felt like she had no voice.

She confided in me when we first met at Balmoral in 1980, 'I think I'm out of my depth.' It was an odd statement to make, as Diana was a descendant of King Charles I and of aristocratic lineage.

She hadn't yet learned the rules of engagement. It would take her a while to establish herself. Charles's duty was to choose a wife, have children and secure the Windsor dynasty. He had known Diana Spencer for most of her life. She had grown up on the royal estate at Sandringham as part of one of the grandest aristocratic families and dynasties in England. She subsequently lived at Althorp in Northamptonshire, her ancestral home. Johnny Spencer, her father, was heir to the family estate at Althorp and would be Earl Spencer one day. His three daughters, Sarah, Jane and Diana, were all titled ladies and were among the most eligible in the land. Diana knew what was expected of her as wife of the future king because duty, respect and loyalty ran through her DNA.

The Spencer family were highly regarded by the Royal Family so it wasn't a surprise to anyone when Charles began dating a Spencer girl. But it wasn't Diana, it was Sarah initially.

Despite having spent barely any time together, Lady Diana Spencer was the choice for the prince. He proposed on 6 February 1981 at Windsor Castle. Diana would later say that she had only met him thirteen times before they became engaged.

'He never wanted a lover, he wanted a mother,' Diana told me.

She always loved Charles, come what may, but she despised Camilla Parker-Bowles, the 'other woman' who was constantly in Diana's life.

'Did you see me on my wedding day walking down the aisle of St Paul's Cathedral?' she said to me one day.

'Of course I did,' I replied.

'You saw me looking from side to side. You know what I was doing, don't you? I was looking for Camilla. And there she was, on my wedding day. Even on my wedding day. As I reached the altar, I knew that she would always be there. It was the proudest day of my father's life. He never thought that he could do it as he was recovering from a stroke.' She stopped short of saying that it was her proudest moment too.

I remember that day well. Tall Paul was sat behind the Queen on the carriage drive to St Paul's Cathedral. I was on duty with the Queen in her apartments with Christopher, her page. As she left for the wedding, dressed in blue, the Queen said to me, 'Watch the wedding on my television and then you'll know when we're coming back.'

She was always very practical.

So I took nine corgis for a walk around the lake in the garden and hurried back to watch the rest of the ceremony on the Queen's television in her sitting room.

I will never forget thinking how creased Diana's dress looked on her arrival at St Paul's, but it was still magnificent. I was witnessing the future of the monarchy, our queen in waiting ... or so I thought. I waited at the end of the Queen's corridor for Her Majesty to return from the balcony appearance but it wasn't Her Majesty who appeared first; it was the new Princess of Wales.

Her train rolled up into a ball under one arm and her wedding slippers in her hand, she was running barefoot towards me, her satin dress billowing like the sails of a majestic galleon. The sunlight was streaming through the windows on the Duke of Edinburgh's corridor, and her diamond Spencer tiara was sparkling. She was radiant, filled with love and hope for the future. But she confided in me that inside she was a mess: 'My stomach was tied up in knots.'

I said to her, 'You may not remember, but I actually served you your wedding breakfast on that day in the ball supper room. There were twenty round tables. Mine was the Queen's table and you were sitting on it. You didn't eat or drink anything.'

'I know,' she said. 'I couldn't, Paul. It was all too much to take in. At times I thought I was going to faint.'

She thought like any newlywed bride that she could change her husband. She thought that she was a power for good and that he would turn away from previous loves, be faithful and fulfil his marriage vows.

How wrong she was.

While Charles was still a bachelor he had desired a country house of his own, despite knowing that he would one day inherit Sandringham and Balmoral. That would be long into the future. He looked for a suitable country house within striking distance of Bolehyde Manor where the Parker-Bowles family lived. He found Highgrove House in Tetbury before he had decided to marry Diana, but he gave her free rein to decorate it and furnish the interiors in her own style. With the help of her designer friend Dudley Poplak, she chose a very Laura Ashley palette of floral and chintzy aesthetics. That was all the rage in the 1980s.

Charles might have given full control to Diana but he did visit the California store within Home Park at Windsor Castle, where there is a vast repository of antique furniture collected over the centuries – an Aladdin's cave of antiques. He chose a few pieces to be sent to his country home and also borrowed some fine silver from the collection at Buckingham Palace for daily use. Diana railed against his wishes and bought a collection of stainless steel cutlery from John Lewis and a set of everyday china from Thomas Goode which she and the boys would use in the nursery. After all, she wanted to give her sons as normal a life as possible.

Of course, her husband had been raised in the nursery on the second floor of Buckingham Palace, spending his early years with his siblings and nannies away from his parents. When the Queen did go to the nursery it was more like a formal state visit at an appointed time. As a result of this, Diana vowed that an isolated nursery wouldn't be appropriate for her children, even though Charles wanted everything to stay the same. He even wanted his old nanny, Mabel Anderson, to look after his children. Diana had different ideas and won that particular battle. The nursery would be part of their household and they would have access at all times.

William arrived on 21 June 1982. They hadn't even been married a year and Diana was still finding her way in the Royal Family, in her marriage and in her life.

Charles mistakenly took her mood swings for post-natal depression but she was unhappy, even in these early days. Meanwhile Charles had achieved his goal, a son and heir, and that was paramount for him. Diana told me that it came at a price – her own wellbeing.

Her baby, whom she loved dearly, had become the full focus of attention. This was the moment when Diana realised that she would have to fight for her survival. It wasn't until Harry was born on 15 September 1984, some two years later, that her fate was confirmed.

Charles came into the hospital room, looked in the cot and said, 'Oh, red hair.'

Diana replied, 'But Charles, you know that's the Spencer gene, we all have red hair.'

Then came the damning blow: he said, 'Well at least I've got my heir and spare now and I can return to Camilla.'

She told me, 'I cried myself to sleep that night knowing that my marriage was over and that he'd gone back to Camilla. Four years, Paul, I gave him four good years and he was gone. And for the rest of the time I had to pretend and put on a façade for the world, act as if nothing was wrong.'

Years later, in the autumn of 2017, I would come face to face with Harry and William in their mother's old apartments 8 and 9 at Kensington Palace and I would tell them what their mother had said to me. They asked me when and where I thought it had gone wrong with their parents.

And I said I thought it was at that moment.

Harry stared straight at me, poker faced. He couldn't believe what I was telling him. I was in floods of tears but he never flinched. I remember this moment distinctly because it looked like he was bearing his mother's pain. I think it was the first time that he had heard that story.

I said, 'Harry, it's the truth. I wouldn't tell you that unless it was exactly what your mother told me. And I think you know that. You're old enough to know that now.'

I think this bombshell, understandably, was difficult for the princes to hear.

This happened just before Harry became engaged to Meghan. I think that powered him, and put fuel in his tanks to go forward with everything that he felt. It may have contributed to what happened after and is probably the reason he called his book *Spare*.

People didn't know that I had contact with William and Harry long after the death of the princess. I was grateful that the boys reached out to me. I could fill in the gaps for them, especially during the years when they were at boarding school. I still loved them; they were Diana's boys.

William told me, 'Harry and I always knew that Mummy was safe because she came home to you. When we were at school, we knew that she was OK as you were watching out for her.'

He added, 'There are three people sat here right now who truly loved our mother.'

William recognised the fact that I did love his mother, and I was touched that he acknowledged this.

He said, 'I wish you could have run things through us and done things differently.'

I told him how I couldn't get to him in those 'wilderness years'. They were in their father's world and I wasn't allowed anywhere near them as it was felt that I might sway them by telling them the whole story. Instead, Diana's name was not spoken and she was being erased from royal life.

Even in death Diana caused conflict for Charles.

But when she was alive, she knew she had to balance being a dutiful wife to Charles, a Princess of Wales to the Royal Family and the country and a mother to her boys. She tried her best to be everything to everybody.

Of course, I had moved to Highgrove and the Waleses for the good of my family. My two boys, Alexander and Nicholas, virtually grew up in the royal nursery on the top floor of Highgrove House and the rooms within apartments 8 and 9 at Kensington Palace.

Diana once said, 'We will be one big happy family as William, Harry and I will be there every weekend.'

I often found myself serving sausages and baked beans to the two princes and my two boys who were similar in age and had common ground. They had birthday parties together throughout the years and day trips to Alton Towers, Thorpe Park and Bristol Zoo were commonplace.

I will never forget my youngest son, Nicholas, wandering alone through the kitchen garden and the long meadow which led to the front door of Highgrove when he brushed past a suited and booted Prince Charles in black tie as he was leaving for a public engagement.

'Oh, you look smart, Prince Charles. Are you going somewhere nice?' he enquired as he bounded through the door and up the stairs.

'I am so sorry about that, Your Royal Highness,' I said.

'He's a strong, spirited young fellow,' the prince responded.

The lines between butler and father were beginning to blur.

In the mornings at Highgrove, I waited for Prince Charles to appear for breakfast where he would be served a freshly boiled egg cooked for exactly four minutes.

He was obsessed with his eggs being perfect so I would be on guard to say, 'He's coming. Put one in.' Sometimes we would misjudge the timing and there would be false alarms when we thought he was coming but he wasn't, so there could be several eggs in the bin by the time he appeared. Talk about waste – it was madness.

To vent his frustrations and displeasure, the King's spidery scrawl in the form of a memorandum, often in red ink, would land on my desk in the butler's pantry at Highgrove. Once he sent me one such memo asking that I cancel the *Sunday Times* as he didn't want to see it in the house again! He also wanted the tabloids cancelled and said that if anyone – including the princess – wanted to read them they would have to source them themselves. Needless to say, Princess Diana did want to read the tabloids, especially the Sundays, and I would squirrel a selection into my pantry where she would read them in private.

On one occasion, I was summoned to the library for a meeting with the Prince of Wales. I was there in a flash, remembering the princess's words as I ran to see what Charles wanted.

'Run, Paul, run! You don't run that fast for me,' she would say with a giggle.

I walked across the rush-matting floor, which Wendy the housekeeper had to water once a week to stop it becoming too brittle. The prince was sitting at his desk behind an explosion of lilies, his favourite, the scent filling the air.

'Close the door behind you,' he said in a stern voice. Not 'good morning', as his welcome often was.

'Did you speak with the princess last night?'

'Yes, I did, Your Royal Highness. Why? She rang late at 10 p.m.

and wanted to speak with you but I couldn't find you as you must have been out.'

I suddenly realised that I'd had the audacity to presume that he wasn't in the building.

'Why did you say that I was out, Paul?'

His temper was beginning to flare.

'Because you were out, Your Royal Highness,' I answered.

'Why couldn't you just say that you couldn't find me?'

He was beginning to turn puce. I was snookered. Perhaps I shouldn't have been so honest. 'Are you asking me to lie for you?' I said, knowing that almost everyone else around him did from time to time.

The prince replied, 'Yes, I am. Yes, I bloody am.'

His voice was angry as he stood and banged the desk with his fists. He was behaving like a petulant child, shouting, 'I will be king of this country one day and you WILL do as I say!'

He picked up a book from his desk and threw it towards me.

'Get out, get out,' he screamed. I dodged the book, exited the room and stood for a few seconds on the other side of the door, my heart in my mouth. I was caught in the crossfire, caught in the line of duty. My cards were marked. My world was beginning to implode. I felt sick. What would happen now? What about my job, my home, my family? How would this conflict impact my life? Nobody was irreplaceable and it seemed that I had fallen from grace.

I never had problems like this with the Queen. My duty with her was clear. I knew what was expected of me. But then, she wasn't needy or insecure like her son.

I never had a conflict personally with where my duty lay when I was at Highgrove; it seemed clear to me at the time – my loyalty would always be with Diana. And she in turn performed her duty by playing happy families and persevering for another ten years, even though it was clear to everyone that her marriage was over.

She stayed silent during those years, turning to her eating

disorder, bulimia, to help with the pain. She would call it 'my old friend', explaining that 'my old friend understands me. It's where I go to control my feelings.'

She suffered and was being squashed into the ground as the war raged on. She was complaining to the Queen and Prince Philip and getting messages of support. They were writing to her and taking her side. People don't realise they supported Diana against their own son. They said they knew who Charles was. They knew that he was spoiled and could be petulant and had a temper. They knew what was going on behind the scenes and they felt compassion for her. They were exasperated by the problems their son was creating and couldn't understand why they couldn't make their marriage work. Prince Philip wrote to the princess and said that neither he nor the Queen could understand why Charles would prefer Camilla over her and went on to be even more damning by saying that they did not agree with either Charles or Diana having extra-marital affairs.

During a conversation I had with the Queen shortly after the death of the princess in 1997, the Queen was very forthright and told me, 'I did try and reach out to Diana but I didn't always succeed.'

'Could I be so bold as to say, Your Majesty that you spoke to the princess in black and white and the princess spoke in colour.' I always thought that there was a subtle difference.

And despite the support of her in-laws, it was not enough. Diana had to take matters into her own hands.

'Paul, could you give me a hand with something heavy?' she said one weekend at Kensington Palace in 1988. She led me into the master bedroom. 'Help me push this' – pointing to a large chest of drawers – 'over there in front of this doorway.'

It was the door to the prince's dressing room and bathroom. My duty as butler was being compromised. I said to her, 'Does His Royal Highness know about this?'

'Not yet but he'll soon find out,' she replied.

For me this was shocking behaviour. I wasn't used to going into the marital bedroom and I felt uncomfortable. I had no reason to go in there but she took me in because she wanted this chest of drawers to go across the door. She was metaphorically and physically blocking the way to her marital bed.

I thought, Oh my goodness, this is just madness. I had not realised that it had come to this.

That night the prince was furious and there was much plate smashing. From then on, he slept in his dressing room in a single bed whenever he came to London. Of course he hated it. It felt like a demotion. After all, he was the Prince of Wales. But he never came back into the marital bed. In fact, that bed was sent back to the California store and Diana asked her interior designer to make her a new bed which would be hers. It wasn't a Victorian bed but a modern bed for her new life. After a while the prince stopped coming to stay.

In a way she was shedding a skin and trying to move forward without him. Diana secured her position on the battlefield with that move. There were many battles fought and she often had to retreat, wounded, to regroup to fight another day. Her troops were small and ill-equipped and were often caught in the crossfire.

Perhaps I shouldn't have been so clear as to where my loyalties lay.

The Prince of Wales would often swim in the outdoor pool at Highgrove and sometimes Tigga and Pooh, his Jack Russells, would join him. Crouching at the front door drying the dogs, only inches away from me, he said, 'Are you happy here, Paul? I have noticed that at times you are somewhat melancholy.' I had no idea how to reply. Of course I was concerned about Princess Diana's welfare and I knew that I was treading a tightrope between his world and hers. 'My family are happy and so am I, Your

Royal Highness,' I replied. He wasn't convinced. I was happy to be at Highgrove. My family had an idyllic life there. If Diana and Charles had been happy, I would have been very content, living my life in anonymity. Those years with my boys at Highgrove were the best I had ever been given. He had no idea exactly how happy we were, how happy Maria was, how happy my boys were or what I did when I wasn't around him. But it wasn't as simple as that.

As far as he was concerned, the world of Highgrove, his domain, revolved around him. He never once said, 'Oh, don't bother scrambling onto the roof to put the Royal Standard up when I arrive.' In storm, snow or torrential rain, he didn't think beyond his own needs, so I had to do it.

My conflict was how to please both the prince and the princess and as always, I followed my heart in support of Diana. In the summer of 1988, Charles was away for the weekend with the boys and Diana was alone at Highgrove. 'I have a very special task for you, Paul, which is strictly between you and me.'

She confided in me that she had taken a lover as her marriage had broken down. It was a huge step for her to take and very few people knew.

'Would you go to Kemble railway station this afternoon and pick up a very special cargo for me?'

That special cargo was James Hewitt. Diana had been searching for love and she had found a dashing, handsome cavalry officer who had swept her off her feet and whom she adored. James and I became friends and we had many conversations during their affair. I became a 'go between' and he once confided in me that he felt 'out of his depth'. Theirs was a true love story and he became her every waking thought. Hundreds of parcels and letters were dispatched to him while he was deployed in Afghanistan – socks, chocolate, toothpaste – essentials that were needed on the front line. She wrote to him daily reminding him of her romantic visits to his home in Devon which he shared with his mother. James was attentive, kind and spoiling and gave Diana the love and the bolthole which she craved. He eventually realised that the closer to the flame he became, the more vulnerable he was and the more likely to be burned. Ultimately, he was cast as a villain when all that he wanted to do was love Diana.

We were told about the separation by Lady Jane Strathclyde, the personnel officer, the day before it was announced. Both the prince and princess avoided the staff all day until Diana broke ranks and rang Maria and me. Diana tackled conflict head on and sorted the problems personally; Charles hid away and let someone else do the dirty work.

The prince never spoke to me about the situation. He spent his time with Mrs Parker-Bowles and avoided all the staff at Highgrove until it was sorted and his new reign could begin in Gloucestershire. He didn't want to deal with confrontation. That's one of the things he shared with his mother, the Queen.

So as a result of the separation, Charles released me from my responsibilities to him and I returned to London with the princess. I was the only member of staff to be sent back to Kensington Palace. Diana was delighted. Maria cried for a week at the prospect of returning to London as she didn't want to leave the idyllic world which we had created in Gloucestershire. But the decision was out of our hands.

My duty to Diana was exclusive. It often caused conflict with my home life as it took me away and my family were abandoned. I look back now and think that although I was selfless in my duty to her, I was being selfish when it came to what my family needed. My devotion to her was sometimes to my own detriment.

I'm often asked if I loved her. Of course I did, but in a platonic way. The more she needed me, the more I needed to be there.

We became dependent on each other at times. Perhaps it wasn't healthy to be so close to arguably the most beautiful woman in the world, as complex and as complicated as she was.

She was often in conflict with herself and these were days long before we recognised mental health problems. Diana was certainly suffering. She had been abandoned, neglected and vilified. Stripped of her titles, publicly humiliated, worn down mentally, turning to bulimia for comfort. She must be the most misinterpreted, misunderstood and misrepresented woman of our times but she always knew what her duty was – to crown and country and to her boys.

A letter arrived from Windsor Castle. I recognised the Queen's handwriting and in the corner of the envelope were the initials E. R. I took it upstairs immediately. The princess was sitting at her desk in her sitting room. She saw the envelope and the crest on the back.

'Oh God,' she said. 'What now?' I stood beside her as she opened the letter with a paper knife and read it. Her eyes filled with tears. She handed it to me. 'Read it,' she said. As she sat there sobbing, I read it.

It said that the Queen had discussed a divorce with the Prime Minister, the Archbishop of Canterbury and Charles and that they had all come to the conclusion that it was in the best interest of all parties and the country that there be a divorce.

The princess looked up at me and said, 'Nobody asked or consulted me. Everybody else was but not me. I don't want a divorce, Paul, but I have to do what everybody else wants.'

This letter was signed, Elizabeth R. This was not a friendly letter from her mother-in-law, as many of the past letters had been. It was a royal command. Diana's fate was sealed.

Her Queen had spoken. She realised she needed to end the war of the Waleses and this was the final blow.

She accepted the divorce but her concern was that William and

Harry should be brought up by them both. Diana was also proud to be Princess of Wales and mother of our future king.

Even after the divorce was announced by Kensington Palace in February 1996, Diana still knew her role.

Mentally stronger than I had seen her in a long time, she told me, 'I'm focused, Paul. I have a strong sense of public duty. I am clear-headed and motivated and want to get on without obstruction.'

On 29 May 1996, she set out from Kensington Palace with her policeman to travel to William's school, Eton, for the annual parents' day. Charles would be leaving from Highgrove with his gang of supporters, the Knatchbulls and the Romseys, as they also had children at the school. Diana was dreading seeing them.

Halfway there she had a brainwave: 'What if we arrived together?' That would be a clear signal that they were going to bring the boys up together and be a real show of unity for their eldest son.

The policeman radioed the request ahead to Charles but the answer came back quickly and definitively: 'No way is that possible.'

She arrived on the back foot and by herself, admitting later, 'I was cold-shouldered by everyone, including Charles.'

But she made an effort at the pre-luncheon drinks to mingle and chat to give a show of confidence even if she felt anything but confident. She then noticed the seating plan for the concert and that they were to be sat on different sides of the aisle.

I'm not having this, she thought and approached the provost's wife: 'Excuse me, do you think I could possibly swap places with you so that I can sit next to my husband?'

The provost's wife could hardly refuse and the princess pulled off a little coup that would have gone unnoticed by everyone but her husband.

She hadn't finished and when they were outside the school

where the television cameras were waiting, she rushed to the prince's car, kissed him on the cheek and whispered, 'Goodbye darling.'

Of course this intimate moment and rare united front made all the news bulletins that night and the following day's headlines screamed, 'A KISS IS JUST A KISS'.

'Now Camilla knows what it feels like to be on the receiving end,' the princess commented at breakfast the next morning.

Diana had found her voice at last and was planning on using it. I think the Andrew Morton book, *Diana: Her True Story*, was the start of it, back in 1992. The book caused the Royal Family to realise that they couldn't underestimate Diana, especially after it was established that Diana had had her hand in it, and I think Diana was punished like a child for being naughty.

I don't know if Charles ever confronted her as by now he was keeping well clear. He was allowed to make his own messes but unfortunately his estranged wife, who was alone in Kensington Palace, had made one mess too many and was going to be taught a lesson. The price was her marriage.

Had she not conspired with Andrew Morton to write this book, I believe it would have been resolved in a different way, but the Royal Family were sick of the stories leaking out and Diana was to be silent or silenced. But in order to understand what happened, we need to look at why she decided to reveal the darkest parts of her life in the first place.

8

THAT *Panorama* interview and what happened next

Having been silenced for so many years, Diana, Princess of Wales had found her voice. She had always known how to use the media and had many friends who were journalists, like Richard Kay and Jennie Bond, whom she trusted to get her story across.

But in the midst of the darkest days as her marriage was falling apart, she was emotionally confused; she was also grieving her father, who had died in March 1992. She felt that Prince Charles was leaking negative stories to the press and the balance of truth was being tilted against her. She wanted her version of events to be heard. She found her voice in Andrew Morton and his book, *Diana: Her True Story*, which was published in June 1992.

In later years, she bitterly regretted speaking out in such a raw manner, but at that time she was vulnerable and she wanted the public to know the truth about her marriage.

It may sound strange, but Diana never met Andrew Morton in the process of writing this book. Dr James Colthurst played a crucial role acting as a go between. He had met Diana on a skiing trip in Val Claret, France when she was seventeen and became a lifelong friend.

Andrew, who worked as a journalist, was covering the princess's visit to St Thomas' Hospital, where James worked. The two men met and started playing squash together. Andrew suggested that he could write a book telling Princess Diana's side of the story.

James would ride his bicycle up to Kensington Palace and have a lunch date with the princess. One on one. Just the two of them. She would feed him a huge three-course lunch. She barely ate anything herself but loved to see others well fed.

They would then disappear into the sitting room and he would read out Andrew's questions and make recordings of the answers. The tapes would be put into a briefcase and returned to Andrew Morton. Sometimes the princess would get impatient with James reading the questions and take the page away and just answer them herself.

This method of contact suggested that the princess felt that she had tried to distance herself from the book.

Deep down she knew it was wrong, but she felt like she was fighting for her survival. She wanted people to know that she had been suffering in silence for a long time.

Diana: Her True Story was the beginning of a chain of reactions which culminated in the interview she gave to *Panorama*, but that would not happen for a few years.

First she had to deal with the fallout the book caused within the Royal Family. Initially she said that she'd had nothing to do with it, much as Meghan Markle and Harry claimed about the 2020 book *Finding Freedom*. They denied speaking to the authors of the bombshell biography. But, of course, they did. Meghan later admitted to it in documents lodged with the High Court relating to her lawsuit against Associated Newspapers, saying that she intervened and allowed a friend to speak to the authors because she was concerned that her 'father's narrative' would be repeated, adding 'so the true position could be communicated to the authors to prevent further misrepresentation'.

So while they did not sit down with them, they helped indirectly. And Diana did the same.

It was another point-scoring exercise in the war of the Waleses. She believed it would be ammunition she could use because she was suffering as a wife and a mother behind closed doors while Charles was off playing polo and seeing Camilla.

And the book made her feel like she didn't have to pretend anymore, even if Charles and the rest of the family were furious.

Diana was hasty and hot headed and admitted that some of her desperation to be listened to meant that the book gave a misleading impression of her feelings for Prince Charles and their marriage in general. It had painted over the many happy times they had also had.

The explosive biography, as well as Charles and Diana's split, the Duke of York's separation from Sarah Ferguson and the fire at Windsor Castle caused the Queen to dub 1992 her 'annus horribilis' or 'horrible year'. The Royal Family was in crisis.

Charles hit back. On 29 June 1994, a television documentary about him – made by his friend Jonathan Dimbleby with the royal seal of approval – was aired. It had been eighteen months in the making and was presented as a way to celebrate the twenty-fifth anniversary of his investiture as Prince of Wales, but some of it felt like a personal attack on Diana.

The journalist would claim that the prince didn't want anything to go in that would hurt the princess but Prince Charles did confess on television to adultery with Camilla Parker-Bowles. The princess was only given a few hours' warning that this bombshell was coming.

A year later, on 20 November 1995, an interview was broadcast which would change the course of Diana's life.

There is no doubt in my mind that several factors contributed to her decision to give the green light to the BBC and Martin Bashir in a frank, explosive interview that set her on a catastrophic course that ended in her death.

Throughout the hot summer, Diana had become increasingly frustrated by the tactics deployed by the Prince of Wales's household at St James's Palace. She was 'sharing' office space with her estranged husband. Her office wouldn't move into apartment 7 at Kensington Palace until a year later.

When I think about Martin Bashir now, I realise that the presenter could have been anybody. But it had to be the BBC and it had to be *Panorama*.

I don't think Diana would have wanted to speak to an American network or an American journalist as Harry later opted for with Oprah Winfrey. Although there is no doubt that many of them tried to get the coveted scoop.

There were many reasons why she wanted to go with the BBC. Firstly, Diana felt that *Panorama* had heft. It was the flagship current affairs programme on the BBC. Also Marmaduke Hussey, the husband of the Queen's trusted lady-in-waiting Susan Hussey, was chairman of the BBC and in a way, Diana relished the thought that she was going through the back door of the BBC to make this happen without his knowledge. It would be a blow not just to the Husseys but to the entire Royal Household, especially the 'grey suits' who had taunted her. It would be a 'poke in the eye' for the establishment. For Diana, it ticked a lot of boxes.

It was Earl Spencer, Diana's brother, who had suggested Martin Bashir, whom he had met previously. He introduced the journalist to his sister and vouched for him.

But there was a secret reason that Diana warmed to Martin. This was the summer that Diana had fallen in love with Dr Hasnat Khan, a Pakistani heart surgeon, and the pair were conducting a clandestine affair. Although Martin was British, his heritage was Pakistani. In my opinion, mentioning his heritage was a strong card to play. Diana found that he had much in common with Hasnat and discussed Martin with him, but Hasnat told me that he had reservations about him.

A friendship formed between the Princess of Wales and the BBC journalist over six months. I would pick Martin Bashir up from BBC offices at White City in my car and put him in the back seat with a blanket over him. This was a common practice I had been doing for years whenever we needed to sneak people in and out of Kensington Palace.

I would tell the police in advance that I was picking someone up and not to stop me or check my boot on the way back. As I flashed my lights coming up the drive to Kensington Palace, they were to lift the barrier and let me through, which they did on every occasion. I would drive into Clock Court, where Princess Margaret lived in apartment 2, which William and Catherine have now.

In Clock Court, there were no CCTV cameras; Margaret would not allow them to be pointed at her front door because she valued her privacy. So it was a perfect way to access the back door of apartment 9 without being seen. The princess would know I was coming and she would have the door ajar ready for our arrival.

On the drive to Kensington Palace, Martin, hiding in the back, would make conversation and ask me questions about the princess. It would usually be general enquiries but sometimes he would ask specifically about her love life. I was always tight-lipped – after all, he was a journalist and I did not trust him.

So there were secret meetings for many months while they built up a friendship and an understanding of what the princess wanted out of this.

Diana was very aware of what Martin Bashir wanted from this friendship. He painted a picture of himself as a poor, downtrodden man who wouldn't be given the stories he should have been and wasn't getting the jobs and promotions he should have had. He felt that he was not well regarded at the BBC and he was desperate to climb the ladder there. He told her this interview would be the 'jewel in the crown' and would help his career enormously establishing him as a major player. He also confided in Diana that he was having marital problems, something to which she could obviously relate.

It was not unusual for Diana to want to help. She felt sorry for him and she wanted to do what she could. In her eyes she would be championing an underdog. She would not be giving this interview to one of the dynastic journalist families like her husband had done with Jonathan Dimbleby, son of Richard and brother of David, who had both presented *Panorama* in the past.

I noticed that each time that he visited, Martin became more self-confident and more assured. I would serve him a glass of cold, crisp Chardonnay on a silver salver on his arrival which he came to expect. There is no doubt that he was excited by and loved the cloak-and-dagger aspect of the whole operation. He was visibly high on the secrecy of him being inside the palace with a royal princess – and not just any princess but Diana, the most photographed and beautiful woman in the world.

He became cocky knowing that he had Diana's full attention and he, like Andrew Morton before him, could provide something she desperately wanted: a voice – and to be heard on the most prestigious heavyweight programme on the BBC.

Diana needed convincing that this was the right step but Martin was very persuasive. He had nothing to lose and everything to gain from making this interview happen.

It was a work-in-progress throughout the summer, culminating in filming on Bonfire night, 5 November 1995.

I didn't know when the interview was actually being recorded because she sent me off duty on that Sunday afternoon.

She said, 'You go and see your family. You've not seen them all week. Don't come back until the morning and have a nice evening.'

I thought it was very odd at the time as she wasn't usually that generous with my time off duty. When I came back to work on Monday morning, I walked through the room which used to be the Prince of Wales's study and I realised that furniture had been moved.

I asked Diana, 'What's been going on?'

'Oh, I had an exercise class with Jenny. She came last minute on Sunday night. We pushed the furniture back to make room. That's all.'

And then she avoided me for the next two or three days and I thought, Something is wrong.

I confronted her: 'Is there something you should be telling me? Is there something that I don't know?'

She confessed she had given the interview and that it had been recorded in that room.

I never thought she'd go through with it. I thought it was all bravado and bluster and that she wouldn't actually do it.

She did it when I wasn't there because she knew that I wasn't totally on board.

I remember saying, 'I hope you didn't say too much.'

She replied, 'I think it will be OK.'

And I had to wait with the rest of the world to find out what she had actually said. Once I had seen it, I thought, Oh, my goodness, this is far too personal, far too raw and far too controversial and there are going to be repercussions. The Queen will not be amused!

Diana had no idea of the impact it would have or the consequences.

I try to remind myself that she wanted her side of the story to be heard. After all, Charles had spoken with Jonathan Dimbleby.

This was her retaliation for the mortification she felt over him admitting to cheating on her. She felt ashamed that her husband had been unfaithful and she believed that she had been downgraded in her position in the Royal Family and in the eyes of the British people.

Of course she had long known that Charles was committing adultery, but she didn't want the whole world to know.

Perhaps that's why she did the same.

Martin had provided the questions in advance. It wasn't a scripted interview but Diana knew what was coming and had rehearsed her answers. She did not want any surprises so everything was vetted and she was open about what she did and did not want to discuss.

While she was open to discussing her bulimia, her marital woes and Charles and Camilla's affair, the one sticking point of this interview was her relationship with James Hewitt. Their affair had lasted from 1986 until 1991. I became aware that he was her lover when I first arrived at Highgrove in 1987. This was two years after Harry was born. Like I was to do with Martin and Hasnat, James would be collected and smuggled in. I felt sorry for Diana and understood her problems and her position, so I helped to facilitate their affair. This was really the beginning of our closeness because she knew I could be trusted implicitly to keep her secrets.

Martin wanted her to open up about what had really happened with James Hewitt. There had been rumours but no one knew for sure. Of course, the princess didn't want to.

But Martin said to her, 'You must because you have to be open and frank. This can't be a hagiography of you and your life. You have to show the light and the dark. The way to do this is to be honest about James Hewitt.'

She told me that Martin had thought it was a good idea. Of course he did. He was certainly Machiavellian. He knew exactly which buttons to press and knew what he wanted to achieve. He was thinking of the sensational headlines and the plaudits these exclusives would bring him.

Months later she admitted to me that she should never have spoken about James.

She said to me, 'What would my boys think? What would they think when they find out that I loved another man who wasn't their father?'

When the programme was shown on BBC One, nearly 23 million people in the UK tuned in to hear her speak frankly about her marriage and her life, including the famous line 'There were three of us in this marriage'. It was estimated that 200 million people across a hundred countries watched worldwide. The National Grid in the UK reported a 1,000-MW surge in demand for power across the country at the end of the programme as millions of people turned the kettle on and made a cup of tea to digest what they had just witnessed.

I watched it at home with my family. The next morning, I thought, Did that really happen? Was that a dream?

Diana watched it alone in her bedroom. At first she was jubilant but then then took herself to bed for several days after realising the implications. She was mortified by the fact that Martin had persuaded her to talk about James. She bitterly regretted the interview. It was her telling the nation private things that shouldn't have been shared. We all watched her unravel afterwards and it was uncomfortable viewing.

Then she emerged trying to behave like nothing had happened when a bomb had gone off and she was surrounded by the collateral damage.

That was when the doors of Buckingham Palace slammed shut. They didn't understand it. They couldn't comprehend why she had done it. The press office went into meltdown.

The BBC's board of governors had been deliberately kept

unaware of the interview by the *Panorama* executives and by the director-general of the BBC, John Birt. The official liaison between the BBC and the Royal Family, Jim Moir, had also been kept in the dark.

Nobody at Buckingham Palace knew that this was happening and they were completely caught off guard by it.

After the broadcast they were all left reeling for days, not knowing what they should do about it. How could they control this uncontrollable being in their midst? How to solve a problem like Diana was ringing through the corridors of Buckingham Palace.

Patrick Jephson, Diana's private secretary, was blindsided by it as well. His position was compromised. His credibility had been undermined and he was no longer welcome in the corridors of Buckingham Palace.

The link between Diana, her household and the Royal Family was severed for good. Patrick handed in his notice saying his position had become untenable and if he didn't know what his principal was doing and she didn't take his advice, then his job was redundant.

Martin Bashir poisoned the waters around the princess. He whispered untruths in her ear and alienated her from her close allies, household staff and members of the Royal Family. Diana began to believe that she could trust no one ... only Martin. Diana's personal chauffeur, Steve Davies, believes that Martin Bashir's lies ruined his relationship with the princess. In March 1996, Martin told Diana that Steve was feeding information to journalists. He wasn't; he was devoted to Diana. This was part of Martin's scheme to make Diana feel insecure. The travesty is that she died feeling that she had been betrayed by her favourite chauffeur, someone of whom she was very fond.

John Birt later wrote in his memoirs, 'In effect the Diana interview marked the end of the BBC's institutional reverence – though not its respect – for the monarchy.'

The BBC also lost its sole production of the Queen's Christmas broadcast, though Buckingham Palace denied that the *Panorama* interview was the reason, instead saying new arrangements were made to reflect the change in composition of television and radio industries.

The fallout continued and things were never really the same again. Now the public understood Diana's plight, and it had caused a massive ravine to open up between her and the rest of the Royal Family.

At the time it was hailed as 'the scoop of a generation' and the interview is still causing issues nearly thirty years on.

In 2021 the Dyson report found that Martin Bashir had obtained the interview through deceit after forging bank statements that appeared to show that members of Diana's household staff were being paid by the security services to spy on her. This was a clear breach of the BBC editorial code of conduct.

Earl Spencer has also claimed that he would never have introduced the journalist to his sister if he had not seen the forged documents.

I did not know about these forged bank statements at the time. I never saw them. I had no idea she (and the Earl) had been duped.

She trusted Martin Bashir and she considered him a friend. After all, she had helped to propel him into high regard in his workplace. She had given him the best interview he could have ever wished for. In return, she expected him to be true and loyal.

She kept in touch with him after the broadcast, strangely enough. That might have been a case of 'better the devil you know'. He wasn't the outcast that people might have presumed. He always felt that despite the consequences it was the best thing that she had ever done. She didn't think that; she wished she hadn't done it. Even though everything she had said was true, it was a step too far. And while the public supported her, the Royals didn't.

I think Martin just used the documents as another persuasive weapon in his armoury. If it hadn't happened, it would have been a different journalist at *Panorama*. She wanted her say.

In May 2021, both of Diana's sons released statements about the interview, and Prince William suggested that the lies told to his mother contributed to her sense of 'fear, paranoia and isolation'.

William has said that they will never allow the interview to be shown again. You might expect me to agree with this since I know she regretted it but I don't.

In his 2022 Netflix series, *Harry & Meghan*, Prince Harry said: 'She was deceived into giving the interview but at the same time, she spoke the truth of her experience.'

It is not often that I agree with the sentiments of the Duke of Sussex but I do here. These were Diana's words. Why should she be silenced? This was what she fought for. It is what she wanted. She was a mature woman in charge of her own destiny. She wanted to be heard.

There is no doubt that some of the revelations were misguided but she was brave and she felt it was the right thing for her to do at the time.

I worry that her words will not be heard by a new generation who were not around at the time of the interview. They will only know Camilla as queen and Charles as king and may not be aware of the history that went before.

I understand William's point of view that she was vulnerable, alone and misrepresented. She had dismissed her personal protection officer, Ken Wharfe, a man in whom she had confided and from whom she sought advice and he often gave her the unfiltered truth and his honest opinion; he was devoted to her. She didn't trust her private secretary. There was no one around to advise her properly. She didn't trust anyone. She felt at war with her husband and his family – and she was losing.

I am a divorced man who is a father of two boys and I have great respect for my ex-wife, particularly as she is their mother. I wish Charles had treated Diana that way, and I believe if he had, none of the events towards the end of her life may have happened and she would have been alive today.

So while I relate to William wanting to protect Diana and her legacy, I do worry that William is silencing his mother just as the Royal Family did. All she ever wanted was a voice and yet again even in death, hers is being silenced.

Of course back in 1995, the interview set Diana on a dangerous path. The Palace did what it always does and regrouped in order to protect itself. The shutters came down, the drawbridge went up and the Royal Family closed ranks. It was a self-preservation mechanism.

But the Queen knew that this war between Charles and Diana could not go on because it was damaging the monarchy. Divorce was the only option.

It was an incredibly difficult time for Diana. She was very lonely yet never alone. She was always trying to turn her pain into strength. She once told her estranged husband in a letter that she appreciated him being so hurtful towards her because it made her stronger.

But she also became more paranoid and felt she could trust no one. She was battling the Royal Family and she found herself fighting with the people closest to her. She dismissed staff along the way: personal aides, dressers, her policemen and even her long-term chef, Mervyn Wycherley, who had been totally devoted to her and a loyal servant since she was married in 1981. The household was shrinking in an attempt to prevent anything leaking out.

And then she turned on me. She was advised by a medium not to trust or confide in anyone whose name began with the letter

'P' but I was one of the last ones trying to keep things together for her.

At times, I was distraught. I couldn't sleep. Sometimes she would fall out with me on her way out to an engagement and I would sit there at my desk staring through my window. The next thing I'd hear would be the car returning two hours later. I had been sitting there for two hours in my own little world, dazed and thinking, I'm not in the wrong here. I never thought about being dismissed. I was worried about her.

The announcement came in July 1996 that the prince and princess were intending to divorce. The divorce was negotiated by Anthony Julius and Lord Mishcon from Mishcon de Reya of Southampton Row. Lord Mishcon would have an audience with the princess every Tuesday evening at 6 p.m. to talk through the finer details. He would always be very respectful and would bow and shake the princess's hand on arrival.

He would say, 'Ma'am, do excuse my cold hand. It's cold hands and a warm heart.' He was devoted to the princess. He advised her that her original demand for £40 million was not negotiable but a lump sum of £17 million was.

There were caveats, of course. Charles wanted some watercolours, a pair of paintings of his distant German relatives, a pair of 1780 chairs from the drawing room and all the George III silverware which was used daily.

Diana told me, 'He can have the lot. Even if we don't have any knives, forks or spoons. It will be worth it.

By August 1996, she was finalising the details of her divorce. 'That's enough to take us all to Australia and begin a new life,' she told me in a surprising statement. 'The boys will love the outdoor lifestyle.' She imagined herself on the New South Wales coast, enjoying its endless beaches.

'Do you like Australia, Paul?' she asked. 'Would you consider living there?'

'It's a long way from home,' I replied. 'But you know that I would do anything for you. I'll have a think about it.'

I do love Australia and its people but it would have been such a change in lifestyle for us all and I had to think about Maria and my boys.

Of course, Diana had an ulterior motive. Having contacted the Victor Chang Heart Research Centre in Sydney, she felt that it would be a perfect place for Hasnat to work. And then we would all be together.

Of course, it wasn't realistic. She would never have been able to take the future king to live in Australia and she would miss them too much if she went without them.

The boys adored Diana and loved being with her at Kensington Palace on the few occasions they were not with their father and the rest of the Royal Family.

'I know that I have to give them up . . . they are royal princes and this is their heritage, but I miss them so much,' she would say.

I would regularly set up a camp bed for William beside his mother's huge bed at Kensington Palace, while Harry would jump right in to snuggle with his mother. He'd fall asleep with her arms wrapped around him.

I didn't know it at the time but during the separation talks the prince had asked Diana to make a list of all she needed to fulfil her life in London and she was also told that Highgrove would no longer be her home. We were all to be cast adrift.

She had asked to take me back to London to live and work with her solely at Kensington Palace. She rescued me, Maria and the boys from the sinking ship.

Although we were devastated to return to the city, she told us that she would take care of us for which we were so grateful. I realised that we were collateral damage from the split. We were now to be two separate households and our world in London was going to be very different.

The decree absolute was granted in the divorce on 28 August 1996 and terms were agreed. The Princess was to receive a lump sum settlement of £17 million. I wrote in my diary, 'A great change today. HRH The Princess of Wales becomes Diana, Princess of Wales.' I will never forget that hot summer's day when the princess returned from her solicitors waving a piece of paper above her head. She walked triumphantly towards me down the corridor from the front door of apartment 8. 'I'm a rich lady now,' she said. 'And the first thing I am going to do is double your wage.' She kept her promise and did exactly that one month later; I became the highest-paid butler in royal service. I was flabbergasted, but little did I know that that pay day was short-lived as it would end a year later on the death of the princess.

Sir Robert Fellowes, the Queen's private secretary and Diana's brother-in-law, rang her on the day of the divorce to wish her good luck on what he thought would be a difficult day, adding, 'It is a tragic end to a wonderful story.'

She replied, 'Oh no, Robert. It is the beginning of a new chapter and remember, Robert, I do still love my husband.' He was lost for words but it was true. She did love him – she just couldn't live with him.

Her focus was on preparing for the next chapter and new life as a divorcee, and another plan was being hatched. 'Come with me over to the wardrobe room,' she said. I had no idea what was coming next. 'Open the doors and let me see them. Look at all these dresses. How many do you think there are? Go on . . . count them.'

She stood in the middle of the room giggling as I went from the rows of black cocktail dresses through every colour of the rainbow, finishing with the white gowns.

'There are sixty-two excluding your wedding dress,' I informed her. This did not even include the dresses that hung in the wardrobe on the first floor.

'Each one of these is a memory and an old friend but now is the time and I'm going to sell them all – not my wedding dress though. I will give the proceeds to AIDS Research. I could make a million dollars if I sell fifty dresses. I will never wear them again so it's time to have a clear out.' I pulled out a silk taffeta evening dress printed with blue chintz flowers and Diana's eyes lit up as she said, 'I remember wearing this dress in Melbourne when Charles whizzed me around the dance floor.' This would become lot number eight in the auction. Then there was a light blue chiffon evening dress by Catherine Walker, lot number six. 'Ah ... this is my Grace Kelly dress,' she said. 'I loved wearing this at the Cannes Film Festival and at *Miss Saigon* in London. I felt like a movie star.' Then she spotted what would become lot number two, a black silk crepe cocktail dress by Christina Stambolian: the revenge dress. This dress took me back to a time when I was closer to the princess than I had ever been before. She constantly needed encouragement and support and she trusted me and my judgement one hundred per cent. On the invitation of Lord Palumbo, Diana was to attend a dinner given by *Vanity Fair* at the Serpentine Gallery in London in 1994 on the same evening that the explosive interview given by Prince Charles to Jonathan Dimbleby was to be broadcast. That afternoon Diana discovered that Charles had admitted to committing adultery with Camilla Parker-Bowles in the interview. Her initial reaction had been to cancel the engagement and stay at home. 'How am I going to face everyone?' she sobbed. 'Everyone will think that my marriage to Charles was a sham. It's all so embarrassing. Why has he done this to me?' There were many anxious tears but I consoled her and gave her encouragement. 'You have to go,' I said, 'You have promised Lord Palumbo and there are so many people waiting for you. This is the time to face your critics.' Sitting in my pantry on the ground floor, I could hear the princess pacing up and down. 'Paul, are you there?' she called over the banister of the first-floor landing and I bolted up the three flights of stairs. As I arrived, she was standing there with her hands on her hips, dressed and ready to go. She was wearing a midnight blue cocktail dress with a white satin collar and cuffs (which became lot eleven in the auction).

'Well, what do you think?' She gave me a twirl.

Now, don't get me wrong, she looked spectacular – but my expression must have let me down.

'You don't like it?'

'I love it', I replied, 'but it's not the right dress for tonight. Tonight you have to pull out all the stops.' I always gave her an honest opinion, sometimes to my detriment, but she knew she could rely on my word.

'I don't have anything else to wear,' she said. 'Find me something!'

The challenge was accepted and she followed me into her dressing room. I instinctively went to the black evening section in her walk-in wardrobe. 'What about this?' I asked, holding up a sequined number.

'Oh no. That's too much of an old friend.'

Then I came across something that didn't look spectacular on the hanger but I knew would be transformed by the princess.

'This one! Amuse me and try it on.' I handed her the Stambolian dress.

'Do you think so?'

'Yes,' I replied. 'Go on. Let's see.'

When she re-entered the room two minutes later, she looked incredible.

'Zip me up. Don't you think it's too much?' She pointed at her cleavage.

'That's the one for tonight … with sheer tights and heels.' I was confident in my choice. We then went to the safe to find the right jewels.

'What do you think?' she said.

'It has to be the pearl choker with the Queen Mother's sapphire.'

Time was now paramount. 'You get ready. I will go and check to see if the car is at the front door.'

Five minutes later, a vision appeared on the staircase with her arms outstretched. 'Ta dah!' She giggled.

'Wow.' Mission accomplished. 'You will knock them sideways. Just one more thing: when you get there, stride towards Lord Palumbo, shake his hand, hold your head high and say to yourself, "I am Diana, Princess of Wales and I am here to stay".' I followed her out to the waiting car. 'Remember, you are the mother of a future king.'

By now we were outside the front door. I opened the car door for her and stretched the seat belt across her.

'Night, night perky Paul. Don't wait up.'

I stood to attention, smiled at her face beaming back at me and bowed. She was perfect.

I watched her arrival in Hyde Park on the news that night and as she strode towards Lord Palumbo, I could almost hear her thinking, Stride … head high … I am Diana. It was a triumph. I scribbled a note and put it on her pillow: 'Well done. I am so proud of you.' Then I left the bedroom door ajar with the landing light on as I always did.

And then there was that wedding dress. Her plan was always to donate her Emanuel ivory silk taffeta and antique lace wedding dress with its 25-foot train and 153-yard tulle veil to the Victoria and Albert Museum for its national dress collection. But after her death, the dress was taken by her mother, Frances Shand Kydd, and put on display at the Diana exhibition at Althorp.

I had devised a plan for a museum at her home which would offer visitors a walk through Diana's life from childhood to include her inspirational charity work and culminating in her wedding dress in a huge glass case.

Selfishly I hoped that there might have been a role for me to curate the collection, which would offer me not only a job but somewhere for my family to live. There was no place for me there in the end, but the Diana exhibition did become a great success.

When William came of age, he wanted his mother's 'chattels' back. The museum closed and all of Diana's belongings were returned to the royal collection. Occasionally individual pieces, including the famous wedding dress, are put on public display in Kensington Palace.

The Christie's dress auction in June 1997 was inspired by a conversation with Prince William and Elton John. Diana was always thinking about how she could help others.

But there was a lot to do. She asked me to fetch my wife, Maria, and her mother, Betty, to help with the sorting. The Prince of Wales's former study resembled a second-hand clothes shop.

Even William was brought in to help with the tough decision-making process as Diana regaled us with the tales and memories of each dress.

But, of course, not all of the dresses were destined for auctions or museums. During her lifetime, Diana's unwanted designer wear was often given by her to female staff including Maria and Lily, our Filipino maid, while bagfuls were also given to her sisters and close friends. I was often sent to take her clothes to second-hand shops in Knightsbridge or Chelsea, where they would be sold at a fraction of their original cost. Diana loved having a little stash of fifty-pound notes in her desk drawer: her pin money for magazines, books and treats for the boys.

Christie's sent its costume expert, Meredith Etherington-Smith, to catalogue and describe each dress. There was no lot thirteen so seventy-nine dresses went under the hammer raising almost £2 million for AIDS and cancer charities on both sides of the Atlantic.

Diana was delighted by how much money was raised by the auction in New York. It gave an incredible boost to HIV/AIDS causes, which were important to her. Nowadays Catherine and other Royals are seen recycling dresses and helping them find second homes, but Diana was the first.

Times were changing and moving fast. Out with the old and in with the new.

No longer bound by the shackles of royal life, she was exploring new opportunities and there were plenty who wanted her to be involved with their causes, businesses and companies.

Diana had a way with people. They loved to be in her company. Richard Branson became a good friend of the princess and she was afforded the luxury of his sanctuary Necker Island in the Caribbean where she took William and Harry on occasion. She was often spotted wearing his Virgin Atlantic Flying Lady sweatshirt on the way to the gym to work out at the Harbour Club, an endorsement many companies could only dream of.

But there was another advertising stunt that didn't work out the way Richard Branson wanted.

He had asked Diana to launch one of his 'Scarlet Lady' aeroplanes, part of his Virgin Atlantic fleet, by wearing one of their red cabin stewards' outfits. She politely declined the request.

Life is funny, because who could have predicted that the King's eldest son's mother-in-law, Carole Middleton, worked as an air hostess with Richard's rival airline British Airways at the same time.

Diana also declined an offer to move into the professional sphere of her future daughter-in-law, Meghan, and become an actress. She was approached to appear in *The Bodyguard II* alongside Kevin Costner.

I put the call from Mr Costner through to her sitting room and heard fits of giggles with her saying, 'But I can't sing! What would I be expected to do? I'm not sure but yes, OK, send it and I promise I will have a look.'

She told me at the end of the call that he had offered her the lead role in a follow-up to the smash hit which had starred Whitney Houston as the lead. She was to play a princess and Kevin would be her bodyguard and save her life. He promised it would be tastefully done and that he would look after her.

Diana chuckled. 'He was so charming but he cannot be serious.'

But he was extremely serious, and the script arrived for *The Bodyguard II*. I'm not sure that she ever read it but she was flattered. She politely declined the opportunity, saying, 'It is simply impossible.'

In the midst of all of this, almost like the plot of the Hollywood star's movie, the princess was worried that somebody was trying to kill her. This was something that she had never mentioned before. She was becoming paranoid. She was worried that people were following her.

On occasion, she would ask me to crawl underneath her car to see whether there was anything suspicious. 'Is there anything leaking? Is there anything dripping? Can you see anything that shouldn't be there?' she would say.

I said, 'Well, I'm not a mechanic. I don't know what I'm looking for. I'm a butler.'

But I did think it was strange.

The princess had written a letter to me in the autumn of 1996 in which she prophesied her own death. Her usual practice was to write notes to me at night and leave them on my desk to read first thing the following morning.

It read: 'This particular phase in my life is the most dangerous – my husband is planning "an accident" in my car. Brake failure and serious head injury in order to make the path clear for him to marry.'

And I sat back in my chair and thought, Do you really think that? That your husband wants you out of the way? Was she thinking that the Royal Family had had their fill of her and wanted her erased?

It appears that they were her thoughts at the time – she feared for her life.

When she came back from the gym that morning, I asked her, 'Why did you write that last night?'

She said, 'Well, that's what I was thinking last night. That would be the perfect scenario, wouldn't it? If I disappeared, if I died, then that would solve all of their problems. I am the one that's upsetting them the most and if they got rid of me, they wouldn't have to deal with it anymore.'

I said, 'Don't be ridiculous. Who would possibly want to kill the mother of the future king?'

We discussed her worries and I did my best to convince her that this could not be true.

Surely no one would kill her – and certainly not her ex-husband. After all, he was the father of her two children and she was the mother of a future king of our country.

Despite what happened, I remain of the opinion that no one would order such a heinous crime. It would be the end of the monarchy if it was proven to be true.

I still have that letter.

I have thought about it a lot through the years. If I had been at the Tudor court and Anne Boleyn had written a letter to me to say 'I believe that my husband's going to chop my head off', I would have addressed it in the same way by saying 'Don't be ridiculous. That cannot happen.' But it did.

It is chilling to read Diana's words, seemingly prophesying her own death, in her own hand, on her own stationery.

But I don't honestly think that she thought that Charles would kill her.

Agatha Christie couldn't possibly have written that script because you wouldn't believe it but Diana did write it.

And in the last year of her life, with these thoughts in her head, things accelerated out of control. I remember saying to her, 'Slow down! You are moving too fast and I can't keep up with you.'

School had broken up for the summer of 1997 when Mohamed Al Fayed said to Diana, 'Why don't you come out to the South of France with Heini [his wife] and myself and the family as we are all out there? We will get jet skis for the boys and you'll have fun in the sun.'

Perhaps this shows how much the divorce had isolated Diana. She had nowhere else to go so she accepted Mohamed Al Fayed's invitation despite never being a huge fan of his.

During her lifetime, Princess Diana met interesting, and sometimes controversial, people, none more so than Mohamed Al Fayed. I saw this particular relationship develop at first hand. Mohamed Al Fayed was no stranger to the princess, the Queen or the Spencer family. He donated generously to the annual Windsor horse show, whose patron was the Queen. She was often photographed with him there. He befriended the Spencer family, especially Raine Spencer, the princess's stepmother, whom he made the director of a Harrods subsidiary. He made no secret of the fact that he craved a connection with the Royal

Family. But who was the man behind the mask? He wore many disguises: pharaoh, grand vizier, showman, puppet master and even god. Diana always told me that God lived on the fifth floor of Harrods, such was his power.

Mohamed Al Fayed was one of the richest men in London. He sought fame and fortune and was the owner of arguably London's finest department store – Harrods. He was proud to display on the corner of his store every royal warrant. Here, royalty and celebrities met to shop and we gazed in awe. Nobody came close to him but beyond the carefully crafted image, he was licentious and forceful and there was a darker side to him which he hid successfully.

In 2024, a BBC investigation exposed allegations against him from more than twenty women in relation to decades of serious abuse. The billionaire businessman, who died in 2023 aged ninety-four, was accused of multiple counts of rape and attempted rape by several women who worked for him – many felt they were unable to report what had happened until recently. Since the BBC documentary *Al Fayed: Predator at Harrods* aired, the Metropolitan Police have revealed that a further forty victims have come forward with new allegations covering offences including sexual assault and rape over a period from 1979 to 2013. It is now thought the number of victims could be more than four hundred.

Princess Diana was a victim in his game too. They met in 1986 at a charity polo match at Smith's Lawn in Windsor and he was dazzled by her beauty.

Harrods was one of her favourite stores in Knightsbridge and it was around the corner from her favourite restaurant, San Lorenzo. It was only a short drive from Kensington Palace but it was rare that she could shop without Mr Al Fayed popping up beside her.

The security guards on each door were adept at notifying the fifth floor as soon as she or any famous personality entered the store and seconds later he would appear. The princess found this annoying as it made her shopping trip feel like a state visit.

So she started going to see him on the top floor for about five to ten minutes when she arrived at Harrods, and then he would leave her in peace to go shopping.

She didn't want to be alone with him more than she had to be. There was a sigh of relief when the meeting was over. But they were friends of sorts and in 1996, Al Fayed gave her permission to park in the Harrods depository (the princess called it the Harrods suppository) on the opposite side of Brompton Road and use the service tunnel to enter the store. On one such occasion, she returned to the car waving a black plastic credit card. 'Look what he gave me.'

'What is it?' I asked.

'He told me that it was a limitless Harrods card. I can buy anything with it and there will be no charge!'

By the time we had returned to Kensington Palace she had thought carefully and placed the card face down on the pink blotting paper on her desk

'What do I put on the back?' she said, staring at the strip where her signature should be.

'Diana, of course,' I said.

'That's too obvious.' She took a pen from the pot on her desk and signed it 'Wales' – 'After all, that's my surname'.

She never used the card herself but gave it to me in case I ever needed to use it to shop for her. She preferred to pay her bills, not wanting to be beholden to him.

'I don't want to have to return the favour,' she said.

A green-liveried Harrods van would arrive at Kensington Palace on a daily basis with the latest gadgets and computer games, which Diana sometimes sent back only for a lackey to return in the van with even more parcels. But at Christmas 1992,

Al Fayed solved a particular crisis. The most popular toy of the year was Tracy Island, the home of the Thunderbirds, and it was impossible to find. However, two arrived in the Harrods van for William and Harry. 'The boys don't need two,' said the princess. 'Would your boys like one of them?' Needless to say, my boys were delighted.

It felt like he was trying to soften her up and exploit her vulnerability. An invitation from Al Fayed to dine with him at Harrods arrived on 5 July 1996, followed by the premiere of the new Tom Cruise movie, *Mission: Impossible*. Mr Al Fayed wrote to Diana advising her that although Tom Cruise knew her, he had asked Al Fayed to invite her as he was too shy to invite her himself.

Indeed Diana had met him with her sons the previous September to watch the film being made. She liked Tom Cruise but it amused her that she towered above him and that he was very shy.

She turned down the invitation to go to the premiere with Al Fayed and met Tom privately afterwards instead. He was besotted.

On another visit to Harrods, she returned to the car red faced and blushing. 'You will never guess what Mr Al Fayed just said to me.'

I had absolutely no idea what she was going to tell me.

'He said, "I want you to marry my son." I told him, "I don't know your son," and he said, "But you will know him and fall in love with him – and marry him".'

In fact, Diana had met Dodi Fayed in April 1992 when she had shaken his hand unknowingly at the premiere of the film *Hook* starring Dustin Hoffman. She couldn't remember the meeting as he had made no impression.

She then revealed that Al Fayed had made an even more shocking statement: 'I want you to marry my son because in

Egyptian tradition, the father goes first. I'm going to sleep with you.'

He was in his sixties then and double her age. Unsurprisingly, Diana was not impressed with the indecent proposal. She said in shock, 'Can you imagine me making love to Yoda?' That's what she called him, as he was a doppelganger for the wrinkly green character from Star Wars. I was appalled by his behaviour. He thought that it was his right and that it would actually happen, that he would sleep with the Princess of Wales. That was on her mind throughout her romance with Dodi.

On other occasions she branded him 'creepy' and 'slimy' and complained that 'He's always putting his hands on me.'

People probably wondered why she didn't stop seeing him. But at this time after her divorce from Charles, she chose to play along because she said to me that she needed security.

He gave her something the royals didn't give her. He facilitated an escape for her and he knew what he was doing. He gave her an avenue to explore that she thought was safe. She said to me, 'Like Jackie Kennedy, I need to find an Onassis who'll keep me safe.'

Al Fayed always had intentions to matchmake his son with the princess. It was during that trip to the South of France with Diana and the boys that he forced Dodi to pursue the relationship. He was already engaged to Kelly Fisher but his father said to him, 'You are going to marry Diana. Tell Kelly whatever you want but you need to invite Diana back after she's taken the boys back to England. You invite her to come back. I'll buy the yacht, the *Jonikal*, and you can entertain her on board in private.' His son and heir of the Harrods empire had to obey his father.

So they returned to England and on 1 July 1997, her last birthday, Diana split with her lover, Hasnat, with whom she had been in a relationship for two years, over a silly row at a meeting on Wandsworth Common. He could not contemplate forfeiting his professional career to become Mr Diana Wales.

In early August 1997 I sat with Diana with her diary and between us, we decided when would be best for me to take my family on our annual holiday. 'Let's both go away in the last two weeks of August,' she said. So the dates were fixed in both of our diaries. 'There is no point in me being here if you are out of the country,' she said.

I planned to take the family to Naas, a town in Ireland that we knew well. Diana said that she was going to disappear off somewhere and we would all be back together at the end of August before the boys went back to school. Once the boys had returned to England from their trip to the South of France, she had planned to spend the next two weeks with her friend Lana Marks but Lana's father had become ill and she had to cancel. Diana had nowhere to go when the invitation from Dodi arrived.

On the rebound she agreed to meet Dodi on the yacht; from the moment Diana met Dodi to her death was only thirty days. History has been rewritten by many to make the romance between Princess Diana and Dodi Fayed seem like a great love affair, but this was not the case. They were together for just a month. The actual romance really only lasted two weeks.

When Dodi flew Diana to Paris on the Harrods helicopter, they visited the faded glory of the Villa Windsor in the Bois de Boulogne, where the Duke and Duchess of Windsor had lived in exile. Al Fayed had bought the villa and its contents. Dodi tried to woo the princess by taking her to the villa in the last month of her life. 'This could all be yours,' he said.

She confided in me that she could never live there. 'It was filled with ghosts,' she said. This reminded me of the generous gifts that Al Fayed had also sent to the Queen, one of which was a pair of brown leather riding boots. 'Open that door and look what's on the other side,' the Queen once said to me pointing to her dressing room doors at Windsor Castle. I opened the doors and found the boots complete with stocks. 'Oh I am so sorry, Your Majesty,' I said. 'Did I forget to clean your boots?' They looked identical to the ones that the Queen wore for riding. 'Oh no, they are not mine. They are Uncle David's. Mr Al Fayed has sent them to me as a gift but what am I going to do with them?' I picked the boots up and examined them. They were only size five. Very small for a man.

In the end, Mohamed Al Fayed's world imploded when he died and the truth surfaced. If only Diana had trusted her instincts that he was 'creepy' and stayed away from him then maybe she would still be here today.

I don't think that Diana would have been surprised by the recent allegations against him, because he propositioned *her*, the mother of the future king.

If she could, I think she would stand by his victims and say, 'Well, it could have happened to me. It didn't. Thank God. But I'll be with you all the way.'

I wish she was here to do that.

Dodi promised Diana the world. His father would have bought it for them.

Al Fayed was playing high stakes. Nothing was out of reach for him.

Unfortunately she accepted that invitation in the summer of 1997. She was in the Mediterranean posing for cameras on a diving board and kissing Dodi on the deck of the yacht. It was a holiday fling.

Diana would ring me most days and say, 'How's Hasnat? Have you seen him?'

I would reply, 'Yes. He has seen the newspapers and he's furious with you.'

'Oh good,' she said. She was playing games with another Muslim man to taunt her lover. This was a complete no-no. She was playing with fire.

But she was missing Hasnat. She wasn't enjoying the time on the yacht. She said to me, 'It's freezing cold downstairs with the air conditioning then it's roasting hot on deck. Paul, I am crawling the walls. I can't wait to come home.'

Then right at the end of the trip, she rang me and said, 'You won't believe it. I should be coming back on Sunday as the boys should be coming to me on that day. But we can't come home directly as Dodi has to go to Paris to do some work for his father so we are going to stay at the Ritz in Place Vendôme. I'm going to be a day late because I'm on the Harrods jet and I can't get home any other way. Appointments have been made for William and Harry to see the tailor and the hairdresser so can you please arrange for them to come the following day?'

She also asked me to call Balmoral and inform the boys that she was going to be a day late. I did as I was asked. That final call and her last words to me still haunt me. 'Promise me you will be there, Paul,' she said. 'Go on, say it. I want to hear you say it.' So I did. 'If it makes you feel any better, I promise that I will be there.' She took a deep breath and said 'Night, night, perky Paul.' Then she hung up.

When I saw the footage of her in the lift with Dodi, I realised that the princess was going out late at night reluctantly. I knew her body language. She stood there with her back to the wall. I could sense that she was thinking, Have I got to do this?

She was ushered through the back door to avoid the paparazzi and into a car where she didn't put her seat belt on.

That has always puzzled me as every time she got into a car, whether driving or as a passenger, I would follow her and stretch the seatbelt over her and be inches away from her face, so close that I could smell her Hermès perfume. She always wore her seatbelt.

Then she was gone into the night and life would never be the same again ...

I was in my apartment at the Old Barracks in Kensington Palace, waiting for the princess to come home. It was just past midnight on Sunday 31 August 1997 when the telephone rang. I thought it might be the princess with more instructions but it was Lucia Flecha de Lima, the Brazilian ambassador's wife and one of Diana's closest friends. She was ringing from Washington to where her husband had been posted. She said, 'They've just announced on CNN that the princess has been in some kind of accident in Paris. Paul, I've tried to ring her but she's changed her number again.' [She did this on a weekly basis at this time.] 'You've got her number. Can you ring her and see if she's OK then ring me back.'

So I did. It rang. I imagined the screen lighting up with 'Merlin', the nickname given to me by her friend Susie Kassem. She and Diana joked that I was like a magician who always knew what was going to happen next.

But that particular night I had no idea what was going to happen next.

When I rang her mobile, there was no answer, which was unusual. I thought how odd it was because she never left her mobile phone anywhere. She always had it with her.

The paramedics later found it at the crash scene in the footwell of the car.

Two hours passed by and there was still no answer. What should I do? By 2 a.m. I decided to go to her office in apartment 7, next to her home in apartments 8 and 9. Perhaps news had reached her office. Michael Gibbins, her comptroller, Jackie Allen, her P.A. as well as secretaries Jo Greenstead and Jane Harris had heard the news and – concerned – had made their way to the office to await developments.

Michael Gibbins, chain-smoking as usual, was fielding calls from Balmoral where he was in touch with the Queen's private secretary, Sir Robert Fellowes, Diana's brother-in-law.

It was confirmed that Diana had been in a road traffic accident and had been injured. I was told that she had sustained a broken arm, possibly a fractured pelvis but nothing more serious.

The best thing I could do, I thought, was to be in Paris to take care of her.

I asked Michael Gibbins to book me onto the first flight to Paris. My friend and the princess's driver, Colin Tebbutt, agreed to accompany me at Michael's request.

Within the hour, there was a second call. It was serious. Dodi was dead and the princess had suffered serious injuries. I needed to get there for her.

I decided to pack a few essentials, as I thought she would be in the hospital with nothing.

I went to her dressing room and collected a nightdress, a dressing gown, underwear, her wash bag, lipstick and powder and as I passed by her dressing table, I grabbed a recent photo of the boys that could sit on her bedside table in the hospital. I then went into her sitting room and stood at her writing desk where I spotted the rosary beads given to her by Mother Theresa hanging on a miniature alabaster statue of Christ the Redeemer and slipped them into my pocket.

I went home and showered and dressed in a suit ready for the journey to Paris.

I returned to the office by 4 a.m. with my bag and her bag and met up with Colin.

By now, the mood was very sombre. Everyone looked glum. Jackie approached me, took my hands in hers and said, 'Sit down, Paul – I have something very difficult to tell you.'

The penny still hadn't dropped. I hadn't thought the unthinkable.

'I'm afraid that the princess is dead. Did you hear me, Paul?' She repeated the word: 'dead'.

She had been pronounced dead at 3 a.m. British time, 4 a.m. French time after failing to survive emergency surgery.

Almost in slow motion, I stared into the room which seemed to grow longer with the people in it moving further away. If I had screamed, no noise would have come out.

Jackie began to cry. I realised it was true but my emotions hadn't surfaced yet.

'Even more reason for me to be in Paris,' I said. 'I will need to get there to protect her, keep her safe and look after her in death the way I did in life. Colin will help me. He will be by my side and look after me. I couldn't be in better hands.' Colin took charge of the transport arrangements as I was in a complete daze. I had already begun to protect Diana's world. Colin and I had sealed all the doors to the princess's rooms securely so that their contents would not be disturbed.

I said goodbye to Maria, who was waking our boys up to tell them the heartbreaking and life-changing news. Little nine-year-old Nicholas was sobbing. 'But she told me she would take me to the crystal factory,' he said. All our lives were about to change. I looked around our cosy home and the world in which we lived. I instinctively knew that we were about to lose everything we had. But first came my duty. I left to head to Heathrow, from where I flew to Paris at the break of dawn, to fulfil my duty to be there in death, the way I was in life.

9

The Death of a Princess

Everyone of my generation remembers where they were and what they were doing on that Sunday morning, 31 August 1997. Some had been to weddings and celebrations the night before and had awoken with a thick headache, only to be greeted by this unimaginable news.

And even now, almost thirty years on, people still say, 'Where were you when Princess Diana died?'

You are probably recalling what you were doing right now.

It felt like the world had stopped spinning for a brief moment.

People were glued to their televisions and radios – not just in the UK but around the world. Personally, I was functioning on auto-pilot. I was numb and almost oblivious to the world around me. I would be consumed by the series of events to follow and I lost touch with reality. In the heart of everything, I felt that nobody understood this tremendous grief which I was carrying as it was so personal.

Our British Airways flight touched down in Paris and Colin and I were met by the ashen-faced British ambassador, Sir Michael Jay, after we had been ushered by the kind crew from the plane.

We drove to the British embassy and the butler brought in a tray of tea and biscuits. The ambassador's wife, Sylvia Jay, took my hand. 'Is there anything you need, Paul?'

Aged eighteen months on my rocking horse in the living room at Chapel Road, Grassmoor

Having ice cream with Mum and Dad on the beach at Cleethorpes in 1961 before my two brothers arrived

Posing with a monkey on a day trip to Skegness in 1963, in a red tank top Mum had knitted for me

With Mum, Dad and a two-year-old Graham at Derbyshire Miners Holiday camp in Rhyl in 1969

In full state livery in the Pages Lobby at Buckingham Palace before the state drive for President Ceauşescu of Romania

With Tall Paul on the deck of the *Britannia* sailing down the Kiel Canal during a state visit to Germany

Waiting for the Queen and Princess Margaret as they disembark from *Britannia* in Aberdeen in 1978

At the age of nineteen, standing beside the purple-liveried Royal train before departure from platform 1 at Euston Station

The Queen at a fancy dress ball in the staff canteen at Balmoral with Tall Paul dressed as Buzby in 1978

Prince Charles at the same fancy dress ball in the staff canteen at Balmoral in 1978

Dinner in the dining room at Sandringham

With Maria and Chipper, my favourite dorgi, at Balmoral in early 1980s

In day livery in the Green Corridor
at Windsor Castle

Sitting behind the Queen and Prince Philip
on the carriage drive at Royal Ascot

Beside the Irish state coach waiting for the
Queen at the state opening of Parliament

Carrying Piper off the Queen's Flight
on arrival in Aberdeen in 1979

With Princess Diana at a shooting lunch
in the fields at Sandringham in 1988

At the presidential guest house in Islamabad
in Pakistan with Princess Diana in 1991

Princess Diana barefoot on a visit
to a mosque in Egypt in 1992

Princess Diana at Philae temple
on the Nile in Egypt in 1992

Princess Diana, Maria, William, Harry,
Alex and Nick with nanny Barbara Barnes
on a day trip to Bristol Zoo

A family outing with Princess Diana
to Alton Towers in Staffordshire

Harry, Alex and Nick in the back of a
Land Rover on the estate at Highgrove

On the steps at Gatcombe Park with Apollo

Former study of Prince Charles at Kensington Palace where the *Panorama* interview took place

Princess Diana's desk at Kensington Palace

Princess Diana's day wardrobe in her dressing room at Kensington Palace

The Cambridge lover's knot tiara given by the Queen to Princess Diana

A tray of earrings and bracelets worn regularly by Princess Diana

With Graham at our wedding in the Lake District in 2017

Receiving the Royal Victorian Medal from the Queen at an investiture at Buckingham Palace in November 1997

Shutterstock

With Joe Pasquale and Fran Cosgrave at the final of *I'm A Celebrity . . . Get Me Out Of Here* in 2004

Me today

Being practical and thinking of what I might encounter in the hospital, I said, 'Do you have a full-length evening dress, possibly black, that I could borrow?'

I assumed the princess would have no clothing with her that would be suitable and she would need something dignified for her journey home.

She led me into her dressing room and opened a large armoire containing dresses.

'This one,' I said. It was an elegant black three-quarter-length cocktail dress. Perfect.

'And some black shoes?'

I had no idea whether she was even the same size as the princess. I was just thinking off the top of my head.

'These will do.'

Then we drove to the Pitié-Salpêtrière Hospital. As I entered the eight-storey building, Mrs Jay, who had seen the princess in the early hours of the morning, squeezed my hand and said, 'Be brave.'

Diana had arrived at the hospital at 2.06 a.m. that morning and was pronounced dead on arrival.

I spoke with the paramedics who had attended the accident at 1.18 a.m. They told me that Diana was alive but critical when they reached her.

They said that her final words were, 'Oh my God – what just happened?'

They continued to explain to me that they were on the way to the hospital when Diana suffered a cardiac arrest and they pulled their ambulance over to try to stabilise her. In the end, they performed emergency surgery to try to fix the problem and found that she had suffered a tear to her pulmonary artery which was so severe that it could not be mended.

The paramedic told me that he had done everything he could to save her including massaging her heart. It was futile. She could not be saved.

I remember the muggy heat as we were led down numerous corridors that all seemed to be empty. Then we got to the second floor. The lift doors opened. Another long corridor which was like any other in a hospital but this one was filled with people.

At the end of the corridor were two gendarmes in uniform standing either side of a door.

In the room adjacent was a Roman Catholic priest, an Anglican priest and a wonderful nurse who I later learned was called Beatrice Humbert. She spoke little English but in this solemn situation, gestures seemed to matter more than words. There was a peaceful air in the room as both priests prayed.

'Would you like to see the princess, Paul? I will take you in,' said Nurse Humbert.

The door opened and with Colin on one side and Nurse Humbert on the other, I entered the sunlit room. The large windows on one side had no curtains, which alarmed Colin, who immediately called for paper, which he taped to the windows to prevent the peeping eyes of paparazzi getting a grandstand view from the building opposite.

I noticed a screened-off area in the corner of the room; a man and a woman stood silently in the corner. I was told later that they were the embalmers.

The smell of formaldehyde filled the air as we three approached the simple hospital bed.

There she was – the woman I knew so well. It looked as though she was sleeping.

A white sheet covered her from her neck down to her ankles. I could see her toenails painted in Chanel Rouge Noir, her favourite. Her hair was wet and combed back off her face and there was a wound in her hairline.

I moved closer, supported by Colin and the nurse as my legs turned to jelly and began to buckle. The enormity of what I was witnessing began to sink in. I started to cry. I couldn't stop the tears.

The reality had struck me, although I kept saying, 'I just can't believe it.'

I touched her hand. She was warm, nothing like my mother's dead hand a year before. She had been cold and as hard as marble.

Perhaps she isn't dead, I thought.

I looked closer, and I saw her eyelashes and a wisp of her blonde hair move.

Then I realised that it was just the breeze from the electric fan on the bedside table, whirring away.

'Open your eyes,' I said. I was in shock. I wanted more than anything for her eyes to open and to see her looking back at me.

I was struggling, crying, not believing what I was witnessing.

'Why didn't you take me with you? Who's going to look after you now?'

So many thoughts, so many questions.

I kissed her brow.

I didn't want to leave her there alone. I was a mess while Colin remained composed and in control.

Two dozen roses had arrived from the former French president, Valéry Giscard d'Estaing, and his wife.

I tried to remember the spiritual belief that Diana held. She had not been afraid of death since she witnessed the passing of Adrian Ward-Jackson in 1991. She told me when my mum died, 'When a person dies, their spirit stays for a while and watches.'

So I thought that she was in the room then and could see us. That was my only comfort. I wanted to believe that her spirit was still there. The atmosphere in that room was heavy. I truly felt that the princess was watching me. I didn't want to leave her alone with strangers but Colin and I went to attempt to collect the princess's belongings from the Ritz. But we were told Mr Al Fayed was too busy to see us and that her possessions had been dispatched to England via his country estate in Oxted.

Back at the hospital, a telephone rang on a side table and on answering I recognised the voice of Prince Charles ringing from Balmoral.

'Are you all right, Paul?' he enquired.

Despite being anything but, I replied, 'Yes, Your Royal Highness. Thank you.'

I had never felt so awful in my life.

'Paul, you will come back with us on the Queen's flight. We will be with you at about six o'clock. Jane and Sarah [Diana's sisters] are coming with me. William and Harry send their love and the Queen wants me to extend her sympathy to you.'

I went back in to see the princess again. This time I was more composed. I knew what I was going to see but she looked more like herself now, dressed in the black dress and shoes with her hair beautifully styled (just as she liked; her one daily luxury in life was a blow dry) and, wound between her fingers, the rosary beads I had brought from her study. She looked peaceful.

Prince Charles arrived that afternoon with Diana's sisters. He walked up to me and touched the lapel of my jacket. 'Are you sure you are all right, old thing?' I managed to hold back the tears and nod.

I embraced Lady Jane Fellowes and Lady Sarah McCorquodale. A future king, two titled ladies and a butler offering comfort to each other.

They went in to see her and Prince Charles left looking shaken. She was now in an oak coffin; it is a sombre sight to see someone you love in the confines of a coffin. I have never seen him look so sad.

I boarded the Queen's Flight BAe 146 with Prince Charles, Colin Tebbutt, Lady Jane and Lady Sarah. All of us bringing the princess home. I hated the thought of Diana in the hold and how cold and lonely she was. I kept thinking, It's just not fair. She was reduced to precious cargo.

The plane touched down at RAF Northolt, west London and I stood on the apron of the airfield and watched as eight RAF airmen carried the coffin from the belly of the aircraft almost in slow motion and moved in unison towards the hearse. The Royal Standard was draped across the coffin.

At least they brought her home as a royal princess, I thought.

The prince said his goodbyes and boarded the plane for Balmoral back to his boys while I was charged with ensuring the princess reached her next destination. We drove to an undisclosed underground destination where I was greeted by Dr Peter Wheeler, Diana's physician, who explained to me that he was there to oversee her autopsy. I left her there and returned home. She was later taken to the Chapel Royal at St James's Palace.

The next day, still grieving and in disbelief, I went to the only place I could imagine being. Apartments 8 and 9, Kensington Palace. Butler to a palace with no princess. Michael Gibbins came to see me armed with the difficult task of collecting my keys.

Less than twenty-four hours after bringing Diana home in a casket, the suits were locking the doors. I refused and wasn't challenged.

That week was one of the most distressing of my life. Maria was concerned about me and on occasion came up to the palace to find me asleep in the bottom of the princess's dressing room wardrobe. Duty carried me through and I tried to think what the princess would want me to do. Knowing her so well, I followed what I imagined would have been her instructions.

It was a critical time for the Royal Family too. The Queen had not yet travelled south from Balmoral. While Her Majesty, who rarely put a foot wrong, thought it best to hunker down with the boys, the public felt they needed their Queen. The outpouring of grief was something we've not really witnessed before or since – even with the Queen's own passing in 2022.

One person who was grieving more than most was Hasnat Khan. His heart was broken. He was in pieces.

The day before the funeral, I went down to meet him as he sat in his car outside the Royal Garden Hotel. I wanted to get him into the palace where he could see her privately one last time but security was so tight. So I gave him a piece of the princess's clothing. I probably shouldn't have done, but I thought it was the least I could do and what Diana would have wanted. I knew how much they loved each other. I wanted him to have something of hers that smelled of her perfume and that she had touched. My heart was breaking for him too.

I also ensured that he was included on the guest list for Diana's funeral, which he attended accompanied by Susie Kassem.

But he was a broken man. He couldn't stay in London so he went back to Pakistan and married. It was an arranged marriage and it didn't last. No woman could ever match Diana. She was an impossible act to follow and he was living with her ghost. I know he is back in London and back at the Brompton Hospital. I've tried to reach out to him but to no avail. I would love to put my arms around him and talk to him and tell him I understand. I'm sure he regrets the missed opportunity as a result of her stubbornness.

Kensington Palace was Diana's home and it was where she spent most of her adult life so it seemed fitting that she should leave from there for the last time.

She spent the night before her funeral in the inner hallway on the ground floor. I had the police bring some of the flowers in from the street and spent hours arranging them alongside those sent from friends. I prayed with my family's Roman Catholic priest, Father Tony Parsons, who left as the Royals arrived. The princess's relatives had visited by 10 p.m. and after they had all left, I closed and bolted the front door ahead of my vigil with the Bishop of

London in attendance in the corridor outside. I couldn't let her be alone, even though there must have been 30,000 people outside the palace gates. I felt then, as I still do, that Diana came home to me for the last time.

It was a beautiful morning on 6 September 1997, the day of her funeral. The King's Troop gun carriage pulled up outside the front door of apartments 8 and 9 and eight soldiers in scarlet Welsh Guards' uniform filed in, lifted the coffin and took the first steps of their two-mile journey to Westminster Abbey. It was time to let her go, time to share her with the rest of the world. I couldn't count how many times I had stood in that spot and waved goodbye, but this was to be the last time. I looked over to my wife and sons whom I loved very much and felt their grief as they shed tears for the princess who had played such a huge part in their lives.

I stood inside the front door while Maria, Alexander and Nicholas huddled with the rest of the household staff as we watched the horses pull the carriage away. It seemed surreal that just two weeks earlier I had waved the Greece-bound princess off in her BMW. There was no waving this time as she left. I simply bowed to my princess and said, 'Goodbye, Your Royal Highness.'

At the funeral with the world watching, Earl Spencer made his speech and rattled the Royal Family with his accusations. I could not help but think about how he had rejected his sister while she was alive as he delivered his emotional, carefully crafted eulogy that was packed full of punches. She had wanted a bolthole at Althorp and a home to which she could take William and Harry at weekends. She asked to rent the Garden House. Having originally agreed to it, he later reneged on the deal saying that it would no longer be possible for many reasons including the press and police interference which inevitably followed Diana wherever she went. His letter had driven Diana to despair as did the follow-up request for her to return the Spencer tiara which she had worn on her wedding day.

Although Charles Spencer had withdrawn his offer of Garden Cottage as a weekend retreat much to Diana's displeasure, he did give her alternatives. This incident led to their relationship reaching an all-time low but Diana's brother never gave up communicating with her whether he was at the ancestral home at Althorp Park or at his estate in South Africa. Letters and faxes arrived at apartments 8 and 9 on a regular basis. He constantly told his sister that he loved her and was loyal to her but he was always honest with her, as only a brother could be, about her relationships with people who he said told her only what she wanted to hear.

While he spoke at the funeral I stared at the coffin draped in the Royal Standard with a wreath of white roses and a card saying 'Mummy' written by the princes on top. My heart broke for those boys. I stared at our Queen, her head bowed for much of the service, and Queen Elizabeth the Queen Mother nodded in my direction and smiled in acknowledgement of my service and duty as she struggled on her sticks past me in the choir stalls.

When Diana arrived back at her childhood home, the Royal Standard had been removed and replaced by the white, red, black and gold Spencer flag. Earl Spencer had made the swap. 'She is a Spencer now,' he said. There's no doubt in my mind that Diana would have wanted to be buried as a Royal.

Later at the graveside, Diana's mother, Frances Shand Kydd, grabbed my hand so tightly it hurt and whispered in my ear, 'At least she was mine for nine months.'

I always thought it an odd thing to say, particularly at that time.

But this was the Spencer family claiming Diana back as one of their own. To the world she was a royal princess but to them she was Lady Diana Spencer and she had come home.

She is buried in an unmarked grave on an island that was a pet cemetery during her childhood. It is surrounded by water so she is as isolated in death as she was in life. It feels like a Shakespearean tragedy to me. I didn't – and still don't – think it a respectful burial site for her. When I said goodbye to her that day, I knew I wouldn't be back and I haven't been since.

In fact, I think more fervently now as I get older that she should have been buried in St George's Chapel at Windsor Castle, which would be a fitting resting place for the mother of a future king.

It was the politics of the time but, interestingly, King James I was so appalled that his mother – Mary Queen of Scots – was buried in Peterborough Cathedral that he had her exhumed and brought down to London to be buried in Westminster Abbey. I don't think William would do that but he could. I just wish there was a public place where she could be respected in death by all walks of life the way she was when she was alive.

Over the years, I have been told by some that she is not buried on the island in the grounds of Althorp but with her father in the local church. I was at the private interment after the princess arrived at her childhood home – she is buried there and not in the church as some people speculate.

There have been many rumours that the princess was carrying Dodi's baby when she died. This is also not true. I read the autopsy report and know for a fact that she was not pregnant when she died.

People say she was engaged to Dodi, but again I found no engagement ring among her possessions when they arrived at Kensington Palace from the Ritz in Paris.

But there was a simple gold Bulgari band, which Dodi had given to her the night before; he showered her with gifts.

'He is very generous,' she told me on the phone from aboard the *Jonikal*. 'He has given me a bracelet, a watch, earrings and a necklace.'

'Be careful,' I warned. 'He will be giving you a ring next.'

There was a sharp intake of breath. 'Do you think so?'

'I know so . . .'

'What do I do then?' she asked.

'Put it on the fourth finger of your right hand, then it's a friend-ship ring rather than an engagement ring.'

She repeated it twice as if to memorise it.

'Things are moving so fast. Now I'll know what to do.'

When the princess died on the way to hospital, she was wear-ing that band on her fourth finger but on her right hand just as I suggested to her. She listened and took my advice.

Much has been said over the years about the crash but I have to believe that the princess's death in Paris was an accident.

Nobody could have known her route that night and predicted that she would have been killed in a simple road traffic accident.

If she had been wearing her seatbelt she may have survived.

Still today there are conspiracies about what actually happened and the internet is full of videos of people claiming that she was murdered.

'There are forces at work in my country of which even I have no knowledge,' the Queen said to me, standing alone in her sitting room in September 1997, weeks after the tragic accident in Paris.

I had just described the scene in Pitié-Salpêtrière Hospital in Paris where I saw mysterious suited-and-booted men standing in the shadows.

I told the Queen that I thought that they must be police-men or secret service. She nodded. I do not know to this day whether I was right or wrong, who they were or what they were doing.

Prince William I believe, is also confused about what actually happened on that tragic night which robbed him and Harry of their mother.

*

I know much time has passed but I still think about Diana constantly. I am sixty-seven now. I have lived for almost double her years.

She comes to me in my dreams. Sometimes I am in Paris. I always think that if I had been there, she would not have died. I have to live with that. Sometimes I dream that she is at Kensington Palace at her desk writing and she looks up and says, 'We need to tell people that I'm not really dead.' I am sure people think that I am mad when I tell them that.

When she died and I saw her in hospital, I held her hand and wished she had taken me with her. I can see now that it was probably the most selfish thing I have ever thought. I have a duty to my family to be here, but at that moment, I wanted to die and go with her. I had devoted my life to her and in her passing, I was lost. Not many people understand that.

I sailed through that period of my life on autopilot. I got through with no therapy, no counselling and I wonder now if I should have sought some professional help.

My life was never the same. I was never the same. People will say, 'Look at you now!' And they are right. I've done some unbelievable things, but it is a double-edged sword.

I live with the memory of an icon that I loved and I live with a lot of guilt over how her life ended.

She never got the chance to show us all that she had to offer. She could have done so much more if she had had a long life like the Queen.

I feel a pressure to preserve her memory and keep it alive for those who didn't know her or prefer to forget her.

Today Diana is the ghost that will forever haunt the House of Windsor.

Almost thirty years after her tragic death, she still casts a long shadow over the monarchy.

Her husband married his mistress and she became a queen, but her son waits in the wings with his own future queen, and one day the sapphire surrounded by diamonds that the Queen and Charles chose for Lady Diana Spencer in 1981 will sit on the finger of a queen.

Camilla is not my queen. She never will be. I am waiting for Queen Catherine and I know Diana would be so proud when her son is finally king.

10

Whatever Love Is

The immortal words uttered by Prince Charles when he was standing in front of his eighteen-year-old fiancée Lady Diana Spencer will forever haunt him. She was left bewildered when journalists asked them after their engagement in 1981 if they were in love. 'Of course,' Diana responded, while Charles added, 'Whatever "in love" means.'

The nation watched and took a deep breath in disbelief; the moment heralded that the union was off to a rocky start.

When it comes to love in the Royal Family it is never straightforward – even the unlikely ascent of Princess Elizabeth to the throne was linked to love. Her uncle, the never-crowned Edward VIII, abdicated as monarch in December 1936 so that he could follow his heart and marry his love, American divorcee Wallis Simpson. Love means different things to different people. It is worth taking a look at some of the love matches within the Royal Family.

Prince Andrew and Sarah Ferguson

Nobody was more delighted than the Queen to see 'favourite son' Prince Andrew settle into married life. His choice of bride pleased

Her Majesty and Prince Philip as they were familiar with the daughter of Ronnie Ferguson; he and Prince Philip had played polo together many times. He was a horse man who became polo manager for both Prince Philip and Prince Charles. His extensive knowledge of horses thrilled the Queen and younger members of the family often joked that 'RF' loved being related to the 'RF'. I often heard the expression, 'Ronald-ty' used as that's what Ronnie thought he was. He was so transfixed on occasions when sitting next to Her Majesty at lunch or dinner, as was Captain Mark Phillips, partner of Princess Anne. They were favourites as they could talk about horses for hours, which enchanted the Queen.

Sarah, who was given the nickname Fergie, was from a middle-class background, much the same as Mark Phillips. Although she was not as aristocratic as Lady Diana Spencer, her lineage could be linked back to royalty; she was a descendant of King Charles II and one of his mistresses. Fergie was also related to both Princess Alice, Duchess of Gloucester and Robert Fellowes, the Queen's private secretary, but to put it simply, Fergie was a gung-ho farmer's daughter which suited Andrew's boisterous personality.

Their wedding, on 23 July 1986 at Westminster Abbey, a week before Charles and Diana's fifth wedding anniversary, was my last state ride behind Her Majesty and Prince Philip on the magnificent 1902 gold state landau.

Fergie was twenty-six and like a bouncy, uncontrollable red setter puppy. Unlike Lady Diana Spencer, who had had her own separate suite before marriage, Fergie moved into Buckingham Palace a few months before the wedding and shared second-floor rooms with Prince Andrew, the same rooms in which the Prince and Princess of Wales had spent the early days of their married life. Eyebrows were raised within the Royal Household as it was quite a scandal at the time.

She was not as popular or as well received downstairs as Diana had been. Fergie may have been a breath of fresh air for the Royals but the staff preferred the gentleness of the established Princess of Wales whom they had known for almost five years. Fergie was a newcomer and she had to earn the trust of the staff. She was far too familiar for her own good but the staff could be snobs at times. When the men were out stalking, the ladies would meet them on the hills for a picnic lunch. A page would enquire in advance what people wanted to eat and compile a list. On one occasion, Fergie sent one member of staff into a rage having failed to comply with his request. In a voice heard by all the ladies assembled, including the Queen, he boomed, 'What does that red-haired mare want for lunch?'

It was accepted with silence as if it was never said. No reprimand. The staff had formed their opinion based on gossip and her behaviour.

Andrew was besotted with her. She could do no wrong but the staff were up in arms early in the marriage. From the beginning, the royal newlyweds refused to leave their marital bed. The maids weren't allowed to go into the bedroom to make the bed for days. When the couple did surface, they held lavish dinner, lunch and tea parties with all their friends. The kitchen staff were run off their feet. Even the Queen didn't entertain so extravagantly. The royal chefs were furious to be making food like it was an à la carte restaurant. They were used to serving food to the Queen and the Royal Family at set times. It was too much. The staff rebelled and protests were made to the Master of the Household who informed the Queen of her staff's unhappiness. She had to intervene and put a stop to the lavish gluttony. After all, she despised waste, deciding in advance which food should be cooked for her each day.

So why should Andrew and Fergie be different? It is fair to say that Andrew was never an easy Royal to get along with, especially for the staff, to whom he was inconsiderate and rude at best. He was so demanding that he kept a photograph of his collection of soft toys in a drawer in his bedroom to which the maids had to refer to ensure that they were in their correct place after they had made the bed.

Fergie formed a friendship with Diana, Princess of Wales from the beginning of 1982. They shared regular lunch dates and became confidantes. They called themselves 'the Wives of Windsor'. They would discuss the dour men in grey suits within the Royal Household, nicknamed 'the enemy within'. Diana having been in the Royal Family for five years was able to offer Sarah some sage advice on the dos and don'ts, whom she could trust and a rather lengthy list of those with whom she should be cautious. It was tragic that the relationship between them disintegrated after the publication of Sarah's autobiography, *My Story*, in 1996. Although Diana supported Sarah's decision to go public and become an independent woman, her support came with conditions. Diana requested that Sarah didn't talk about her, her boys or their relationship but it was too much to ask. When the book was published, Diana was furious that throughout its pages, there were references to her, William and Harry. Many thought that the fallout was caused by Sarah suggesting that she had contracted verrucas from shoes given to her by Diana, but that was not the case. Diana felt used and refused to speak to Sarah. They resorted to writing letters to each other. The last blow came when a letter arrived purportedly from Eugenie, Sarah's daughter, with the envelope written in a child's hand and addressed to HRH The Princess of Wales. Diana said to me, 'Look at this,' as she held the letter head high. 'She is now using her children to intervene. It's her last resort.' The letter was actually from Fergie with a cruel postscript. It referred to a letter from Diana in which she had assured Fergie that nothing would ever appear from her about Fergie's life. Sarah went on to add a vitriolic swipe suggesting that 'Mr Kay' (the *Daily Mail* journalist) or even 'Mr Jephson' (Diana's private secretary) might not agree with her. Diana was incandescent with rage. The relationship was terminated for good and they never spoke again. Diana's last words to Sarah were that when it came to honesty, perhaps she shouldn't resort to using her child to address envelopes to Diana and that Diana was happier than she had ever been.

Just like Diana, the duchess wanted to be liked by the Queen. When the Queen bestowed Andrew with the royal dukedom of York on the eve of his marriage, it was significant. The title had been long associated with the Queen's father, George VI. Fergie took its poignancy as a sign of acceptance of her, but she misunderstood. The title was bestowed on Andrew, not her. She simply took it as his wife. It is a subtle difference but 'the enemy within' used it as a chance to poke fun at her when she wrote to the Queen to thank her for the honour.

Fergie did not have an easy ride. She was deemed 'vulgar' by some staff and one newspaper hurtfully dubbed her 'The Duchess of Pork'. However, the couple did have happy times welcoming two daughters, Princess Beatrice and Princess Eugenie, into the world.

Traumatic affairs and a toe-sucking scandal followed and the couple split in March 1992 with Fergie citing the demands of Prince Andrew's naval career as the primary cause. However, they remain close, and even live under the same roof thirty years later.

After the separation, Fergie was banned from all royal residences on the order of Prince Philip. On one occasion, Prince Andrew persuaded his mother to let Fergie come to stay for a weekend at Balmoral towards the end of Prince Philip's life. Prince Philip was recuperating from an illness and convalescing at Wood Farm at Sandringham and had no idea of Andrew's plotting with his mother.

'Wouldn't it be nice, Mummy, if Sarah and the girls could come and spend a weekend at Balmoral? They would love it. And you would love to see your grandchildren.'

So the Queen agreed without Prince Philip's knowledge.

The Yorks arrived in force with tons of luggage and gifts for all the household and servants but Prince Philip got wind of it at Sandringham the next day and phoned the Queen immediately.

'I'm coming to Balmoral tomorrow and she had better be gone.'

What would the Queen do? She had to explain carefully to Andrew that Fergie was not able to stay in the house under the same roof as Prince Philip. So Andrew had to tell his ex-wife that she had to go. She didn't cause a fuss but simply packed all her bags and left before Prince Philip arrived so as to avoid a royal contretemps.

Towards the end of the Queen's life, after Prince Philip had died, Fergie saw an opportunity to open a door into the Queen's world. The Queen had decided not to have any more corgi puppies. She said, 'Who's going to look after them when I'm gone? It's unfair.'

But Fergie didn't listen.

She and Andrew bought two new puppies, a dorgi (a dachshund-corgi mix) and a corgi, Sandy and Muick, and presented them to the Queen as a gift during lockdown in 2021.

The Queen was not happy. 'What did I tell you all? I said that I didn't want any more dogs.'

I have no doubt that Sarah's actions were well intended. She was always kind and thoughtful to everyone around her and often showered both the family and staff with gifts but of course the dogs were then left after the Queen's death in 2022. They now live with Fergie and Andrew at their home at Royal Lodge.

The favourite son is probably feeling the loss of his mother more than most. Prince Andrew is the son of a monarch, a royal duke and a knight of the garter. He demands and expects respect for his position and will reprimand anyone who forgets to bow when introduced to him.

The Queen was always there for her son to save him from himself and from his mistakes. He had complete access to her and used it regularly. When financially strapped, he would always ask her for help. His only income was a naval pension which was not enough to run his residence and pay the wages of a regiment of household staff at Royal Lodge in Windsor Great Park. It was heavily subsidised by our late Queen.

But now she is gone, what next? Well Andrew has never been realistic. He hasn't come to terms with the fact that he is no longer a working member of the Royal Family. He grew up in a closeted situation as the son of the Queen and his whole world is a bubble.

This is where he differs from his brother King Charles, who wants him to see sense.

As siblings they have a good relationship but as king and prince things are different.

Charles knows that Royal Lodge is far too big, too grand and too expensive for Andrew and Fergie to occupy. He has the expense of a butler, a housekeeper, a chef and a driver, all of whom are run ragged. His butler came from Buckingham Palace and is answering the phone, setting the table, waiting on lunches and has even been persuaded to help to tend to the vegetable garden. It has gone way beyond what he should be doing. The Queen would never have expected members of her staff to do anything outside the remit of their job description.

In my opinion, Royal Lodge should be handed over to William and Catherine for their family. Prince Andrew is better suited to Frogmore Cottage, which was refurbished for Prince Harry and Meghan (and has the added bonus of being directly adjacent to the golf course!).

Andrew is living a lifestyle which is far too grand and far too expensive for him and Royal Lodge is not befitting for his station within the Royal Family now. He is well down the pecking order at eighth in line to the throne, as well as being a non-working

Royal. Royal Lodge is more befitting to the heir to the throne but Andrew is stubborn and will just not let go.

The future for Prince Andrew looks bleak because while he is on relatively good terms with his siblings, the same cannot be said for his nephew. Prince William sees Andrew as a liability to the Royal Family. He thinks he is someone who should be side-lined and quietened. He, like his father, is unlikely to take on the expense of running Prince Andrew's life. My advice to Andrew would be to move to Frogmore Cottage, accept that he is no longer a working member of the Royal Family with no way back and retire gracefully. He should disappear for the good of the House of Windsor.

Despite living together, rumours that Andrew and Fergie will remarry are unfounded. It's not on the cards. It just serves them to live under the same roof because they're joined at the hip by their daughters and grandchildren. It may be considered a strange arrangement, and Prince Philip could never understand it. He was heard to say, 'Didn't we already pay her off once? Didn't we have to give her lots of money to go away? And then she comes back again.'

Fergie received a substantial divorce settlement so Prince Philip could not understand why at Andrew's insistence she was brought back into their lives.

Prince Edward and Sophie Wessex

When I arrived at Buckingham Palace, Prince Andrew and Prince Edward were still living in rooms adjoining the royal nursery. Andrew was sixteen and Edward was twelve.

Prince Edward, as the youngest son, was spoiled by his nanny, Mabel Anderson, and was a petulant child. Anne and Charles had lived in the same nursery with the same nanny. At the time of writing, Mabel is ninety-eight years old and living in grace-and-favour accommodation in the grounds of Frogmore Cottage in Windsor Great Park.

Edward grew up in the shadow of his extrovert brother Andrew, a war hero from the Falklands.

He joined the Royal Marines, based at Lympstone in Devon, in 1986 but lasted only a year – much to his father's disapproval. He was never made of strong military material.

He tried but it was just too combative for his gentle nature. Major Hugh Lindsay was the Queen's equerry at the time and took him on regular yomps through the heather-clad hillsides of Balmoral. I regularly found them both exhausted and sweaty in the front hall. On one occasion, I saw Edward sobbing, completely broken. 'I just can't do it,' he said. 'I don't want to go back to the Marines.' He dreaded going back to camp so he left.

He was more interested in the arts and theatre so a new career in television beckoned and the idea of *It's a Royal Knockout* was hatched in 1987. It was a complete disaster and cast a shadow over the dignity of the House of Windsor. He was severely reprimanded by his father and it never happened again.

The saving grace was him marrying Sophie Rhys-Jones in 1999 at St George's Chapel, Windsor Castle when he was thirty-five. He is the only one of the Queen's children not to have divorced. The couple went on to have two children, Lady Louise Mountbatten-Windsor and James Mountbatten-Windsor who is now Earl of Wessex. They live at Bagshot Park, eleven miles south of Windsor, which is owned by the Crown Estate and is a rather grand 120-room mansion. They have lived there since 1999. It was originally built for King Charles I in 1609 and has been in the family for two hundred years.

There was always a question mark around Edward's sexuality. He had a penchant for dressing up and particularly enjoyed wearing ceremonial uniforms. Sophie has been forced to say, 'My husband isn't gay.' Why a wife should have to say that, I have no idea.

Although Queen Elizabeth II made Prince Edward the Earl of Wessex when he married Sophie and then Earl of Forfar in 2019, he did not become Duke of Edinburgh until after his mother died. King Charles III granted him the title on his fifty-ninth birthday.

Even now when people talk about the Duke of Edinburgh, I think of Prince Philip. The title was bestowed on him by the Queen's father, King George VI, the day before he married Princess Elizabeth on 20 November 1947 at Westminster Abbey.

The original Duke of Edinburgh was Frederick, Prince of Wales from 1726 to his death in 1751.

The title has always been a special one and there is no doubt in my mind that it had always been intended for Edward. It had been ear-marked by Charles, but the Queen remained Duchess of Edinburgh until her death.

It is a lifelong peerage, not hereditary, and remains a gift of the monarch so will not pass automatically to Edward's son, just as Zara Tindall will not inherit her mother Anne's title of Princess Royal which was bestowed on her by Queen Elizabeth II in June 1987. In my opinion, King William V will eventually bestow the title of Princess Royal on his daughter Charlotte and the Duke of Edinburgh on his son Louis and, of course, his son and heir George will follow him to be Prince of Wales.

Prince Edward has assumed the duties and responsibilities of his father's successful Duke of Edinburgh's Award scheme, which was founded on 1 September 1956 and was designed to attract boys (and later girls) who had not been interested in joining one of the main British youth movements such as the Scout Association.

At last he has found his niche and that is partly due to the influence of his wife, Sophie, who is now the Duchess of Edinburgh. She has survived and blossomed by being embraced by the inner circle of the Royal Family along with their children. Prince Philip taught Lady Louise to drive 'four in hand' in the Home Park and left her all his carriages, which was his real passion. They are housed in the Royal Mews at Windsor Castle. Sophie gave great comfort to our late Queen in her later years and could often be found at Windsor Castle in the Queen's company.

Their supportive role to the family has long been recognised. Sophie is a safe pair of hands and complements Edward perfectly. She has been deemed a valuable asset to the Royal Family and was even proposed as mentor to Meghan Markle when she joined the family – although the American actress rejected the offer.

Princess Diana and Hasnat Khan

Although Princess Diana and Hasnat Khan never married and Diana was no longer part of the Royal Family at the time of their relationship, in my opinion Hasnat Khan was *the* man in Diana's life. This was the man she wanted to marry.

Diana first met Hasnat when she was visiting the children's ward at the Brompton Hospital in the summer of 1995. The doors of the elevator opened and Hasnat was standing there in his white coat surrounded by students. The princess just stared at him and he stared straight back and smiled.

When she got back to Kensington Palace, she told me, 'Oh my goodness. Something profound has just happened to me. I have met Mr Wonderful [her nickname for him]. He didn't speak a word but he stared straight through me. He put his foot in the lift door to stop it from closing then he smiled at me. And I knew then that he was "the one".'

For two years they had an affair and no one knew about it. I was the go-between to sneak him into Kensington Palace. I would go out in my car and tell the police, 'Don't stop me on the way back. I'll flash the lights halfway up the drive and just lift the barrier. You don't have to check the car.' I would hide him underneath a blanket on the back seat of the car just as I did with Martin Bashir. But this was different. It wasn't about an interview, it was love.

We used to go through the back door so the police cameras wouldn't see him. I would turn right into Clock Court opposite Princess Margaret's apartment which is where William and Catherine live now. Diana would be waiting at the back door of apartment 9. She would know when I was due back and would have the door open so he could slip in.

Princess Margaret got wind of this as she saw these comings and goings. She would often stand in her window watching him arrive. Diana said, 'I've had enough of this. I'm just going to acknowledge her.' So one night she waved to Princess Margaret and shouted 'Good night, Margot'.

Princess Margaret was the Diana of her day. And I think as a lonely old woman inside Kensington Palace, she remembered those days when she had fun and lovers used to call on her. She was jealous as she watched their love affair unfold.

I would organise candle-lit dinner parties for Diana and Hasnat as they could rarely go out for dates. Most of the time there were clandestine meetings confined to the rooms at Kensington Palace or Hasnat's flat. Sometimes I would ask the chef to do double portions for dinner 'because the princess was hungry' and I would serve a romantic dinner for two in the dining room or in her sitting room. On other occasions, I would send the chef away and tell him to 'leave something cold in the fridge'. No one knew of the dinner guest (well, except Margot!). Not even the chef or the maids. On occasions Diana would spend whole days in his flat playing 'housewife', vacuuming and dusting and washing and ironing his clothes. She loved that.

For two years we kept it completely private and under wraps but then it started to go wrong.

One day the princess said to me, 'I want to marry Hasnat. How can I do this?'

She sent me out to talk with Father Tony Parsons, my family priest at the Carmelite Church in Kensington Church Street.

She said, 'Get him to come in and perform some kind of ceremony and marry us. Then when we step out onto the world stage and we tell everyone we're married, they'll have to accept it.'

But when I asked Father Tony about this, he said, 'It's absolutely impossible. I can't do that. The church won't allow me to do that. She's the mother of the future king.'

Tragically the next time Father Tony would come to Kensington Palace would be to bless the room in which Diana would lie overnight before her funeral. He turned to me and said wistfully, 'If only things could have been different.' I took that to mean that if she had been able to marry Hasnat, she wouldn't have gone on that fateful trip to the Mediterranean. She wouldn't have gone to Paris.

They hadn't been getting on when Diana took Princes William and Harry on holiday to Greece with Mohamed Al Fayed and his family in the summer of 1997. But when she arrived back in London with the boys, she arranged to meet Hasnat on Wandsworth Common. They drove out there separately and they had a massive falling out.

Diana said, 'That's it, if you are not going to marry me then I'm off. I'm done. I'm done with this. I've wasted two years of my life. You are the one for me but if you can't marry me . . .'

But Hasnat said, 'I can't marry you because I'll become Mr Diana. What will happen to my valuable work? What will happen to my surgery? What will happen to me as a person?'

They could not find a compromise so on the rebound, she accepted the invitation to go to the South of France and join Dodi Fayed as his guest on board the *Jonikal*.

Diana would ring me most days and say, 'How's Hasnat? Have you seen him?'

Over the years I had got into the habit of going out for a pint with Hasnat to the Anglesea Arms or another pub in Kensington. As two friends we could sit in the corner and have a drink and discuss our world completely privately between ourselves. I used to give him Diana's news and he gave me his for her in return.

I continued to see him throughout the Mediterranean romance.

'What does he think?' she would say. 'Has he seen the newspapers?'

I would reply, 'Yes. He has seen the newspapers and he's furious with you.'

What she was doing was parading herself beside another Muslim man in front of the world's media to get a reaction. And it worked as it did really rile Hasnat. He was hurt. He would go to the newsagents every morning and buy all the newspapers. He kept them in a box underneath his bed.

He was getting angrier and angrier and he would say to me, 'Wait until she gets back. I will have something to say to her.'

And she was saying to me, 'Oh just keep Hasnat sweet because I'll be home soon.'

She was playing games and taunting her true love. She wanted to know what he was saying, which to me didn't seem like she was over him or moving on with Dodi.

Hasnat is such a lovely man. He is extremely kind, considerate and generous. He was a complete surprise as a partner for Diana because he wasn't conventionally good looking although she considered him to be the best-looking man she had ever met.

He used to say, 'She could have anyone in the world!'

But she didn't want them, she wanted him. In their time together she never looked at another man until the very end when she wanted him to be jealous.

Her death left him broken. I really think that if she had lived, they would have got back together and he would have made her happy.

William and Catherine

I do think that the Middletons realised that William was going to St Andrews and if Catherine had to go to a university, why not go to St Andrews to be in the best company? But Carole Middleton could not possibly have foreseen that Catherine would actually meet William or that they would fall in love and get married. It is difficult to make the stars align but she may have pushed her daughter in the right direction.

William was infatuated by Catherine from first sight. Anyone could see early on that he was smitten with her. It is not very often that you find somebody that you can trust in those circles and he had found it in Catherine. From a friendship and being able to trust her, a seed grew into love.

Of course what concerned him most was how Catherine would cope with the Royal Family. His world was so different from the one in which she had grown up.

Similar to the concerns Prince Harry would later have about Meghan, he wondered how she would deal with it. The Royal Family is a difficult environment for those who have not been in it since birth. Studying the history of incoming brides and grooms, the chances of survival are not that great – William's own parents served as a cautionary tale. So he must have considered this when he was thinking about a life with Catherine. He had to make sure she understood the Royal Family to which she was gently being introduced and the characters within it because that would be a huge part of Catherine's future if she were to marry him.

William is always conscious of the fact that one day he will be king. Ever since he learned to walk and talk, he has been aware of his destiny. He knew that Catherine would have to be patient and understanding. She would have to put up with a lot if she was going to marry him.

He knew that there was only one shot at it and he wanted to

get it right. And Catherine had to consider if she actually did want that life – many girls did not. Charles had experienced that too. He had dated the likes of Sabrina Guinness and Amanda Knatchbull and while they enjoyed the close connection, when it came to anything serious, they were gone. Young girls read fairy tales of being rescued by princes but the reality of being in the Royal Family is quite different, and your needs are often sacrificed for the good of the monarchy.

William always knew that it would take a special person to understand not only him but his future role as monarch too – and I don't think there is any doubt that Catherine is the right person.

The fact that she came from a middle-class (albeit relatively wealthy) background and that she is not from aristocratic stock makes her refreshingly different. She brings something new and normal into William's world.

His and Harry's lives had already been dramatically reshaped by the tragedy of losing their mother so young and so they were both looking for security in the future. They found it in different places but both needed a partner who could help them cope with this world, which they knew all too well could destroy normal people.

William is like his mother Diana and looks for loyalty, honesty and trust.

Diana did not trust people who wanted something from her. I never asked her for anything and in return I was given a great deal.

Catherine never asked for a thing either, and didn't want anything from William except his love. That was and is a very solid foundation for the future of the Royal Family. They have built that between them. The Queen told me years ago, when I was a single man, 'Once children arrive they are the cement that holds a marriage together.' That is what William and Catherine have found with their three children.

William has always known that the Royal Family is not the real world. Catherine brought with her a family who were grounded and understanding and that is what William liked. He has often spoken of enjoying Sunday dinners with his in-laws and even in a family home video from September 2024 there is a glimpse of Carole and Michael Middleton playing games with their grand-children. This is the normality that they offer to the family.

Incoming Royals often suffer and don't last. They are the people who are scrutinised the most. Thankfully Catherine is made of strong stuff and William recognised that she could cope with a world that is so far removed from ours. They have been together for more than twenty years. Of course, every relationship has its ups and downs and goes through sticky patches. It doesn't matter who you are. It happens when you live with someone for twenty-four hours a day, every day. You get used to each other. I am sure that that has happened with Catherine and William too but I have no doubt that this relationship will last, come what may. There have been rumours about William's infidelity, as there were about Prince Philip, but in both cases, I firmly believe that they have been loyal and faithful to their spouses.

Of course they have had a difficult time dealing with Catherine's cancer battle but I think it will have made them stronger. William was suddenly confronted with the fear that he might lose his wife, and would have realised that she is the most precious thing in his life; being with Catherine and the children is what he cherishes the most. He prioritises his family, unlike the Queen, who was monarch first, mother second. William is father first and when the time comes he will be king second. Times are very different. I salute William for putting his role as father and husband before that of Prince of Wales and eventually, king.

11

My Sexuality: My Truth

I have struggled with my sexuality all my life. It is only now that I am at peace with it; I have nothing to hide and I can be honest and true. This has been a battle over the years.

I didn't always know what 'being gay' meant but I knew that I was different. As a child I had saved a dolly from being thrown away by my female cousin. In those days boys didn't have dolls. It would have been frowned upon for a boy to have a 'girl's toy'. Thankfully children can play with whatever they like nowadays.

I kept the doll hidden in a Clarks shoebox under my bed. I liked the idea of her being there while I slept. It was a comfort blanket for me. Sometimes I would move her to the gas cupboard alongside my mother's knitting as I was constantly trying to keep her existence from being exposed. I thought it was my secret but of course my brothers found her. They teased me. They sniggered. They didn't understand.

That was really the beginning of me thinking that I might be different from other boys but the word 'gay' wasn't in my vocabulary – not in that context, not in the tough mining village in which I grew up.

As the eldest child, I had already assumed a motherly role for my two brothers while our parents were at work. My little brother would crawl into bed with me at night for comfort.

Even as children we were at opposite ends of the spectrum as to what we liked and what we wanted to do in life. My brothers loved to play rough but I certainly didn't. I often got dragged into a fight with my brother Anthony. We would fight until someone drew blood. That was how we fought. But I wasn't a fighter. I really wasn't.

Rather than rough and tumble I dreamed of other things. I couldn't pass a net curtain without wanting to be a bride. I didn't know why. I look back now and think it was probably obvious.

I didn't realise I was gay going through school either. Perhaps others like my friend Kim Walters, whom I met at William Rhodes, sensed it and that's why he protected me. But then I was eleven years old and at an all-boys school and just trying to survive without being picked on by the bigger lads.

At the age of sixteen when I left to go to catering college, I was still a virgin. I was extremely naive about the world. I did not experience anything sexual until I arrived at Buckingham Palace and – as I revealed earlier – that was quite a traumatic experience, with older men trying to win a bet by getting me into bed.

Religion played a big part in my childhood and as I have said, I wanted to be a priest at one point. During my teenage years, I would pray to God every night to 'make me straight'.

I was praying to be a straight man with a girlfriend. I didn't want these feelings which would happen when I looked at an attractive man. Even when I arrived at Buckingham Palace I still looked to the skies and hoped God would make me 'like everyone else'.

But I was dropped as a young lad from the north of England into Buckingham Palace, which really was quite a gay world. And I didn't have a clue.

The theatre and spectacle of royal life was very flamboyant. Alongside all the partying I had entered into a make-believe world of dressing up in all those different uniforms and I secretly enjoyed it. It all hit me between the eyes at the age of eighteen and I was loving it.

I don't think that anyone should be judged by their sexuality but back then, people were, so I had to appear to be straight. I did have girlfriends at Buckingham Palace but perhaps deep down I knew it wasn't a girl that I wanted to embrace.

On my arrival in London, I wanted to explore its nightlife. In my mind the city was exciting but I was scared. I discovered that on Monday nights, there was a disco called Bang held in the Sundown Club in the basement of the London Astoria near Oxford Street.

Dare I go by myself? I thought.

I couldn't discuss this with anyone else. I didn't want to tell anyone at the palace. I didn't feel comfortable being labelled as gay by other gays. I wanted to be straight. I wanted everybody to know that I was 'straight'. I didn't want to be gay. If I had asked just one person, it would have gone around the palace like wildfire. I had already been warned by my good friend Martin Bubb, the deputy sergeant footman. He said to me, 'Paul, be careful' and always reminded me to keep my door locked.

But I was young and I wanted to explore so I went. I circled the block two or three times watching people entering the club. I was terrified that I might see someone from the palace there and my cover would be blown. But I was brave and I went in. I had fun and I met someone.

This was one of my first ever sexual encounters, with a young man called Greg Pead. He was an Australian on holiday in London. This was all long before I was married.

I was the Queen's footman but it was a six-foot Australian man who mesmerised me and turned my world upside down. I was unsure and naive but impressed and besotted by this good-looking human being who came from an exotic land so far away and who acted and spoke like no one I had ever met. We began a close relationship, an impossible reality as he lived on the other side of the world. I entertained him in my room at Buckingham Palace and he was so impressed. After he returned to Australia at the end of his holiday in London, we kept up correspondence.

I have always been a man of letters. I prefer the written word and of course in the late 1970s there was no such thing as social media, the internet or mobile phones. So writing letters was the only way of maintaining contact.

The Queen would be at Sandringham for six weeks over the Christmas and New Year period. Tall Paul would cover one half and I would cover the other. So I went to visit Greg in Australia during my three-week break. It felt new and exciting. I had never been to the southern hemisphere before. It was an adventure and I owed it to the boy who lay in bed in Grassmoor dreaming and looking at world maps and pictures of Hollywood stars to have that adventure. So I escaped a cold winter in Britain for a hot beach holiday in Sydney. The Queen's face was a picture when I arrived at Sandringham on my return to duty in January.

I had got quite the tan over the Christmas break so when I met her in the corridor to feed the dogs on my first day back on duty, she exclaimed, 'Good gracious! Where have you been? You are as brown as Princess Margaret!'

She was very amused.

Of course deep down I knew it had to end because the distance was just too much. It was impossible to maintain a long-distance relationship in the late 1970s. The letters, of which there had been many to start with, became less frequent and eventually stopped.

But this relationship made me realise that it was not the world I wanted. I didn't want to be skulking in the corridors. I didn't want to be hiding in the shadows. I wanted to be married and to have a family.

Then an incident happened that solidified my need to settle down with a wife once and for all.

Gossip was rife downstairs. It was 1981, the year Charles and Diana had married, and the Royal Yacht *Britannia* was raided by the military police, which happened from time to time. Lockers had been broken into and evidence seized including personal letters. Photos were found showing gay parties happening on board the yacht. Those poor naval ratings who were involved were arrested, court-martialled and dismissed from service having been accused of 'disgraceful conduct of a cruel, indecent or unnatural kind'.

The newspapers carried the grave news that 'gays' had been found and would face severe punishment.

At this time, no service women were allowed to spend the night aboard Her Majesty's ships and homosexuality in the armed forces was illegal and punishable by dismissal for indecent conduct. This law was only changed in 2011.

Of course, everyone (including Her Majesty and Prince Philip) knew that discreet homosexual behaviour happened on board ships. Vice Admiral Sir Peter Ashmore, who was our Master of the Household, had to have known, but everyone turned a blind eye. But on this occasion it had become public knowledge, so something had to be done.

I was young and single and by now Her Majesty's personal footman. I talked to, served and was in the presence of the monarch on a daily basis. I felt sick to the stomach from what I saw and heard members of staff discussing. They were gossiping and revelling in other people's misfortune, especially the 'older gays' at the palace, who were loving the drama of it all and questioning who would be implicated next.

I was naive and had formed a friendship with a 'yachtie' whom I had seen regularly both off duty and on duty whenever I had been accompanying Her Majesty on a Royal tour. I had written to him fondly and we had become incredibly close. I had no idea that it was a crime.

The newspapers carrying the report on the incident were placed on the breakfast table for the Queen to read. Unbeknown to me, she had already been briefed on the matter but it wasn't long before the rumours started and I was asked to attend a 'meeting' with Michael Tims who was assistant to the Master of the Household.

Private letters written by me had been discovered in a locker during a general raid by the military police and I was to be suspended and relieved of my duties pending further investigation. It was a breach of my privacy but naval regulations overrode personal rights.

My whole world collapsed there and then in that office. I sobbed uncontrollably and Mr Tims kindly passed me his white starched handkerchief to dry my tears. I had let everyone down: my parents, the Queen, myself. What would I do? The shame of it all.

I went to my room on Pages' Lobby and cried for a whole day, stuffing my head into a pillow to drown the noise. My dearest friends, Rose and Pauline, tried to console me but there was nothing they could do. A junior footman assumed my duties for the day and I felt that I was doomed.

After two days of what seemed like solitary confinement, I received a message that I would resume my duties the following day. I would report on duty, as normal, as if nothing had happened.

The Queen had been briefed and had decided to save me from my worst fate and reinstate me against all the odds. She liked me and saw no reason why I should be punished. After all, I had committed no crime.

It wouldn't be the last time that she would save me.

Of course, I had to thank her. So I had to have an awkward conversation with her which took place as we fed the corgis with bowls of Pedigree Chum.

Awkward for me but strangely not for her.

'It's been a difficult time for you,' was her opening line.

'I can't begin to tell you ... or to thank you, for what you have done for me,' I replied.

This was the most traumatic moment of my life so far, and I was in a confessional with our monarch – head of our church – it was a humbling experience.

She was expert at turning a negative into a positive – a diplomatic genius. She kept glancing at me, over her spectacles, as she dolloped out dog food with a silver fork and spoon.

In between, she offered pearls of wisdom and advice like a mother.

'You're getting far too fond of one of the stewards on *Britannia*. You do know he's married, don't you?'

I said, 'Yes, Your Majesty, I do.'

As another dollop of Pedigree Chum hit the yellow Tupperware dog bowl, she continued: 'Paul, it's not a wise path. Have you ever thought about getting married?'

I said, 'Your Majesty, I'm only twenty-two. I've not thought about my life yet.'

'Well, think about it. There are some lovely young girls in the palace. And I can see you being happily married to one of them. Then when children come along, you will find that it's a wonderful institution. And they're the glue that holds it all together. I know you'll be happy. Will you promise me you will try?'

'Your Majesty, I will.'

I always knew that I was in the presence of someone very special but this time, it was different; she really cared. Afterwards I thought, Wow! That was my telling off?

She filled me with encouragement and hope and as I took the dogs out of the garden entrance that afternoon, a huge weight had been lifted. I could breathe again.

It was the most devastating thing that had ever happened to me in my life to that point. I thought that I would lose everything. I would lose this incredible job I had and this environment in which

I lived. I could not return to the coal fields from where I had come. I had escaped and was working in Buckingham Palace. I was so proud of what I had achieved, as were my family. At the time, the only thing I could think was that I had brought shame on my family. And it was all because of my sexuality; I had always strived to keep it hidden and it had been exposed to none other than the Queen.

I went back to my room and thought, I don't believe what has just happened. I don't believe that my Queen could be more compassionate than anybody I have ever known in my life.

Of course, it brought us closer because we had no secrets. Well, I had no secrets from the Queen. None. And she embraced that. I was her footman. I was with her for much of the time. She knew me. And I wanted to please her so I did look around the palace for a prospective wife.

Armed with the Queen's advice, I didn't have to look far. In 1983 I went to the Queen and said, 'Your Majesty, I want you to be the first to know that I am to become engaged to Maria Cosgrove, Prince Philip's maid.'

Maria was actually introduced to me by my old friend from High Peak College, Rose Smith, who was a housemaid on Princess Anne's floor. Maria had worked in the linen room then the Belgian suite then moved up to work for the duke.

Despite not liking me on first meeting – she called me a 'tuppence ha'penny toff' – she fell in love with me and I, who adored her infectious laugh, sharp wit and stunning brown eyes, felt the same. I thought that that was the end of my gay world. And I was happy. I thought I'd exorcised it.

The Queen was thrilled by our impending union. She said, 'Oh Maria. How wonderful. Paul, I am so happy. And this brings both our households together. Mine and Prince Philip's. There'll be a downstairs wedding.'

This was long before *Downton Abbey* was on our screens; it was all real.

She then asked about what we had planned for our honeymoon and I told her we were considering going to Rhyl in Wales.

'Oh no,' she said, shaking her head. 'I think you should go to Balmoral and you should get married in the Chapel Royal.'

But there was a slight problem in that Maria was Catholic so could not get married there. Instead we tied the knot at St Mary's Roman Catholic Church in Wrexham on Saturday 21 July 1984. The Queen found a solution by sending her chaplain to my wedding. The Queen's chaplain had to explain to the Roman Catholic priest that Her Majesty wished them to share the service together so we were to have two men of the cloth marrying us. The Queen's wish was put into effect and Canon Anthony Caesar drove from his residence alongside the Queen's Chapel in St James's to Wrexham to help officiate. The Queen even gave Tall Paul and Peggy, her dresser, leave of absence so that they could attend ... and the corgis sent us a telegram too!

She and Prince Philip gave us the most wonderful wedding gifts. We were called to the sitting room together. The Queen was fond of me and Prince Philip thought equally as much of Maria.

The Queen said, 'We wanted to give you something as a memento for your wedding. I thought, what better to give you than a clock because you give me your time. It will just tick away through the years.'

The clock had her cipher on one side and Prince Philip's on the other.

Then Philip said, 'I wanted to give you something as well, especially you, Maria. And I thought, candlesticks. They are something a little more practical. You can stick a candle in them and they will light your way.'

We left the sitting room with a pair of candlesticks and a clock. This was unprecedented for royal servants. Can you imagine how much jealousy there was? My goodness, we were the chosen ones. It caused a lot of issues through the palace that we were favoured.

Unfortunately years later during one of our many house moves, one of Prince Philip's beloved candlesticks was smashed to smithereens.

'I wonder if Coalport could make us a replacement?' I pondered.

We did end up going to Balmoral to complete our honeymoon. We went first to Llandudno and then on to Scotland. When we arrived at the castle, the housekeeper was most indignant and unhelpful.

She looked at us and said, 'Hmm I don't altogether agree with this.' And I thought, 'Well, you don't have to because it's Her Majesty's wish, not yours. It's her home and she makes the decisions.'

She said, 'And anyway, you'll have to sleep in staff accommodation. As you know, Paul, we have no double beds there as there are no married couples in Royal service but I suppose we can give you the best room in the female quarters above the Pend door at the back. It is nice but it is only a single bed.'

We told her not to worry and it would be fine. Nine months later we welcomed our first-born son, Alexander.

One day the Queen was giggling and she said, 'Isn't it funny to think that Alexander was made at Balmoral? I suppose if you broke him in half, he would have Balmoral written all the way through him like a stick of rock.'

Thirty years later, when the castle grounds were opened to the public, I took Alexander there and showed him the room above the Pend door where he was conceived – perhaps we should have called him Balmoral Burrell instead. He wasn't amused at the thought of either the room or the name.

Another problem caused by our marriage was that Maria would have to give up work when she became my wife because married couples were not allowed to work together in royal service.

I went to the Queen and said, 'It's such an awful shame, Your Majesty, that Maria has got to leave service as soon as we're married. It's an old rule that the woman leaves service to look after the home. She is expected to be the homemaker.'

And she said, 'Well, that's an old-fashioned rule. What can we do about it?'

'Well, you're the Queen. You could change that rule.'

So she did. She spoke with the Master of the Household who changed the rule so that Maria stayed in service with Prince Philip and I stayed with the Queen. We were the first married couple to work and stay in royal service after getting married.

It felt like life was on track. I never wrote to Mr Pead again. He continued his life in Australia and I in England. I hoped that he found happiness, a career and a family as I did.

I didn't hear from him again until our innocent love affair came back to haunt me thirty years later at the lowest point in my life. During my trial at the Old Bailey in London, when I felt like everyone was against me, he sold my entire correspondence with him to the now defunct *News of the World* newspaper reputedly for £50,000. They ran headline after headline pummelling me at the trial, undermining my position of trust and respect in Royal service. I felt betrayed.

I was married to Maria at this time and had my two boys, so my whole family were also subjected to the sordid details of something which should have remained private, a wayward youth finding his way in life. I was so ashamed.

I have always maintained that nobody should be judged by their sexuality but I was. I had to keep thinking, as my mother would say, It's tomorrow's fish and chip paper!

Or – as it was when I was growing up – cut into squares to be placed on a rusty nail to hang on the back of the outside toilet door to be used as toilet paper.

I really wanted to be married and have a family. We were very happy and I was aware that I had made my parents happy and fulfilled by being married and giving them grandchildren.

Being gay wasn't an option for me in my circumstances. I know I would have brought shame on my family, my community and everyone I knew. It was a different time. I couldn't have survived the shame all those years ago.

Maria and I have no secrets. Ours was a true relationship. She knew when she embarked on this adventure with me that I had a past and she fell in love with me regardless. I fell in love with her. We had a full marriage in every way possible. There was never a time when I doubted it because it was real.

I thought I'd put my sexuality to bed. I had nothing to hide. It never haunted me during my married years. I felt safe in my marriage. I was totally devoted to my wife.

I didn't know anything about other closeted gay men. I thought I was the only married gay man. I had been approached by gay men but I was dedicated to my role as a faithful husband.

I had some gay friends, but no sexual relationships. I thought that was wrong because in getting married, Maria and I made a pact to bring up the boys in a family unit. I wanted children more than anything in life, and that was my sole focus during those years; I didn't really think about my sexuality because I was happy. I was happy in the world which we had created. We would have children and bring them up to be decent human beings. I was married for more than thirty years but everything changed shape when Diana died in 1997. Nothing would ever be the same again.

My marriage was different in the wake of her death.

When I lost Diana, my world was turned inside out. Those feelings which I had kept buried for two decades started to resurface and I just wasn't happy anymore. But I stayed with my wife. I said to her, 'We have to grow these children and make them into fine young men.' They were on their path in life and I had been selfish in the past and neglected them. I knew then what my duty was; my responsibility as a father will last for the rest of my days. I wanted my boys to have a strong, dependable home environment and I embraced the opportunity to be a father. I'm still with them every step of the way.

In fact, towards the end of our marriage, I honestly thought we would have another child. Maria thought so too. We had a moment when she thought she was pregnant again and I often wondered what would have happened if she had been because I'd have stayed in my marriage. I would have brought up that child in the same way that I brought up my others. Then I wouldn't have thought about myself. I'd have thought about that child. I couldn't have abandoned Maria and my children. I couldn't. That's not the person I am.

Before the princess died, she had been talking about a move to the States and excitedly told me that Maria and I and the boys could come too. So, some time after her death, I decided to still make a home for my family in America and start anew. I took my family across the pond and applied for green cards. I wanted them to have a settled life. I built a home in Clermont, Florida where I would join my family whenever I could.

But after two years, I realised that I couldn't live in America – the culture just wasn't right for me. So I said to them, 'What do you want to do? Do you want to come back to England with me or do you want to stay here?' They all wanted to stay so I left them there and returned to my flower shop in Cheshire. In the wake of Diana's death and after a short spell as the fund-raising manager of the Diana, Princess of Wales Memorial Fund, I had set up a florist's, with the legacy of £50,000 I had been left from Diana's estate. I would keep the flower shop for twenty years as it would bring in a regular income for me and my family. But on returning from the States, I was lonely, rattling around in the flat above the shop. I had little contact with anyone other than my customers.

It was 2004 and I had just signed up to go on *I'm a Celebrity...* for the first time. I had gone to London to sign the contract and was on the train from Euston to Crewe. I was on a later train than originally intended and halfway through the journey, when I glanced down the aisle a man smiled at me. I thought it odd: Is he a policeman? A journalist? A private investigator?

I looked again and he smiled back at me again. And I thought to myself, Oh, something's just happened but I don't know what it is.

We pulled into Crewe station and this man, to whom I had not spoken for the entire journey, reached for his briefcase and his coat from the rack and started to walk towards me.

I thought in that instant, OK, you want to know who this person is. You'd better be quick as this could be a sliding doors moment.

They happen rarely in life and this was one of them. If I'd let him leave the train I might never have seen him again. All I could think was that I was in a dilemma. I didn't know what to do. He could have been anyone.

But as he passed my seat, I looked up and said, 'Are you going to leave me your card?'

He turned his hand over and showed me that he was clutching his business card ready to give me. He placed it on the table and left the train. I stayed on the train and disembarked in Chester. That man, Graham Cooper, became my husband.

We were strangers on a train; it was just like the film *Brief Encounter*. I couldn't help but think of my days with Princess Diana in Kensington Palace after she had separated from Charles. We would spend a Saturday afternoon sat at either end of her pink and cream striped sofa with a box of Kleenex tissues and watch Celia Johnson and Trevor Howard have their brief encounter at Carnforth railway station. We watched that VHS many times over the years. Rachmaninoff's Piano Concerto

No. 2 came back to me and I thought, This is not a coincidence. She has sent him to me.

I honestly thought that. She sent him to take care of me because she was not here and I was at a crossroads in my life. I realised that she had become the captain of *my* ship and our roles had been reversed. I knew that I should pursue it. So I phoned him the next day and said, 'I think we should meet up.' He agreed and we went for a drink. Then we met again at Bodelwyddan Castle, a beautiful hotel in north Wales, with a table in the window in the restaurant overlooking the valley. It was the perfect lunch and I was sold. In fact, I was gone at the first look on that train on that fateful day.

I knew immediately that this man would be instrumental in my life. That was twenty years ago. I was still married but I realised my future path had been presented to me.

My family had gone, Diana was gone and my world was empty. I felt that I had to try to live an honest life and be true to myself. So I had to make the difficult journey to America to tell my wife. I said, 'I don't want to lose you. I don't want to break up this unit. We four are very important. We've come a long way together through thick and thin. I feel so selfish doing this but I have to do this for me. I have to do it for you and I hope that we will always be friends as we are now.'

We both cried and she said, 'We can just live together. We can just carry on as we are.'

But I said, 'It wouldn't be fair on you or me or anyone else involved. I will always be here. I will always be your best friend. I'll be here for you to turn to.'

The greatest gifts I have in my life are my two boys. I always say to my wife, 'I love you very much because you gave me our boys and we grew them together. It was the best thing we ever did and we should be proud of that.'

It broke my heart to say goodbye to her and goodbye to my marriage. And then I had to tell my boys. How do you even go about telling them that you are divorcing their mother and are now in a relationship with a man. Fathers shouldn't have to tell their sons about their sexuality. Children don't want to hear it. But suddenly there I was. I was a public figure now; I had to tell them before anybody else did. And I did. And again, my heart broke.

My heart's been broken so many times. I had been so happy in my marriage and so happy with my boys and I had to say goodbye to that to have the love I have now. It was not easy.

There are men out there who will understand this. There are women out there who will recognise this. They will feel the same and some day they may have to tread the same path. My only advice is to always try to be true to those you love. No matter how painful it is. It's the best course and hopefully they will understand and respect and love you for being honest. You think you can try and hide it but you can't. I've tried all my life to be truthful at my own expense. So I hope that my atonement is that my children and my wife will know that I love them just the same as I always did. I haven't changed. My heart aches knowing that I've caused them pain and upset. I would have done anything to keep it all together but I couldn't. It was beyond me. It was a force stronger than me and it broke me.

Coop put it back together again. He takes care of me and looks after me. He was sent to me and I think he knows it.

I have never spoken about any of this in this way before. It is a cathartic experience for me to share this with you now and be honest; it is my journey and it is who I am.

The Queen's advice shaped my life. I know I was protected and looked after inside the Royal Household and because of that I survived it all. I really believe that marrying Maria in July 1984 saved me. Throughout my life, I have been saved by women. Women have always stepped up and saved me: my mother, my wife, the Queen, Princess Diana. In return, they had complete trust, loyalty and respect from me. My mother, the Queen and Princess Diana are all gone now but Maria is still here. And now my husband and I watch over her. She is still very important in my life.

We continue to have a relationship and I remember Her Majesty's words of wisdom: 'Children are the glue which holds it all together.' Understandably, Maria was upset at first but now our relationship has changed. I still love her and tell her that we did something right. We have two amazing boys and an amazing grandson and none of that would have happened without our union. We are blessed. Perhaps in the next life, we can all love each other equally and not have any complications. That's an idealistic situation but that's what I would like to hope.

My faith has made me struggle with my sexuality too. For a long time I thought being gay was an affront to God. I asked him for help so long ago as a teenage boy but perhaps he gave me help to live a life which was true and full with Maria and our boys. Maybe that was my time. Perhaps I should have listened to Him when I was eleven and become a priest, but I'm thankful for the blessing of my sons and grandson.

I often take stock of how circumstances place you in certain places at certain times. That day on the train changed the direction of my life. It was like someone had switched on a light and no matter the pain it was going to cause, I had to pursue it.

I was never really convinced about destiny or the spiritual world, although Princess Diana believed in it all. She gave me many books on spirituality and the afterlife. She was obsessed with death and the thought of what was on the other side. Over the years she regularly sought advice from clairvoyants, psychics, mediums and astrologers. Rita Rogers in Derbyshire was her favourite medium and the spiritual healer Simone Simmons and astrologer Debbie Frank were influential in her life. I was always a little more sceptical about it all and sat on the fence. Diana would giggle and say, 'You don't believe it, do you?' and I would say, 'Well I'm not sure.' Even the Queen believed in spirits. 'There is a light burning in Edward III tower,' she said to me late one night at Windsor Castle. 'Could you please go up there and switch it off? I don't like going up there as there is something in the Casson Suite which I can't quite explain and the dogs don't like it either. They started growling and their hackles went up the last time I was there. So would you go up there and turn the light off?' I did, of course, but I couldn't help but think of the Queen's warning. And at Balmoral, the Queen never wished to stay the night at Allt-na-Guibhsaich, the lodge on Loch Muick where Queen Victoria and Prince Albert would stay in private. 'The dogs don't like it and they have a sixth sense about these things. It definitely has a spirit in residence,' she once said.

I took part in a television programme in 2023 called *Celebrity Help! My House Is Haunted* in which experts came to our home in Cheshire. I took it all with a pinch of salt. I thought, It's just entertainment. We're making a television programme. I know how to do that.

Long before she died, Diana used to say to me, 'You don't believe, I know you don't believe, but one day you will. One day you will believe this.' She was right. Something happened to me during the making of that show while I sat in our kitchen. There was a medium on the other side of the table and she stared at me and said, 'Oh my goodness, I think you should know, Paul, that there's somebody standing behind you with a hand on your shoulder and you will know who it is.'

I said, 'Yes, I do. I know. I know who it is because I can feel that.'

I'm not crazy and I'm not dramatic, but I know that even today there is some force that's with me. I know that she's with me. I just know it. I know it. I have signs. Things happen. I may see a picture, a book, whatever is in front of me and it means something to me; it's a sign from another place.

The medium said to me, 'That's what we have to recognise in life. We have to see the signposts and if you don't read them you will never understand.'

I became very emotional.

We then made a recording of sounds that are so high pitched that they are beyond the human ear. The medium told me to ask a question.

I said, 'Did you send Graham to take care of me?'

Nothing. Not a sound other than the whirring of the recording device.

I asked another.

'Are you happy?'

Again, no response.

She switched off the recorder and said, 'Now I'm going to replay it. You'll hear lots of high-pitched white noise which is from this plane but you may hear something else from another plane as well.'

So we heard the white noise then my voice asking the question.

And then I heard, 'Possibly.' And a giggle.

It was Diana's voice.

And then I asked if she was happy and I heard her say, 'Yes.'

I know many people won't believe it but I feel that she still guides me and that Coop was sent to save me. Diana and I had no secrets. She never asked me outright if I was gay but I was married at the time and had a family. I always assumed that she knew but we never discussed it openly. We did not have to – it wasn't necessary.

I lived a double life for a time but now my sexuality is in the public domain. Many people don't have to share that side of themselves with the world. I chose to share the truth about my sexuality partly because I wanted my children and my wife to understand. I wanted them to know that my love for them is unconditional and that it will never die. Had I met Coop when I was eighteen, I probably wouldn't be here now. I trod the path that was safe and right for me, for my life and my circumstances at that time. I played the hand that I had been dealt.

Coop and I married in the Lake District in 2017. It was the most perfect day made even more wonderful by the fact that my sons Alexander and Nicholas were there to share the occasion with us. I wore a tartan kilt and as a nod to my Royal past, my treasured set of blue cufflinks Diana had given me bearing a crown above the letter 'D' as well as the Royal Victorian Medal that was awarded to me by the Queen in 1998 for my service to her and to Diana.

I said on the day, 'There's no more hiding my unbridled happiness now. Life is about being true to who you are and, for the first time ever, I'm able to stand proudly beside my husband and say, "This is who I am".'

And while my first marriage was marked by a Buckingham Palace telegram and a present from the Queen, not many people know that she also bestowed a gift on us to celebrate my second marriage.

It was delivered to me by her trusty page Tall Paul, who came to stay one weekend and said, 'Her Majesty thought you would like this as a wedding gift. Don't get too excited because she was looking through her cupboard and she had some things that were left over from staff Christmas presents. But she thought of you when she saw this because she thought it would be useful.'

He said, 'I'm to give it to you with her very best wishes for your future together.'

We were very grateful. I wrote to the Queen to thank her. That letter is now, no doubt, in the Royal Archives. The Queen would write in red pencil across the top of every personal letter she received as to how she would like it to be answered. Then it would go into a box beside her desk. For more than seventy years, even when she was Princess Elizabeth, that box sat there. There would be letters from heads of state like Nelson Mandela and Ronald Reagan, celebrities like Grace Kelly and Marilyn Monroe and ordinary people or members of staff. They were all there. Including mine. I always felt that it was important to keep in touch with the Queen, to keep her informed and make sure that she knew the truth about everything. And that's what I did throughout my working life and afterwards. Even when I wasn't the flavour of the month at Buckingham Palace, I still wrote to the Queen because she bore no animosity. She never had a bad word to say about anyone and she enjoyed hearing news. So when I received the gift I knew that she was happy to hear of my marriage to Graham. It meant so much.

Pride is something I have felt often in my life. I was proud of the job I did with both the Queen and Diana and I have so much pride when I look at my sons and grandson. But pride also has another meaning for me now. Gone are the feelings of shame and social stigma. Pride is a celebration of embracing your own sexuality and supporting the LGBTQ rights movement.

Each year cities around the world hold events, marches and parties to celebrate the community's achievements. On 1 July 2023, which would have been Diana's sixty-second birthday, it was Pride in London. I was asked to walk in the parade for Prostate Cancer UK along with thirty others who had been affected by prostate cancer directly or indirectly. Matt, who walked beside me, was there to support the charity as his father had the disease twenty years ago.

I wasn't sure what to expect. It was my first Pride march ever and as we were led into formation between representatives from the Royal Opera House and Fortnum & Mason, I felt vulnerable. Despite the support around me, I was feeling exposed in a way I hadn't felt before.

That morning, I had been upset as my thoughts were with the princess, as they always are on the anniversary of her birthday, but as I met our group in Grosvenor Square, I was lifted by the noise of whistles and invigorating music. On the parade itself, there were thousands of people from all walks of life showing support and giving encouragement. It was an assault on the senses.

'Paul, Paul,' someone shouted. I went over to them as they wanted to have a selfie and a few words. 'Thank you for all that you have done,' she said. Another said, 'Thank you for helping to raise awareness around prostate cancer.' There was encouragement all the way from Park Lane to Whitehall.

As we walked past Fortnum & Mason through Piccadilly Circus and into a mass of humanity in Haymarket, I felt a strong ownership of not only being a gay man but being a survivor of prostate cancer. For the first time in a long time, with my husband by my side, I felt invincible. I also felt the strong presence of Diana. People associate me with 'their princess' and so she was walking beside me, encouraging me. This was the right thing to do. All the apprehension disappeared. What would she have said, I wondered, as I marched with pride. 'Go on Paul. You are doing a great job,' I think.

For one brief moment, I was standing with her on a hillside in Sarajevo, Bosnia in August 1997. She smiled as we entered a dimly lit makeshift house built in a shanty town to house a large family. They had nothing.

We noticed a curtained-off back room. The princess pulled the curtain to one side. Behind it was a small child, perhaps two or three years old, lying on a soiled mattress. Without hesitation, the princess bent down and picked the child up. She cuddled the bundle of skin and bone and he opened his eyes. At that moment, I could see that the child was blind. There were no cameras to record that simple act of humanitarianism – pure and simple kindness. I was the only witness and it moved me to tears.

That one action personified the woman whom I loved and cared for. That was who she was.

I thought of her as I walked in the parade and the inspiration that she had given me.

Little did I know, all those years ago watching her and admiring her courage and her bravery, that I would have to harness it myself one day.

Here I was, because of her, standing on my own platform harnessing her strength to help save lives.

What an incredible, energy-charged, enlightening day it was.

And I felt proud.

12

There's Something About Harry

I was one of the first people to 'meet' Prince Harry. There is no doubt that Diana trusted me but her first test of trust came at Balmoral when she returned from the Highland Games in 1984. She had been engaged in conversation in the lobby next to the dining room. Then she beckoned me into the dark dining room, closed the door behind her and said, 'Give me your hand.' She placed it on her baby bump.

'Did you feel that?' she said as the baby kicked.

'Yes, I did,' I said. I was embarrassed and worried as if someone should come in and catch us, it would be deemed that I was being inappropriate with a royal princess.

'It's a boy,' she said.

I never told a soul and she knew then that she could trust me. I told Prince Harry just before he became engaged to Meghan Markle that I had first met him in his mummy's tummy.

Once third in line to the throne of the United Kingdom, Prince Harry is now in self-exile in California having abandoned his family, friends, career, duty and country.

Although I had known him from birth, I got to know him better when I moved to Highgrove in 1987 to work for the Prince and Princess of Wales when he was three years old.

He was an adorable, inquisitive and gregarious child, unlike Prince William, who was studious and shy.

Harry knew that he was number two from day one. He knew that his role was to support his brother on his ordained path to monarchy. But while he understood it, he didn't always like it when his brother was given preferential treatment. It was never by his parents but from the servants and staff around him. The boys' nanny would whisper into William's ear as she placed three sausages on his plate at teatime, 'You need to grow up big and strong as you are going to be king one day.' Harry would stare at the two sausages on his plate and wonder why his brother had special treatment even at mealtimes. William received priority even to the point of one of his nannies calling him 'my little prince'. What William wanted, William got. Diana loathed this approach to her sons by any member of staff. In her eyes, they were equal. But William was born to be king, Harry wasn't. William's clothes were all brand new and Harry often wore the 'hand-me-downs'. Deep down it must have registered with Harry in some way. I always adopted Diana's approach. Both boys were the same to me.

For me, William and Harry were very similar to my two sons. I loved their individual personalities, especially Harry's cheeky charm. On one occasion for instance, Tigga and Pooh, his father's Jack Russells, who I was looking after at the time, managed to burrow underneath our garden shed and got stuck. It was Harry to the rescue in his parachute fatigue dress. If one of my boys was saving for something special and was short of money, Harry would come through and give them a five-pound note – 'a blue granny,' he said – to make up the difference. He was generous and kind but at times impetuous and petulant.

I say petulant reservedly as it wasn't always on display, but make no mistake, he expected to be treated like a royal prince and the grandson of a monarch. In a similar way to Prince Andrew, he knew his position and place in the hierarchy of monarchy from a very early age.

We all watched as he struggled with his unimaginable emotions as he walked behind his mother's coffin in 1997, something he railed against until the very last minute. Everyone could see that his world had collapsed.

Earl Spencer, Diana's brother, joined the family behind the cortege. After all, William and Harry are half Spencers. Often Diana's blood family have been neglected in the narrative of this story, but they played an important role in the princes' bereavement. Their uncle and aunts were drawn into this royal catastrophe.

Both sons returned to Kensington Palace in floods of tears. In private, they could find sanctuary with those who loved their mother.

There, Harry ran down the corridor and flung himself into my arms with his broken heart. Interestingly, my arms, not his father's. I've wondered about that ever since.

It's obvious to me that his mother's death triggered what would happen later in his life.

And when a thirty-six-year-old (the same age as Diana was when she died), ambitious, mixed-race American divorcee whispered in his ear, 'You and I could change the world', Harry didn't hear Meghan's voice; he heard his mother's. It was something he had long been searching for, and he knew that his life was about to change.

Six years ago I stood on Castle Hill in Windsor at the wedding of Prince Harry, the boy I had watched grow up, and his future wife, Meghan. The nation rejoiced and embraced the fairy tale. We were all happy for Harry, especially me, having witnessed his pain first hand. Meghan seemed to have saved him.

But how could it have gone so horribly wrong? And how did the couple squander so much goodwill from the Royal Family and the nation so quickly?

In the early days of their engagement, Harry and Meghan were given Nottingham Cottage, a rose-covered, one-level house with two bedrooms, a sitting room and a kitchen, which faced the front door of his mother's apartments at Kensington Palace. It was the former home of Princess Margaret's private secretary and nestled alongside Kent Cottage, a similar residence which was once the home of the Duke and Duchess of Kent. It was small but cosy and enough for a couple embarking on a journey through life.

The fairy-tale cottage wasn't a royal residence though, as Meghan discovered when she and Harry were invited to dinner with Harry's brother and his wife, the Duke and Duchess of Cambridge at their home, apartment 2 in Kensington Palace. This was the former residence of Princess Margaret, the Queen's sister, and was very much a palace. They even had a ballroom. The Cambridges had a corner of the state apartments so that they could entertain. Only the black and white tiles in the hallway remained from Princess Margaret's original interior decoration; it had been entirely refurbished. It was a far cry from the two-bedroomed cottage only two hundred yards away. This may be where the trouble began.

Perhaps the problem was that Meghan never wanted to be a 'supporting actress' in our Royal Family soap opera. She wanted to be the star but she would always have second billing to the future Queen Catherine. While Meghan wanted celebrity status, she did not want to conform to the rules of the House of Windsor. Being American, she struggled to understand the culture of the Royal establishment with its rules and protocols.

But I was shocked and saddened to hear that they were to leave the Royal Family in January 2020. Diana would have wanted Harry to stay to protect and defend his brother and be his wingman all the way to the throne. After all, Diana never wanted a divorce from her husband or the monarchy. She knew that she could do far more good within the institution than outside of it, and here was Harry divorcing himself from the family firm. If only she had been here to advise her second son, history may have been different. They could have had it all.

The Queen was of the same opinion. She wanted them to stay but she was born into an Edwardian court and was nearly sixty years older than Harry. Her Majesty had lived in a different world from her grandson. How could the Queen understand all of Harry's problems? She couldn't.

They did, however, have a special relationship – particularly because Harry was something of a joker. He didn't always adhere to protocol. Everyone was very stiff and starchy around the Queen, which she disliked, but he was relaxed and funny. Everybody else was too busy standing upright and bowing whereas Harry would say, 'Oh, Granny, how are you?' and he would grab her hand. She was very fond of her grandson. The Queen loved the warmth and tactile presence that Harry brought into her life. It was a shade of Diana, of course. The Queen recognised the friendliness that came from Diana's son. William has it too, but Harry has it in spades.

She was proud of Harry and that's why she fought so hard for the couple to stay within the Royal Family. There is no doubt in my mind that she didn't want them to leave. She did not want 'Megxit' as it was dubbed, as she knew they would be estranged from her world.

The Queen even said to Meghan, 'You can go back to acting if you want to.'

She was willing to bend the rules for Meghan, and offered to talk to her whenever she had any problems. Who could forget that it was the Queen who took Meghan on her first engagement and showed her the ropes to make sure she settled into Royal life? I do wonder if Meghan would have had an easier passage if her mother-in-law, Diana, had still been around. Diana had little help. It was like fire and brimstone for her in 1981.

I understand all the complications which Meghan as an

independent, older, divorced, bi-racial American woman will have faced trying to join the establishment. Believe me, I was part of that system. William knew this too and counselled Harry about it. 'Megxit' was inevitable.

I think the Royals learned lessons after Diana's death and must have realised that they could not let a similar situation arise again. But it happened again anyway.

The Queen was generous to say that Harry could keep his titles as long as he did not call himself 'His Royal Highness'. There is also an unwritten rule within the Royal Household that no part of a title should be used for personal gain. But as we know, Meghan uses her title Sussex for most things brand related.

Ultimately the Queen realised that what mattered most wasn't her wishes but Harry's happiness. He thought that this was the best route for him and his family to be happy. So while Harry neglected his duty to his grandmother, his Queen, his family and his country and he should have known better, it was all for love and for Meghan.

I see it differently. Harry was born into a privileged life, one which he could have embraced and used as a platform from which he and Meghan could have done incredible work. William also sees things differently from his little brother. William sees his life as a matter of duty, loyalty and service. Their two worlds collided because Harry was being totally selfish and William was trying to embrace the values of monarchy. So they came to a crossroads. Meghan was standing there and Harry had to decide in which direction to go. He couldn't go in both directions. William turned left. Harry turned right and those two paths may never cross again.

The King has been ill and Camilla does what she can to support him but it is the monarch that must carry the burden of state. There were suggestions that Harry wanted a part-time role within the Royal Family but it was impossible, even if the King wished it, as Harry and Meghan had become an incendiary device within the heart of the Royal Family.

They would do far more damage within it than they could possibly do outside of it.

After all, who will ever forget the Oprah Winfrey interview in March 2021 when in response to a loaded question, Meghan pressed the 'racist' button and it detonated a grenade within the family firm? The entire interview was their truth and not entirely factual.

And of course it prompted the Queen to release a statement which included the now famous phrase 'some recollections may vary'.

Even Her Majesty did not recognise their version of events. The allegation of racism was never corrected or clarified, even when the Queen was dying. She died thinking that there was a racist in the family, something which was abhorrent to her, particularly as she always maintained that her 'family', her Commonwealth of countries, was her greatest achievement. Some members of the Royal Family are still sickened by this and will never forgive them for causing the Queen undue stress and upset towards the end of her life.

After the Oprah Winfrey interview, there was also substantial fallout from Harry's biography, *Spare*. He signed a three-book deal with his publisher reputedly for £25 million and still has two more books to write. It is a big payday so he will need to write something that will be a draw and of interest to the public to make them put their hand in their pocket to buy another book. So he needs to be near the family to know what is going on. William no longer trusts him. The shutters are down for Harry at the House of Windsor.

William has drawn a line in the sand and made it quite clear that his brother is not welcome. He was angry when Harry spoke out about their father and feeling 'trapped' in the book. Harry is now in exile of his own making. He has become an American resident and has severed links with the Royal Family, the crown and the country. His wife is American, his children are American so perhaps he should be American too.

It is such a shame because William and Harry with their wives were the 'Fab Four' and certainly for a time Harry and Meghan were 'the golden couple'. They had everything. I had Harry marked down for Governor General of Australia or Canada and then they could have lived in their own royal domain. It would have been as if they were king and queen in their own country and they could have travelled the world for their own causes.

I think the problems came partially from Meghan being American. It is a different culture, different lifestyle and she had different goals. In the end it really boils down to money. As Royals, they could never be fabulously wealthy like the friends they keep, such as Tyler Perry, although they could be fabulously famous. In American culture, doesn't fame go hand in hand with wealth? And that was the problem. They could never fulfil all of their dreams by being inside the Royal Family. So they thought that they could make a life outside of it and make their own rules where they wouldn't have to answer to anyone.

But has it worked? I'm not convinced that they have got the wealth or the celebrity status that they wanted and all they seem to do is trade on their royal connection – the very thing that they wanted to get away from. It's a dichotomy. They're in a very strange situation. If they are not royal, they have no unique selling point; they need to be royal to retain their value – a total contradiction.

Fortunately the Queen did get to meet both of Prince Harry's children, Prince Archie who was born in May 2019, and Princess Lilibet who was born in June 2021. It was Lilibet's first birthday on the Saturday of the weekend of the Platinum Jubilee celebration in June 2022 and Netflix was in tow at Frogmore Cottage to record the event. Harry and Meghan invited the Queen and all the younger members of the family to a tea party. Her Majesty declined, instead inviting them to tea in the Oak Room in Windsor Castle without the Netflix crew. The rest of the Royal Family were congregating for a buffet tea when the Sussexes arrived. They walked up to Windsor Castle, went through the dog door into the castle and up the spiral staircase into the Queen's apartment. Of course Harry would claim later that he 'wasn't able to get to the Queen' but he knew how to reach her whenever he wanted to see her. He also had a secret weapon. Unbeknown to his father or brother, Harry had sent Granny a mobile phone with the intention of having a secure line direct to the CEO of the family firm, bypassing not just his family but all her courtiers.

When it arrived she said, 'What am I supposed to do with it?' After all, the monarch couldn't be expected to answer it whenever it rang. Imagine it going off in her handbag while she was in a meeting with a head of state or opening Parliament.

So that mobile phone went in the top drawer of a servant's desk at the end of the long green corridor alongside a phone from Prince Andrew, who'd had a similar plan. But even without her mobile phone, the Queen did get to see Harry and Meghan and her great-grandchildren.

When Harry and Meghan appeared in the Oak Room the family parted like the Red Sea so that the Sussexes could take centre stage with the Queen. Some members of the family left the room in disgust and wouldn't return until they had left thirty minutes later. The Queen loved seeing the children but there is a suggestion that she was aggrieved that Lilibet had been given her special family name. She had been asked whether the child could be named after her and she was delighted assuming that her name would be Elizabeth. She had no idea that her great-granddaughter was to be called Lilibet, a name given to the Queen by her father and only used by her closest family. However, she was always pragmatic and realised that she could not do anything about it after the event. She did not like it but she had to accept it. The Queen played with the children and chatted with Harry and Meghan. She thought everything was fine but little did she know.

On the Sunday of the weekend of the Platinum Jubilee celebration, the Queen had arranged for the chef to make her favourite chocolate cake, a Sachertorte, with one candle on top for Lilibet's birthday. She had hoped that her favourite grandson and his wife would join her for tea. But she was left disappointed when she was told they had left already. It might have been a breakdown in communication that Harry and Meghan weren't aware of her plans. And it's a shame the tea didn't happen as Meghan never saw the Queen again while Harry saw her next on her deathbed.

The publication of *Spare*, which was scathing about his father and brother (and also me) has only widened the gulf.

The Royal Family have turned their backs and shunned Harry but the Spencers have embraced them. They see him as having been rejected and have rescued him. William is on the sidelines, being 'half Spencer' and unable to ignore his Windsor heritage.

As he prepares to become king, William devotes his time to following in his mother's footsteps with a focus on homelessness and improving the environment through the Earthshot Prize.

Prince Harry seems to spend most of his days with lawyers and going in and out of court. Of course, he is entitled to tell his story, but I wish that he would stick to the script and tell the truth, the whole truth and nothing but the truth.

In 2003, the *People* newspaper, owned by Mirror Group Newspapers, published an article which referred to Prince Harry calling me 'a two-faced sh*t'.

In his phone hacking claim against Mirror Group Newspapers in June 2023, Harry claimed that those remarks were obtained illegally from a voicemail which he had left for his brother Prince William. Instead of moaning to his brother, why didn't Harry come to me directly if he had any problem with anything I had said or done? I received no direct communication from either of Diana's boys until 2017 when they asked to see me and I met with them with my husband.

In paragraph 99 of Harry's witness statement in support of his court claim which was submitted to the court as an accurate and truthful statement, the Duke of Sussex's truth veered off track. Like his grandmother, the late Queen, so beautifully put it, my recollection may also vary.

In this legal document in support of his claim, he states:

Both my brother and I had very strong feelings about how indiscreet Paul had proven to be with the way he sold our mother's possessions and how he had given numerous interviews about her. ... A 'senior Royal source' is quoted within the article [printed by the *People*], reflecting my exact private feelings, including that I was 'dead against any meeting' and that a meeting would be 'pandering to Burrell's attention-seeking and self-interest'. I also would have used the phrase 'two-face s***' as is reported and believe this could have been lifted directly from a voicemail I had left.

So this statement alleges that William wanted a meeting in 2003 but Harry was against it.

I would have gladly attended a meeting with both boys and knowing that he had called me a two-faced sh*t, I would have confronted him because he certainly did not always view me this way, particularly when I hugged him and comforted him after his mother's funeral.

I was sad and disappointed to read these callous remarks. It really hurt me at such a torrid time when I was battling prostate cancer and dealing with radiotherapy and hormone treatment. I was at a particularly low ebb in my life. I had no idea how the cancer would affect me and whether it was terminal. It was bad timing; he would not have known it but he was kicking a man when he was down.

Prince Harry was, however, challenged in court over discrepancies between his witness statement and *Spare* over whether he wanted to meet with me.

In *Spare* he says that he wanted to fly back and confront me rather than being against a meeting but that Charles and William talked him out of it.

When challenged, Harry couldn't remember whether he did or didn't want a meeting.

But regardless of name-calling or whether or not a meeting took place, it was Harry's repetition of flippant and damning allegations that I sold his mother's possessions that shocked me to the core as they are serious and totally unfounded claims. It is a defamation of my character.

His words are hateful and hurtful particularly as he knows what ordeals I have faced in my life, especially the nightmare of appearing in the Old Bailey where his late grandmother intervened to clear my name and all of the charges against me were dropped.

But why should I be surprised when he seems to have attacked everyone whom he used to hold dear.

He knows that I have loved, cared for and protected his mother's legacy. I have enormous respect and love for her and his brother and I am loyal to the monarchy.

I have been humiliated by Harry. I never wanted to disclose that I met the boys at Kensington Palace. The boys wanted to know about their mother's life from me. However, as a result of Harry's actions since then, I have been left with no choice.

I have been discredited despite being so loyal and I expected more from someone for whom I cared so much.

Things were said in that meeting which gave a very clear indication of how much their mother cared for me and how important I was in their lives.

Harry has no respect for or understanding of what my family and I have endured and suffered. He should know better; his mother taught him better. That is not the Harry I knew or his kindness which I remember so well.

Now he is a petulant prince who has lived a charmed life with every luxury afforded to him.

I was furious that my character was being questioned so I challenged Harry through his solicitors regarding the inaccuracy of his witness statement as I have never sold Diana's possessions. Despite various emails chasing for a reply, there has been no substantive response other than the solicitors informing me that they 'have received no instructions from their client as to responding to you'.

He has a wrecking-ball mentality and seems to be living his own *Truman Show*, a world of reality television, directed, produced and starring him and Meghan. It is presented to show their version of events and their truth.

But what about the *actual* truth?

Not everything Harry says is accurate or a true version of events. He has accused his family of many things which are unforgivable including that the Queen brokered a deal with the media and that his brother made a secret agreement with the press. Mr Justice Fancourt called aspects of his arguments, in a different legal case against News Group Newspapers, 'implausible' and 'not credible'.

Harry is totally aware that it was common practice for Diana to invite celebrities and journalists to private lunches because both he and William attended them. They both knew that there was a 'working' relationship between them and the press but at no time was I ever aware of an agreement.

I think that Harry has seriously over-egged and exaggerated an understanding for his own narrative.

He has burned his bridges with his own family and has had to leave Frogmore Cottage. Even Princess Beatrice and Princess Eugenie have grown tired of his whinging. Eugenie was upset when he and Meghan told the family at Eugenie's wedding in October 2018 that they were expecting their first child. Everyone knows that upstaging the bride in any situation is an absolute no-no.

Harry always knew what his future had in store. His mother taught him that his role was to support his brother on his path to the 'top job'. Diana knew that her son would be king one day and thought that Harry would be beside him. The dynamic duo – what could possibly go wrong? I'm sure that she would be devastated to see her boys, who were such close friends, so far apart now.

Despite everything I still wish Harry and Meghan happiness always and hope that their life in America is successful and filled with everything Princess Diana would have wished for them. They have ultimately chosen their own path, their own destiny and have begun a celebrity life on another continent.

I still believe though that there are many like me who wish that they had taken a different path. Harry is still loved but I very much doubt whether the majority of the British public feel the same about his wife.

If Harry's marriage were to founder – which I believe may be inevitable – he will return to England to seek refuge. Everything he knows is in the country of his birth and once the veil is lifted from his obsession with Meghan, he will want to be back to what and where he knows best – and the King would be delighted to have him back.

But I am not sure if William would be equally pleased. It's such a shame as Harry, who was always one of the public's favourite Royals, could and should have had it all. Instead he has made a right royal mess!

13

Prince Philip –
The Cantankerous Prince

Respected, revered and feared in equal measure by most who knew him, Prince Philip became famous for his 'short fuse'.

Over the years, I saw grown men leave his study in tears but I also saw him being incredibly kind to others. I saw the two sides of this incredibly articulate, devoted, loyal husband and consort.

He was a hard-hitting, no-nonsense man who would shoot from the hip. He never minced his words and was always forthright. He put the fear of God into me at times. I tried to steer clear of him as much as possible.

He admired tough and inspirational men and tried to surround himself with similar-minded people. He sometimes disliked the restraints of the world in which he had lived since he married Elizabeth Alexandra Mary in 1947. He didn't want the fuss or attention that surrounded the court, which engulfed his wife and mother-in-law. The constant fawning and obsequious attitude of servants and their ways, bowing and scraping, wasn't his style.

His two valets and his two pages belonged to his personal household of more than twenty people and suffered the prince's wrath regularly, sometimes for no particular reason. The Duke of Edinburgh was exact and precise about his appearance and always immaculately turned out. His suits and shirts were made to measure in Savile Row and his uniforms were constantly updated according to his rising status over the years. Each night for dinner at Windsor he would wear the Windsor jacket with a cream silk shirt and a black bow tie. The same shirt would be worn for several nights in succession, hanging in his dressing room with the second button undone to signify that the shirt had been worn before. He was frugal. His socks were darned and the collars and cuffs of his shirts, when worn, were reversed by the seamstress in the linen room. He wore military and Hermès ties and always carried a linen handkerchief in his pocket. His shoes were spit-and-polished on a daily basis with the shoelaces ironed flat. They shone like a mirror and if they weren't perfect, they were thrown across the room. He was excellent at spotting what had not been done. His furious parting shots were either 'You are all bloody idiots' or 'It's all a load of bollocks'. His staff were well-advised to stay away from an angry Prince Philip. I was always nervous when passing his door.

One day he came across a footman in tears in his wife's sitting room. Instead of addressing the footman directly, he turned to his wife and said, 'What's the matter with him? I suppose it's boyfriend trouble!'

Not as tolerant or patient as the Queen, he lived in a man's world.

But the Queen put up with it – after nearly seventy-four years of marriage she knew and understood his frustrations. She would let him rant and when finished would simply say something like, 'Well, that's that!' or change the subject completely. The Queen tolerated him on all levels because she loved him. They were a double act – Prince Philip was the outspoken warm-up act, the Queen the main event. In eleven years of serving the Queen, I never once heard a raised voice between them. She had a calming effect on him. Prince Philip might grumble but he always respected his wife and never forgot that she was the Queen. And a queen always trumps a prince – he never had to be reminded of that.

But apart from her, Prince Philip took no prisoners, especially when it came to his children. Charles often caught the rough edge of his father's tongue.

I witnessed an incident one evening when Prince Charles, as he was then, joined his mother and father for a martini cocktail in the Queen's sitting room before a diplomatic reception. He was wearing every order that had been bestowed upon him – the Order of the Garter, the Order of the Thistle, the Order of the Bath, the Order of St Michael and St George ... they were all encrusted with diamonds, emeralds and rubies and sparkling in the light. As soon as Prince Philip saw him he blew his lid, shouting, 'You look like a bloody Christmas tree. You bloody idiot! Look at your mama.' He pointed at the Queen. 'She is wearing only ONE order ... so go back to your room and change. Why do you always have to be so excessive?' And that put Charles in his place. He was of the opinion that his son, his mother's heir, had 'made a bloody mess of everything'. I heard him rebuke his son with that phrase on several occasions.

Equerries, private secretaries, valets, naval officers and generals all suffered the indignations of the Queen's husband. Some were reduced to tears. There was nobody to criticise him – not even his wife.

He was often dismissive to men but kind and courteous to ladies. My ex-wife Maria, who was his maid for eight years, was regularly presented with thoughtful gifts like a box of chocolates or a souvenir from his latest tour. He was always respectful and generous towards her.

It wasn't long before Maria was obviously pregnant.

It might have looked a little irregular back in the 1980s for a maid to be dusting, sweeping and making beds while heavily pregnant – the household didn't like it – but Prince Philip and the Queen saw nothing wrong.

In fact, Prince Philip would often say to Maria, 'Sit when you can', 'Don't stretch' and 'No ladders'. He took great care of her until it was time for her to leave service three months before the baby was due to arrive and withdraw to our home in the Royal Mews.

Prince Philip retired from the royal scene and his duties in 2017, aged ninety-six, having completed 22,219 solo engagements and made 5,493 speeches since 1952.

He spent his last years at Wood Farm on the Sandringham estate surrounded by his household staff, his horses, his carriages and his grooms doing exactly what he wanted to do in retirement away from royal protocols and timetables. During this time, the Queen lived mainly at Buckingham Palace and Windsor Castle.

'Would someone ring Prince Philip and let him know that I'm still alive,' she said to one of her courtiers just before the pandemic hit the country in March 2020. She missed his wisdom and support. Covid and the lockdown brought the couple back together for the remainder of his life.

He returned from Norfolk to join the Queen at Windsor Castle to form HMS Bubble. He never saw his beloved Wood Farm again. He took dinner with his wife at 8.30 p.m. in the private dining room when he was able although he was becoming increasingly fatigued. Like many couples of a similar age, they spent quiet evenings together beside the fire watching television, she with a gin and tonic in hand and he with a glass of Double Diamond beer, his favourite pale ale. The irony was that when he joined the family on becoming engaged, one of his nicknames was 'Bubble' as he didn't quite fit in and was not welcomed with open arms.

He died at Windsor Castle in his dressing room alone as he had been unwell for several months so the Royal couple were sleeping apart. The Queen was awoken by her dresser, Angela Kelly, who told her the sad news. She dressed and with great dignity spoke with the nurses who had been caring for him before spending ten minutes alone with him. She took it all in her stride but when it was suggested that his body should lie in state in St George's Chapel, she insisted that his coffin should be placed in the private chapel at the end of St George's Hall as it was 'a little closer to me'.

Every evening, that lonely figure walked down the carpet of the Grand Corridor to say good night to her husband of seventy-four years.

When the time came to say goodbye at his funeral in St George's Chapel on 17 April 2021, she observed Covid protocol and sat alone, masked, alongside her handbag which contained Prince Philip's handkerchief and a photograph of them on their wedding day.

As the coffin sank into the crypt, he was laid to rest there to await his wife. When Prince Philip died, the Queen didn't have long left to live, although she didn't know at the time. She joined him the following year, on 19 September. Then the two of them, united in death, were laid to rest beside each other in the King George VI Memorial Chapel in St George's Chapel at Windsor Castle.

He was her soulmate, her guardian at the gate and as she once said, 'my mainstay'. He ran her life and kept the family in order. He stopped people getting to the Queen and prevented her from having to worry about trivialities. The rule at Buckingham Palace was always to keep the Queen informed but not to worry her about things that were unnecessary. He was the 'guard dog' and fiercely protective of his wife. But that wasn't always the way. The Royal Family didn't take to Philip in the beginning. They looked on him as an intruder who couldn't be trusted even though he was a prince and a great-grandson of Queen Victoria.

Philip was conscious of that all of his married life. He was an outsider who had radical ideas and had to survive and prove his worth. He was deemed to be a dangerous influence. He thought that his wife and children should carry his name 'Mountbatten' but had to concede to his children being named Windsor as they were part of the House of Windsor. To this day, some members of his family still carry his name.

That is why he so understood Diana and her struggle for survival in an often alien and hostile environment. He realised the pressures of a young eighteen-year-old being inducted into the 'firm'. The Royals see it time and time again when a young, unprepared soul comes into an often cold and hostile environment, with no rule book or guidance, and is told to 'just get on with it' and try and swim in perilous waters.

But unfortunately, once he was gone, there was no one left to replace him or protect the Queen from her family. The family flooded her with their problems. The door was open and everyone wanted something – she had never had that happen before.

I believe it impacted her decline because in the last year of her life, she took family issues on board and she suffered while her children and grandchildren wanted her to solve their issues be it marital, emotional or financial. She missed the protection that Philip had offered her.

In the summer of 1946, King George VI granted Philip permission to marry his daughter Elizabeth, then aged twenty.

During his courtship with Princess Elizabeth, he wrote many love letters from overseas postings. His mind was set on the young princess from the very beginning and in her mind, there was only ever Philip.

When Princess Elizabeth wed her Greek-born third cousin, then twenty-six, on 20 November 1947, they made a vow as man and wife. Six years later at her coronation, the naval officer reinforced that pledge by swearing an oath of allegiance before God to serve the monarch. He took this oath extremely seriously and kept it until his death. Philip knew that he had to earn his place, much as Diana did.

Princess Elizabeth spent the first years of her marriage as a naval officer's wife in Malta. Their home was a grand villa called Villa Guardamangia in Pietà on the outskirts of Valletta. The Queen would later say that these carefree years were among the happiest of her life. Within four years of marriage, Philip had given up his role in the navy, which he loved, to focus on royal life and support his wife as consort.

While he served his Queen publicly, at home, he was the boss in the House of Windsor and made all the decisions. The Queen would often say to me when I enquired of a family matter or arrangement, 'I have no idea. Ask Prince Philip. He will know.'

Throughout her life she depended on her consort just as Queen Victoria relied on Albert. Philip was always the Queen's sounding board and she trusted him above anyone else.

Theirs was a true love story – I saw it on a daily basis. They slept in the same bed, they ate all their meals together and he was the master of her world. I often found notes in Prince Philip's spidery handwriting to his wife in which he referred to her as his 'sweetie pie', 'choux fleur' or 'cabbage'.

While he was often belligerent, bad-tempered, awkward and argumentative, he got things done. He managed the royal estates and their accounts and oversaw the upkeep and running of royal residences. Balmoral and Sandringham were the Queen's private properties and Philip's task was to balance the books and be innovative at the same time. His stewardship of the House of Windsor was very similar to that of Prince Albert to Queen Victoria's world. He very much admired Prince Albert who led the way as the 'first outsider' marrying into the Royal Family. Day-to-day family decisions were made by Philip. He was the head of the family. The Queen deferred all matters to him. He was her mainstay in life and that never changed. I truly believe that they loved each other dearly and that they were devoted to each other. They understood each other completely.

There have been many rumours of Prince Philip's infidelity over the years. It was rumoured that he had an affair with a British actress called Pat Kirkwood in the 1950s. While the creator of *The Crown*, Peter Morgan, followed this theme in the scripts for his Netflix show, the actress never confirmed that an affair took place and there was no evidence to support it. Nevertheless, there is no doubt in my mind that he was a ladies' man. He loved the company of beautiful women – actresses and celebrities including the TV presenter Katie Boyle, singer Hélène Cordet and actress Merle Oberon.

I once heard the Queen Mother discussing Diana and her affairs with a lady-in-waiting in the saloon drawing room in Sandringham. She said, 'Diana is such a silly girl. Doesn't she realise that men have affairs?' Her daughter, Queen Elizabeth, had adopted many of her mother's attributes and may well have turned a blind eye to these rumours. Philip always came home. He was devoted to his wife and would never have brought shame on the House of Windsor. When the Queen came to the throne earlier than expected, it was not easy for him. He was still trying to fit into the system.

Whatever friendships or relationships he had with other ladies, they were very discreet. He knew his lot and just got on with it.

Personally I feel that Philip's life was over-dramatised for effect in *The Crown*, and that the depiction should be taken with a pinch of salt.

And we should not forget that the prince wrote to Diana

when Charles admitted to adultery on national television saying, 'Mama and I do not condone either you or Charles having extra marital affairs.'

The Queen once told me in her sitting room at Buckingham Palace, 'I just don't understand Diana,' and went on to say that she had met Prince Charles on the hillside at Balmoral, walking alone and distraught, who said exactly the same thing.

But Philip saw something of himself in her struggle for survival. He had much in common with Diana as he too had had to fight to be accepted and recognised in the early years.

Interestingly, Diana trusted Prince Philip most of all in the Royal Family. She knew that, in him, she had found a sounding board. She also knew that he was in charge of family business and that the Queen deferred all family affairs to him as she wanted to avoid confrontation at all costs.

Diana once wrote to the duke and said that she had no idea how difficult it had been for him to enter the Royal Family and become consort to the head of state.

Over the years the Duke of Edinburgh survived but he had watched Diana flounder. He realised that he could actually help Diana during the breakdown of her marriage to his son, Prince Charles. He wanted to mediate in what he saw as a catastrophic and sad situation which had far-reaching consequences for the monarchy and the country. He cared for Diana, whom he saw as vulnerable and alone. But how could he help? First, he had to understand how Diana felt. She explained that Charles had told her that he never really loved her and that he had resumed his relationship with Camilla earlier than anyone knew. She was frank and honest and asked Philip if it was true that he had advised his son that if the marriage did not work within five years then he could return to Camilla.

Diana explained that she thought that she had been 'offered' to the Royal Family 'on a sale or return basis'. Charles had told both his father and his wife that he had never really wanted to marry Diana.

But of course, the problem was that Diana had fallen in love with Charles. Diana was too much of a hopeless romantic and thought she had been rescued by her prince in shining armour. She even told me that she kissed a frog and found her prince. But later in life she admitted that she'd actually kissed a frog and found a toad. Philip was on her side despite being her husband's father. Their father/son relationship had always been difficult. They were cut from different cloth. Charles has never had to struggle like his father did.

Diana also realised that Philip had had a rough ride with the press and was often an easy target. They would never get to the Queen but they could get to him. Just as they avoided criticism of Charles, she felt that she had suffered the criticism instead. They were both outsiders. She wrote in one letter to him that it was comforting to her to know that he understood this. Letters from Diana to Philip always started 'Dear Pa' and usually ended 'with my fondest love to you and Mama'. His letters to her always began 'Dearest Diana' and were signed off 'from your loving Pa'.

Diana wanted to set out terms for her continued public service as a member of the Royal Family. While Philip understood her dilemma, he was still consort to the Queen and the father of the heir to the throne so he couldn't always be on her side – he had his own views and responsibilities.

In 1992, she wrote that she did not think that it would be a good idea for her to accompany Charles on a trip to Korea in November. She thought Charles hated joint public events where he was not recognised and often found them 'hurtful and irritating' as most people wanted to see her. But it would be a blow for Charles to have to go by himself and he would have to explain why the princess was not with him. It could have been embarrassing for him. Diana knew that she was holding a winning hand and communication between them was almost non-existent.

As an ally, Philip agreed that Diana had worked hard to establish her role as a hardworking member of the Royal Family but he also accused her of carving out a role as a 'public hero' in the media which had had a significant impact on Charles's position with the public and had undermined him.

In the end Philip persuaded her to go on the trip for the sake of the monarchy and to save face as everyone was expecting to see both of them. Of course it was a disaster and Diana couldn't hide her feelings.

Diana knew that Philip was the only one who talked on her level with authority and knowledge. He saw that her marriage was crumbling and that Charles had returned to Camilla. Philip tried to mediate between the warring couple at this time and to give advice as an impartial judge. He wanted Diana and Charles to work things out and remain married. Both he and the Queen had every hope that they would reconcile and eventually become king and queen.

Diana worried that there would never be a solution with Mrs Parker-Bowles in the equation, but for Charles she was non-negotiable.

Philip agreed with his daughter-in-law, admitting that 'we do not approve of either of you having lovers'.

I remember Philip would rebut some of Diana's claims and correct her at times too.

He reminded Diana, 'You both began to have doubts about marriage after you had become engaged.'

The fact was that both the Queen and Prince Philip were 'anxious' and concerned about Charles's relationship with Camilla.

Diana would write, 'I am completely redundant as a wife and companion.'

Prince Philip's role in the mediation was never to apportion blame or judge either one of them but he realised that both parties had to accept some responsibility.

I doubt whether Philip really ever understood his son's motives; he suggested to Diana that they should both change their ways and stop their public attacks on each other to lessen the bitterness that ensued. He was looking for an amicable solution.

Diana said to me once, 'How many other wives would have to discuss their marital problems with their father-in-law instead of their husband?'

And to be fair he was doing more than his son to try and save the marriage. Charles was putting his head in the sand.

Meanwhile Diana was desperate for a way forward for the couple that did not include divorce. She wanted to live a separate life as they could no longer live together.

In later years, even Prince Philip's patience would run out with Diana and he would say, 'You've made your bed, now you have to lie on it.'

He made it clear that everyone was upset by the biased account of the marriage in the Andrew Morton book in 1992. He told the princess that everyone was suspicious of her involvement. Diana, by then in denial, insisted that she had not assisted the author. I think she was taken aback by the seismic waves its publication created.

There were discussions that a trial separation was necessary but the Queen and Prince Philip did not give their blessing for a split; instead they advised the Prince and Princess of Wales to learn to compromise, be less selfish and try and work through their problems for the sake of the children and of course, the monarchy.

By this time, Diana felt everything was out in the open and

was able to speak frankly to her in-laws about her loathing for Camilla Parker Bowles and her anger. It was a relief for her.

Never let it be said that either the Queen or Prince Philip did not have the best intentions to save the royal marriage.

But when Philip bombarded Diana with correspondence, she got upset and infuriated. She described the letters as 'brutal'.

She made several photocopies of the letters that she dispatched to friends she trusted. I was shown the originals. I remember her sitting on the stairs in Kensington Palace one day in 1993. Over a year had gone by since she had received them and she shook her head over their contents. The letters offered some harsh truths but they were not poisonous as it has been suggested. They were long and rambling over several pages.

The duke was clearly bristling from the revelations in Andrew Morton's book and was wounded on behalf of the family and his son. This might have marred his objectivity. It felt like he was being cruel to be kind to try and jolt her into saving her marriage.

Instead she took it as an attack on herself, especially when he said that 'jealousy had been the cancer within their marriage'.

I cringed at mentions in the book of my involvement as the interfering butler who had let Diana know, after quizzing, where Prince Charles had gone after leaving Highgrove in the middle of the night. Philip said it made his son feel like his wife was 'a jealous spy peeking through keyholes and listening in doorways'.

But I was of the opinion that it would be hard for any woman to know that her husband was continuing to have liaisons with an old flame and that she would want some reassurance as to what was going on.

However hard Diana found her father-in-law's opinions, she respected his honesty and after she challenged some of the comments his letters became kinder.

She also leaped with joy when he expressed his private

thoughts about Camilla: 'We never dreamed he might feel like leaving you for her. I cannot imagine anyone in their right mind leaving you for Camilla. Such a prospect had never entered our heads.'

He also had begun signing off his letters 'With fondest love, Pa.'

More importantly, for the first time since she joined the family, she felt that someone from the House of Windsor was actually hearing her rather than dismissing her as emotionally hysterical. The Duke of Edinburgh might not have saved her marriage but he did break down barriers and brought many unspoken issues into the open.

Away from marriage counselling, Philip was kept busy. His study, library, dressing room and bathroom adjoined the Queen's rooms by connecting doors. He spent a great deal of time at Buckingham Palace sat at his desk typing letters and researching. He wrote all his own speeches and correspondence. He was fascinated by innovation and the modern world, conservation and climate change. This is from where King Charles first got his inspiration too.

Philip had an old London taxi converted into an electric vehicle. He would often be spotted out and about anonymously.

In his later years he became known for his gaffes and certainly Philip was sometimes a little too outspoken, especially on overseas tours. He would make a joke and sometimes in our politically correct world it would seem inappropriate. I witnessed at first hand the fallout from one of his comments when I was accompanying the royal party in Hong Kong when they visited the English Speaking Union. He said to a group of British students, 'If you stay here much longer you'll all be slitty-eyed.' Clearly this is a racist comment bolstered by Philip's alpha male character, and it is unacceptable. However, he would never wish to hurt anyone by his blunt comments. As head of state, the Queen would conduct herself in a stately manner. She was always queen first, so Philip's job was to make everyone feel at ease and relax in the monarch's presence and be as normal as possible in extraordinary circumstances. It is the Queen who said, 'I have to be seen to be believed', and perhaps Philip felt that he had to be heard to be understood.

14

The King and I

I had always known King Charles III as the Prince of Wales. He is nine years my elder but I have always thought of him as much older and from a different generation. I was closer in age to Diana as she was only three years younger than me.

Anyone meeting Charles for the first time will find him charming and amusing but behind that façade is a somewhat complex and complicated character. Charles is exact and precise like his father, expects total dedication and doesn't suffer fools. His routines have never changed. His toothpaste is squeezed onto his toothbrush every morning and he uses a silver key which winds down the tube to avoid any waste. He abhors waste – yet he is excessive. His pyjamas are laundered or pressed every day, the drawstring tapes pressed flat like his shoe laces. He, again like his father, likes his dress shoes to be 'spit and polished' to a mirror finish. He writes endless letters in an almost illegible spidery scrawl with a fountain pen which he never takes off the paper. He always travels with his Balmoral tartan pillow to support his lower back during car journeys. He never eats processed food. Everything is made in his kitchen including pasta and his favourite rosemary herb bread which he has with a sandwich lunch or as toast at dinner. He uses lashings of dressings on salads and adores creamy rich sauces. It's what I call 'wet food'.

His favourites are pasta dishes with truffle and mushrooms and dishes to which he can add ingredients from his kitchen garden at Highgrove. He loves his carefully cultivated fruits which are bottled or preserved to enable him to eat his home-grown favourites year round. Woe betide anyone forgetting to pack a pickled peach or a poached pear for his breakfast when he's away from one of his homes. He loves a cordial drink called 'lemon refresher' made with lemon juice, sugar and bicarbonate of soda. In short, he is spoiled and eccentric.

And perhaps that is why he was always attracted to similarly eccentric characters while Diana was always suspicious of their motives.

Spike Milligan visited Highgrove House several times. Often when Diana was in London with the boys. Charles seemed enthralled by Spike's Irish wit and the two would spend evenings re-enacting sketches from *The Goon Show*. Sometimes as I left for home after a long day's duty, I could hear them singing 'The Ying Tong Song' in the sitting room.

Spike preferred not to sleep in the Georgian four-poster bed in the green guest bedroom but instead in the ceramic bathtub or on the bathroom floor. He later sent the prince a plaque saying 'Spike Milligan slept here' to mark the 'hallowed' spot, which Charles found very entertaining.

While the comedian's behaviour was merely harmless eccentricity, Charles's friendship with Jimmy Savile, in hindsight, was much more concerning.

I have never shared my thoughts of Jimmy Savile, whom I knew for more than twenty years. He was a regular visitor to Buckingham Palace, Kensington Palace and Highgrove, where he was the only person allowed to smoke inside. He regularly came to William and Harry's birthday parties and he also advised Charles and Diana regarding their media relations.

He had us all fooled. It was only after his death in 2011 that hundreds of allegations of sexual abuse were made against him, leading police to conclude that he had possibly been one of Britain's most prolific sex offenders.

But to me, he was a slimy man who was even inclined to stub his cigars out in the princess's Hermès ashtrays, which were really only ever meant for decoration in Kensington Palace. I would find them outside her sitting-room door after he had visited.

'I can't stand the smell,' she would say.

Jimmy Savile could access all areas of Buckingham Palace. His face was so famous, he didn't need a security pass; the police just waved him in. He attended all the staff balls in his string vest and gold tracksuit complete with 'jangle-jangle' gold chains and diamond-encrusted Rolex watch.

'I'm going to be buried in a tracksuit wearing all my jewellery, at forty-five degrees facing the sea, covered in a ton of concrete so nobody can dig me up,' he would say.

It wasn't just the Royals who were in his thrall. *Jim'll Fix It* was a hugely popular television show in the 1980s. Jimmy also had access to Downing Street and Prime Minister Margaret Thatcher. He spent Christmas with her and Denis at Chequers. He placed himself at the heart of British life.

Alongside the Prince and Princess of Wales, no wonder he felt indestructible. He was knighted and raised millions for charity and nobody suspected him even though it was all there in front of us in plain sight.

I once visited Jimmy at his home in Roundhay Park in Leeds. He owned and lived in a penthouse apartment on the fifth floor. It was decorated in a 1960s monochrome style with steel glass-topped coffee tables covered with mementos of his famous life including two red leather-bound albums embossed with 'This Is Your Life' in gold. The walls were decorated with black and white photographs of Jimmy with his white mop of hair surrounded by celebrities and members of the Royal Family. 'Make yourself a cup of tea,' he shouted from another room. The kitchen was immaculate as if it had never been used and the only item in the fridge was a pint of milk. 'I never cook,' he shouted. 'I always eat out. And don't go into the other bedroom. That's Mum's. I have kept it exactly how she left it.' All the signs were there of a reclusive, eccentric and narcissistic man, but I didn't see them. He was even going to be a character witness for me at my trial and I hate thinking about it but I left my boys in his care aged six and nine at the BBC Television Centre where we had been invited to watch a recording of *Jim'll Fix It*.

I ran the London Marathon and the Great North Run with him. We shared the same hotel in Gateshead and the two of us had dinner together on the eve of the race. We chatted and laughed.

'I've got a young nurse coming to see me to give me a massage tonight,' he told me.

'Be careful, Jimmy,' I said. 'She could sell her story to a newspaper.'

'Who's going to believe her?' he said. 'She's not going to talk about having sex with an old man like me.'

We chatted on.

'When are you yourself?' I asked.

'My favourite time is when I am at "Jimmy's" in Leeds working as a porter, especially the night shift when nobody is around. Nobody answers back, especially in the morgue.'

Terrifying to remember now, given what we all know.

I had been familiar with Charles's idiosyncrasies and his legendary temper since I joined the Queen's service in 1976 but I had no idea then that I would end up leaving the Queen to move to Highgrove in 1987 to work directly for him and Princess Diana.

He was a tough and demanding boss whose life has order which must be obeyed and adhered to. In his service, I have experience of this both to my benefit and to my detriment. At one time I was flavour of the month, as many have been in the past, but ultimately I fell from grace. Charles often becomes infatuated with a newcomer, whether that's a servant or a business associate, and showers attention and gifts on them. I received watches, watercolour paintings and presents from overseas tours. Then, once you become accepted and part of everyday life, the infatuation fades and 'today's favour becomes tomorrow's duty'. He loses interest and looks for a replacement.

In the last year of my employment as butler at Highgrove, the prince fell from his horse while playing polo. He broke his arm, injured his back and scarred his face, which is still evident.

After his operations, he convalesced at Highgrove and I remained on duty every single day for three months. Both his valets, Michael Fawcett and Ken Stronach, and I were thoroughly exhausted by the end of it. Poor Michael even had to hold the bottle into which Charles urinated. But there was only one butler. I eventually collapsed one morning while getting ready for duty. I was hospitalised and my consultant ordered that I stay in hospital for two weeks. He said that if my employer had been anyone else but the Prince of Wales, he would have reported him. Of course, the prince never visited me. I didn't expect him to. Another butler took my place so His Royal Highness wasn't inconvenienced.

But every weekend on the way to and from Highgrove, Diana came to see me with the boys. 'Just popping in to say hello,' she would say with an armful of flowers, biscuits and treats and then she'd go and talk to the other patients and nursing staff on the wards.

Charles has always lived in a world where all his household and staff bow and call him 'Your Royal Highness'. Now, of course, it is 'Your Majesty'. Nobody says no. If you do, you're out. He lives in a gilded bubble and is served whatever he wants, whenever he wants and by whom he wants.

The only person that can say 'no' is Camilla. She is and always will be non-negotiable. Perhaps her no-nonsense approach is what Charles needs. She's the steady hand on the tiller of the royal ship now, like it or not. She is at the helm. She rarely asks for anything but is given everything and now has the ultimate position as queen.

Originally Charles went to Queen Elizabeth and said, 'Mummy, if you don't say it, they'll never accept it from me when you are gone.'

Charles persuaded his mother to agree that when he became king, Camilla would be styled as 'queen consort' alongside him. I think that most people were comfortable with that. She would be his wife, the wife of a king, but when Charles ascended to the throne, he dropped the title 'consort' and had Camilla crowned as 'queen' on his coronation day in May 2023.

Most of us had never witnessed a coronation before and perhaps only seen the archive footage of the coronation of Queen Elizabeth II. I watched the coronation of King Charles III like many others around the world, wanting to be part of a moment in history. For me it was tinged with sadness and I struggled to understand why. I realised later that on every state occasion during my lifetime, Queen Elizabeth had been front and centre and now she was missing.

I was surprised to see that at a subsequent State Opening of Parliament Queen Camilla was wearing the sovereign's Diamond Diadem which the Queen wore on the image on postage stamps and contains the emblems of the United Kingdom. It was something that the late Queen wore all my lifetime. For me, it felt a step too far. When I see the word 'queen' I still think of Elizabeth II and not Camilla. I am sure others feel the same. It is quite unbelievable that once the most hated woman in the country, who was allegedly pelted with bread rolls in a supermarket car park in Cirencester, is now our queen.

I often think that if Princess Diana had lived history would have been different. I have no doubt that Prince William and Prince Harry would still be close and there would have been a role at court for their mother. I think it would also have been difficult for Charles to marry Camilla had Diana lived. Although he was divorced, the future king and head of the Church of England could not have a second wife while the mother of his heir was still alive. I imagine Diana would have stayed close to the Royal Family as she was never against them. She always wanted to help and support the Queen. She would have become what she was striving for – to be accepted and as she told me, 'an ambassador for the world'.

Of course it does not help to dwell on 'what ifs'. Charles is king with Camilla by his side, but I don't think Charles's reign will be a long one and if he is survived by his wife, I cannot imagine that she will stay around the court of King William. Once Charles's reign is over, I predict that Camilla will become a postscript and retire from public life to live at Ray Mill House in Wiltshire alongside her children and grandchildren. I believe that she will be gracious enough to do that.

How will the public compare the reign of King Charles III to that of Queen Elizabeth II? Queen Elizabeth wasn't raised with the expectation that she would be queen. She had no idea when she was a young girl that she would be. You couldn't have two more different approaches to being monarch. One, a shock and a surprise. The other, a lifetime in preparation.

Charles has always known, just like his son William and grandson George, that it was likely that he would become king one day. Each one of their reigns will be very different. Charles will emulate his mother, William's reign will be less formal and George will only succeed his father if there is still a public appetite for the monarchy.

Charles has been waiting in the wings to be king for his entire life, much like Edward VII, who spent just nine years on the throne after the death of his mother, Queen Victoria. He has always known it's his destiny.

Charles has waited so long for the 'top job', as Diana once called it, and now that he has it, he is behaving sensibly.

Charles, like his mother, has always been religious and since becoming king, his faith has become important and his mainstay. He is now head of the Church of England and takes that role very seriously. He is devout and God fearing, like his mother. Every Sunday morning at Highgrove I would set up an altar in the drawing room complete with candlesticks, a chalice and a silver salver for the host. The local vicar would arrive and give Charles Holy Communion and absolve his sins. Diana never joined him when she was in residence. She would smile and say, 'It would take far more than that to save him.'

He took his oath before God as his mother did on her coronation day, and is resolute in fulfilling the role of monarch. His coronation in Westminster Abbey followed the tradition and script of that of his mother. Charles, with the help of the then Archbishop of Canterbury, Justin Welby, delivered a slightly slimmed-down version of the traditional pomp and ceremony, which was appropriate for today.

But the transition of power, 'the bridge' between Elizabeth II and Charles III, had been discussed and planned for many years in meetings of which the Queen had knowledge but never attended. They were called 'bridge' meetings. The Queen knew they were happening but she never attended them because she felt that it was none of her business what was going to happen after she died. When London Bridge, the code name for the passing of the reign of Elizabeth II, fell, all was in place and the stage was already set for Charles to succeed his mother. The Royals always have a plan.

So Charles has now got the job he always wanted but Diana used to say, 'Be careful what you wish for.'

She thought that when Charles got the top job, he would find it limiting. Her words may be echoing in his ears. He doesn't have the freedom that he used to have as Prince of Wales and he may not be able to achieve all that he would have wished as king. It has not been helped by him being ill. He is a caretaker king.

The King is not a conciliatory man; he certainly wasn't in the Diana years. I witnessed many arguments and fights between Charles and Diana behind closed doors. At times, they were more than a shouting match. Plates were smashed, tempers raised and even tables overturned. Having set a candle-lit dinner for two on a card table, I arrived in the sitting room to find Charles crumpled on the floor in his silk dressing gown, covered in salad dressing and surrounded by broken china and glass. His explanation? 'I must have caught my dressing gown sleeve on the corner of the table.' The princess was nowhere to be seen. Diana could be just as fiery at times and I suspect, on this occasion, the damage had been caused by her.

When the prince lost his temper, which he often regretted, he was contrite and apologetic. Time has tempered his character. But he still gets frustrated on occasion and you sometimes see it in public. For example, the King was clearly irate as he sat in his carriage outside Westminster Abbey prior to his coronation as he waited for the arrival of William and Catherine, who were late – an illustration of his short fuse.

Charles certainly hasn't always been popular with the public but I think they have warmed to him since he became king. I would credit his mother's legacy for that to a certain extent – but there are people who will never forget Diana.

Some thought him too old and that he should have passed the crown straight to William. But of course that would never have happened because he had waited all his life for this job. The compromise during his short reign is preparing William for all aspects of monarchy. Charles's mother never did that for him. Nobody in his life influenced him more than Queen Elizabeth the Queen Mother, to whom he was devoted. She was born and grew up at Glamis Castle in Scotland as the ninth child of the Earl and Countess of Strathmore and Kinghorne. Born in 1900, she was raised with Victorian moral values and taught those values to Charles; they have been his foundation for life.

Now he has found himself in a serious life-changing situation; he was diagnosed with cancer in February 2024 and began his treatment shortly afterwards.

He withdrew from public events but continued his constitutional role as head of state, completing paperwork and holding meetings in private.

All the ill health in the family has taken its toll on the King and changed him, his attitude and his opinion on life. Dealing with cancer has taught him that life is fragile and could be cut short. While still grieving the loss of his mother and adjusting to the role of king, he is dealing with his own mortality as well as the illness of those around him, including that of his daughter-in-law, Catherine.

I think that he is now seeking answers to questions which have been posed in the past. One of those is undoubtedly Diana. She is the ghost that will forever haunt the House of Windsor. No matter what anybody says, I think that she will still be remembered and talked about in years to come – especially when her son is on the throne – as she had the most tragic life of them all.

King Charles is now grandfather to five children from William and Harry and five more from Camilla's side of the family. Like most grandparents, he is different in that role than he was as a father. He was taught by his mother and grandmother that duty came first and family came second.

When I think about William and Harry's early years, Charles put duty and his personal life first. Diana, on the other hand, always put family first. Charles was often away from home attending engagements in his role as Prince of Wales, playing polo, hunting or on shooting party weekends. Diana was happy to stay at home with the children and that is exactly what William is doing. Nobody mattered more than William and Harry in Diana's eyes. She was there for the boys at mealtimes, bath-times and bedtimes as much as she could.

But when Diana died, there was a change. Charles had to take on board family responsibilities and the public wanted to see that Charles cared. There followed a charm offensive, one that projected the image of a caring father devoted to his boys who were grieving for their mother. Charles organised rooms for William and Harry at St James's Palace so that he could be close to them at Clarence House. There is a door that leads from Clarence House into St James's Palace through which the boys could have access to their father. Charles was concerned to see as much of them as he could growing up and eventually moved them into rooms in Clarence House itself. Camilla has tried to help with this although it's not easy for a stepmother to find her place in an established family. Diana knew that too, having had a difficult relationship with her own stepmother, Raine, Countess of Dartmouth.

Judging by Harry's comments in *Spare*, he still sees Camilla to be an evil stepmother – like something out of a fairy tale – and that isn't about to change anytime soon.

I have to admit that Camilla has coped with this situation well by greeting it with humility, dignity and silence even though she's had so much thrown at her. I think that is a testament to her character and her strength.

Whether you are king or commoner, many parents struggle with the feelings of their children after a remarriage. Charles is no different. He wants a happy life. He wants unity and he has tried hard to build bridges. As head of the Church of England, he is taking instruction from the Archbishop of Canterbury as his mother and father did when they were in the early years of their marriage. They found their faith in the wilderness. Forgiveness is never far from the teachings of Jesus Christ and it is something with which the King is struggling, especially in his relationship with Harry.

There is no doubt in my mind that Charles loves his boys but he dotes on his grandchildren. Like all grandparents, he has learned lessons from the past. The fact is that as we get older, we may have a little more time to spend with our grandchildren. I am sure that Charles would like to see more of Archie and Lilibet but that isn't possible at the moment.

Time is a great healer so perhaps Harry will find a way back to his family, but I am not sure.

Charles's mortality must be playing on his mind as he looks around his disjointed family. He doesn't want to leave this mess behind and wants to sort it out before the end of his time but it is a puzzle which it appears even he is unable to solve.

Harry has only seen his father once since he has been sick and he has not seen his brother and his family. Charles has not been given the chance to be a grandfather to Archie and Lilibet and I am afraid that that may not happen. Although Charles might forgive Harry and welcome him back, William might not be so forgiving.

Apart from his family, Charles is considering where he wants to live as king. He plans to reside at Buckingham Palace. This is not an unreasonable request, although it is currently being renovated and that isn't due to be completed until 2027. The Queen's Wing is the last phase to be completed and has to be totally rewired and replumbed. While this is in progress, Charles has decided to move his office to the Belgian suite which is on the ground floor beside the garden entrance. In this suite is the Orleans room, which is where he was born. However, he has brought his mother's large desk from her sitting room downstairs, thus combining his childhood with the memory of his mother.

Charles has fond memories of living at Buckingham Palace with his mother and father. He grew up in the royal nursery at the palace and spent his formative years there. When invested as Prince of Wales in Caernarfon Castle in 1969, he was living in a suite of rooms on the second floor of the palace next to the rooms occupied by his sister, Princess Anne. He lived here throughout his bachelor years until he was married in 1981 when he moved to his marital home, apartments 8 and 9 at Kensington Palace.

All through his life, Buckingham Palace has been the seat of the monarchy. It will always be special to him.

He sees the occupancy of his mother's rooms at the palace as a link to the past and a bridge to the future. The palace is where he conducts his work and his mother is around him everywhere he goes. He will never escape the long shadow she casts over his reign but he is happy to follow in her footsteps, surrounded by her memories, her monarchy and his upbringing at Buckingham Palace.

Queen Elizabeth II reigned for over seventy years and she is the longest-serving monarch that this country has ever seen. Given that Charles's reign will be nowhere near as long as that of his mother, what will his legacy be as king?

King Charles has certainly followed his father's example when it comes to environmental matters, in which Prince Philip was ahead of his time. I remember helping the then Prince of Wales plant a wildflower meadow down the drive at Highgrove in the late 1980s. It was not usual for a butler to give a hand in the garden but I offered and he was delighted that I did.

We planted a strip down the front drive from the front door to the gate which flowered in the summer and was a haven for butterflies and insects. I was pleased to have had a hand in something so beautiful. It was one of the first rewilding projects in the country. Incidentally, Prince Charles and Princess Diana chose that as a location to have a famous photograph taken of them with the boys for their annual Christmas card one year.

Country life goes to the heart of the man who is now king. He has inherited that from his father, his mother and his grandmother, all of whom loved the countryside. As king, Charles has planted miles of hedgerow and avenues of trees on the royal estate within the Home Park at Windsor which will flourish long after he is gone. He has now inherited his father's title of Ranger of Windsor Great Park. Charles believes that we are all guardians of our environment and should pass on these valuable lessons to the next generation. He encourages the survival and preservation of ancient skills such as drystone walling and hedge laying, and that too is part of his legacy. I think he will be known as an 'environmentalist king', a man who believes in nature and the world in which we live.

Charles's fervent wish is for the monarchy to survive but he knows that it will change shape and that the monarchy of the future will look very different.

His grandmother, born in 1900, saw two world wars, the invention of the jet engine, the splitting of the atom, women's suffrage and a man on the moon. The King will probably not see such dramatic change in his lifetime but William and George may.

Sitting on the throne in the top job he is already thinking about what William is heading towards and the pressures he will face. Currently he is buying William time to watch his family grow and his wife recover before he assumes the huge responsibilities that come with the crown. Charles is keeping the seat warm until William is ready.

Looking further ahead, it is likely that plans are already in place for George to inherit Clarence House as his London home when he comes of age. The Royal Family always wants to be prepared for what comes next.

The monarchy is only there by the will of the people. Charles's wish is that his son and grandson will find their path for it to continue.

15

Read All About it –
Fake News and the Truth
About *The Crown*

Like millions of others, I tuned in fascinated to watch *The Crown* on Netflix. Most of the Royal Family probably did not watch it. I don't think the Queen ever watched an episode because she probably would have dismissed it as entertainment which should be taken with a pinch of salt. Nobody gave it approval. Nobody in the Royal Family checked it for fact. But Harry has admitted to watching the programme. He and Meghan signed a mega-money deal with Netflix so it would make sense for them to see what else they make.

While other people learned something about the most famous family in the world, I was often left puzzled and perplexed because I knew them so well. From 1976 until 1997 I was part of this world. So for twenty-one years covered by *The Crown* through series four, five and six I lived alongside and knew the characters. All of them. But sometimes I didn't recognise the people who were portrayed on screen.

The Crown is not a historical documentary but a dramatisation, a processed, manufactured and carefully crafted version of the truth. Admittedly it has high production values and nods towards accuracy with locations, costumes and some fact is captivating. It does, however, lead you down some scripted untruths rather like Alice in Wonderland down a rabbit hole.

Whatever you may think of my relationship with Diana, Princess of Wales, it is fair to say that I knew her better than most … yet I am nowhere to be seen in *The Crown* and I have wondered how that can be.

I have had to remind myself when watching a television show that is made for entertainment that it is a dramatised version of the truth and just loosely based on fact.

Using dramatic licence is one thing but distorting the truth in a retelling of historic events is another. There will be people watching *The Crown* who were not born or do not remember Princess Diana when she was alive and did not witness events as they happened. After all, she died twenty-eight years ago so you would need to be in your thirties now to have been alive during her lifetime and in your forties or fifties to have really been aware of her. We are in a different era and younger people are being given an inaccurate portrayal of what she was like. I am not convinced that we should be altering the facts and changing the perception of one of the greatest icons of our generation through mass-market entertainment.

I understand how people can be misled about the Queen's character as she was a remote figure during her lifetime and unless you knew her personally, you would only be aware of her public image. I loved Claire Foy's interpretation of the young queen but I was not alive for the events of the Claire Foy era of *The Crown* and have no personal knowledge of the Queen during that time. She was fifty when I entered her service. I can only separate fact from fiction for the period during which I was with the Royal Family. From series five onwards, Netflix added a disclaimer to the programme saying that it was a 'fictional dramatisation', 'inspired by real-life events' but I feel that that gave them artistic licence to depart even further from

what actually happened. The nearer to my era it got, the less acceptable it felt because I had been there and lived the truth. I would get
annoyed watching scenes that I knew were not particularly true
when they gave a false impression of Diana or the Queen.

Of all the actresses who played the Queen, the portrayal by
Claire Foy was the nearest to the essence of the Queen that I
knew. The other actresses, Imelda Staunton and Olivia Colman,
didn't manage to capture the character of the Queen through the
script given to them. They got her measured approach, but lacked
her warmth, her humour and her compassion. I was not keen on
the two-dimensional portrayal by either of them. They made her
appear to be cold, harsh and unfeeling, even in private, which was
certainly not the Queen with whom I was familiar.

I am usually a fan of Imelda's work but her bland and heartless
depiction of the Queen left me cold. Surely she must have noticed
that the character as written by Peter Morgan was way off the
mark. The Queen that I knew was considerate and humorous
whereas the character played by Imelda was cold, plain and dour.
Even the costumes looked like they'd been pulled from a charity
shop rather than the elegant attire designed by Hardy Amies.

Similarly, Marion Bailey, who played the Queen Mother, appeared dishevelled, as if she had been dragged through a hedge
backwards after half a dozen gin and Dubonnets. Of course she
was an actress following direction, but the woman I knew would
never have appeared like that. She was a formidable lady and as
the last Empress of India, she would not have been happy to have
people think she was slovenly and badly dressed.

I found Vanessa Kirby captivating as the young Princess
Margaret but I didn't see the sharp wit or humour of the princess in Helena Bonham Carter's characterisation of her. Instead
she came across as too bitchy and not as elegant as the Margot I
remembered.

Everyone who plays Diana wants to make their own mark on

the character. Emma Corrin, who played her when she first met Charles in 1977, might have looked the part but her Diana fell flat for me. I blame the script more than her because her characterisation was inaccurate. But I will say that Elizabeth Debicki's portrayal of her in her later years was masterful and haunting. It was flawless. She's a little taller than the princess but the way she captured her mannerisms was unbelievable. I had to look away from the screen because I thought I was seeing Diana.

Yet while the appearance was spot on, the character was completely wrong. She looked bewildered, lost, isolated and vulnerable but the reality was very different. Diana had many close friends and confidantes like Susie Kassem, Annabel Goldsmith, Catherine Bartholomew and Lucia Flecha de Lima. If any of them had featured they would have helped to draw out some of the princess's strength of character. And of course, if Peter Morgan had added my character into the mix then she wouldn't have seemed so isolated. I was with her most of the time but he wanted her to be portrayed as lonely and alone.

Inaccurate characterisation of people we have known is not only wrong but unfair on them, particularly when they are not here to defend themselves. As far as Diana is concerned, this does not only happen in *The Crown*. When Kristen Stewart played Diana in the film *Spencer*, her portrayal was very inaccurate. I was appalled by it as Diana was so misinterpreted, misunderstood and maligned. There was one particular scene where she ate a pearl necklace then regurgitated it at the table. I understand the metaphor for her bulimia in the scene, but this just did not happen. People watch a film and the characterisation goes into the public psyche. They begin to believe what they are seeing and that this is who Diana was – someone who was insane. Diana was an intelligent woman and this was an insult to her memory.

In addition to characters being misrepresented, plots are manufactured. In series five of *The Crown* there is a scene where Prince

Charles visits Diana at Kensington Palace after their divorce is finalised. Diana makes them both scrambled eggs and they sit down
and discuss their failings and what might have been. This scene is
entirely fictitious. It never happened. It's a metaphor for the world
in which they lived and what might have been said had they had the
opportunity to sit down face to face. The truth of the matter is that
Peter Morgan has taken one fact and created a new 'truth' out of it.

The true facts, as witnessed by me, are a little more mundane.

Charles *did* drop by one afternoon in the summer of 1996 when
the divorce had just been finalised. He was very early for an engagement and he wanted to kill some time. He rang the doorbell at
apartments 8 and 9, the home he used to live in. I opened the door
to my previous employer and he said, 'Hello, Paul.' I was startled
to see him standing there. He said, 'Is the princess in?'

He entered that familiar hallway and he started up the main
staircase. I said, 'I'll take you up, Your Royal Highness.'

He replied, 'Oh no, don't worry. I know my way.' He mum-
bled something inaudible and continued up the main staircase. I
rushed up behind him. He turned right into Diana's sitting room.
I turned left because I knew the princess was in her dressing room.
I knocked on the frame of the door and she was sitting at her
dressing table making up her face. I caught her attention and said,
'You will never guess who is here?' She said 'Who?'

When I told her she took a sharp intake of breath. 'What does
he want?' she asked nervously. I could see she was apprehensive.

Charles had already asked for paintings and furniture from the
apartments in the divorce settlement. There were gaps appearing
in the princess's furnishings. She was worried that he was coming
to take the rest. She told me she would be through to see him in
a minute so I went to make him a cup of tea which I served to
him in her sitting room. I found him hovering around her desk
looking at papers.

He looked embarrassed when I came in and asked him whether

I could help him with anything. We were engaged in small talk when the princess bounded in like a gazelle. She was upbeat and lively. It felt like she was determined to put on a show. She placed her hands on his shoulders and kissed him on both cheeks. Then they chatted and she giggled a lot. Within five minutes he was gone and she breathed a sigh of relief. 'That was awkward,' she said. 'I don't have anything to say to him. It's a completely different world that I live in these days.'

So no eggs or cosy chats as portrayed by *The Crown*. I have never met Peter Morgan but perhaps he used some of the stories from my book, *A Royal Duty*, and padded them out into scenes for his television show.

The truth is I know who I am and I know what I did and that is what matters to me. Both Diana and the Queen chose me to stand beside them. So I couldn't have better references. I always think about reputation versus character. This is something that Diana taught me. She said, 'Don't worry about your reputation. That's what people think you are. Be more concerned about your character because that's who you are.' That was sound advice.

Nobody can be liked by everyone, not even our dear late Queen or Princess Diana. I have always thought of myself as Marmite. Some people understand me and like me. Others don't. I never asked to become famous or infamous; it just happened to me. But I remain on this rollercoaster because I have always felt a strong loyalty to and need to defend my princess. My duty did not stop when she died.

I can hear her saying to me, 'Don't just sit there. Do something. Say something. You know the truth.' And there are very few of us who do.

So it is up to people like me to stand up and say, 'Well actually that's not true.' I am owning my truth and feel a responsibility to speak out for those who are no longer here to defend themselves.

*

It is not just Princess Diana who has been immortalised on screen. There have been not one but two cinematic creations of Prince Andrew's infamous 2019 *Newsnight* interview with Emily Maitlis over his dealings with Jeffrey Epstein and his relationship, if any, with Virginia Giuffre.

Just like Princess Diana's interview with Martin Bashir on *Panorama*, the original interview was compelling viewing even if I did watch with bated breath. They were both disastrous for the Royals and both interviewers suffered a backlash. While Emily was lauded for the scoop she ended up leaving the BBC to launch a podcast. She told people.com: 'On one hand, I was like, "I've done Prince Andrew. I can do anyone now". And on the other hand, it was like "Oh I can't get anyone now".'

I watched the adaptions with intrigue and thought both were well done. Netflix's interpretation was *Scoop*, based on a book by *Newsnight* booker Sam McAlister, with Gillian Anderson portraying the *Newsnight* host and Rufus as the wayward prince. It felt like Rufus must have met Andrew at some stage before filming as he captured his bombastic nature. He perfectly captured that essence that Andrew is an 'untouchable Royal', living in a world of make-believe.

Amazon Prime released its own offering, *A Very Royal Scandal*, based on Emily Maitlis's autobiography with Michael Sheen taking on Prince Andrew and Ruth Wilson playing Emily Maitlis.

Michael Sheen was excellent as Andrew. He really captured and understood the prince's pompous and arrogant nature as the son of a sovereign with a privileged life: the fact that Andrew lived in a bubble and thought he was indestructible. That is the Andrew I knew.

He made life hell for the people around him. Unlike his mother, who respected the fact that people dedicated their lives to look after the Royal Family, Andrew never did. He thought it was his right.

When on a shooting weekend, he appeared at the door of the staff dining room during breakfast looking for his valet. When no one stood to attention, he said, 'I'm going to do that one more time.' He walked out of the room and back in again so the staff could stand up in the presence of a royal duke.

Michael Sheen portrayed how out of touch and removed from ordinary life Andrew was.

Andrew isn't the sharpest knife in the drawer and he underestimates other people's intelligence, particularly women. A friend who went to a dinner party at Buckingham Palace saw Andrew sat next to a beautiful blonde lady. He didn't speak to anybody around the table that night other than his female companion. He was there to talk about possibilities for business in the community but it was a waste of time. 'I will never go to another dinner with Andrew,' my friend said. 'All he's concerned about is himself and chatting up beautiful girls.'

I am sure that going into the interview with Emily Maitlis, Andrew assumed that he could wing it and win her over with his charm as he had done in the past with many other ladies. He could swoon her into submission. He underestimated her and she caught him out. He ended up telling stories that just did not ring true. He had to defend his position somehow and you could see him sinking into the chair as the interview went on and became increasingly embarrassing. Emily Maitlis's character, as played by Ruth Wilson, came through and actually highlighted Andrew's vulnerability, illustrating to us that she was far more intelligent than him.

It was interesting to think that she knew that she had brought down a prince and she felt guilty. She had a conscience. I think she felt sorry for Andrew because he was so unprepared and so unguarded. She realised how vulnerable he was and what a cosseted and protected world he had lived in.

I thought that it spoke volumes when he said that he didn't regret knowing Epstein and that he didn't have an apology for the young lady in question. It went to the heart of Andrew's character. I winced at certain scenes, seeing Andrew thinking that he could get away with most of his actions as he often did within a royal residence.

Watching it made me feel sorry for Fergie too. Always hanging on to his coat tails, she is her own worst enemy. She gave him his heirs in the two princesses Beatrice and Eugenie. Interestingly though, her divorce settlement with Prince Andrew was said to be in the region of £4 million, and although we don't know the actual figure for the settlement, the rumours are that Virginia Giuffre was paid at least three times that amount. He tried to claim that the famous photograph with Ms Giuffre was a fake but his arguments were not entirely convincing and most people think that they probably did meet. And if so, that was an expensive meeting.

These two television shows have continued to remind people what happened and I don't think Andrew will ever have a public life again due to the scandal surrounding him. He will never come back into the Royal fold or be a working member of 'the firm'. What has happened is far too damaging and I know that William doesn't want the conflict around him and his family. When William is king, there will be no space for Andrew.

Away from on-screen fiction, there is the manner in which the Royals deal with media in real life. It was a regular practice for Diana to invite editors of the national newspapers to lunch at Kensington Palace where she could charm them 'off the record'. Sometimes William and Harry would be there too as part of the charm offensive. As a result, I find it so confusing when Harry speaks out in court and elsewhere about the media as his mother made sure he understood how it all worked.

I distinctly remember Piers Morgan, then editor of the *Daily Mirror*, being one of the editors entertained to lunch. He was a charming man who was a fan of Diana and supported her. I have always found his coverage to be fair. I have known him for more than twenty-five years now and my opinion of him has never changed.

When the serialisation of *A Royal Duty* was bought by the *Daily Mirror*, he invited me into the newsroom to see the process of how the stories were written up. He gave me control over the headlines and layout. I could not imagine any other editor doing that.

While Diana would sometimes court the media, by the early 1990s she had become increasingly aware that she was being followed, monitored and even recorded. She voiced her concerns to the Royal Household but they interpreted her frustrations as paranoia. Newspapers printed articles with information only known by very few people and if it wasn't them leaking this information, where was it coming from?

I vividly remember the princess bringing a newspaper down to me one day, opening it up on my desk and pointing to an article which referred to Hasnat Khan as her lover for the first time. She looked me straight in the eye and said, 'Did this come from you?'

'Absolutely not. You can trust me one hundred per cent,' I insisted. 'I guard your secrets with my life. I wouldn't tell a soul.'

'Well it didn't come from me and it didn't come from Hasnat and you are the only other person who knows.'

It definitely did not come from me and I found myself in an impossible position. I would never do that as it was more than my job was worth. The princess did not speak to me for the rest of the week.

In the summer of 1996, a paparazzo started following her on a motorbike when she was meeting Hasnat secretly at Brompton Hospital. It went on for weeks. She feared that her cover would be blown so she took decisive action. There had to be a confrontation to stop him. On one of her night-time visits to the hospital to see 'Mr Wonderful', she purposely let the man follow her then engaged in conversation with him. Somehow while he was stationary on his motorbike and distracted by her, she stole his keys and crash helmet. She was so excited by her triumph that she rang me at midnight at home. She said, 'I got him. He can't ride his motorbike now.'

The next morning she arrived at breakfast with her trophies of the helmet and keys in hand. 'Ta dah!' she exclaimed, giggling like a naughty schoolgirl.

But it wasn't all pranks. Saturday evenings were always a nightmare for Diana. She had no idea what would appear in the now defunct *News of the World* on Sunday morning. It was then Britain's biggest-selling newspaper with millions of readers. They had the 'loudest shout', as Diana would say.

I would go by taxi at midnight on Saturday evening to Victoria station to buy the first editions of all of the Sunday newspapers. On the taxi ride back to Kensington Palace, I would look through every one. Sometimes stories screamed from the front pages and I was taking an incendiary device back to apartments 8 and 9 as Diana would certainly shoot the messenger if she didn't like the contents.

This continued for years. I can't begin to tell you how devastated the princess was at times, or how many stories nibbled away at her confidence and character. Nobody talked of mental health back then but the princess struggled with her demons and battled with bulimia all her life. She might have learned to control it but she never beat it.

'How do I know who is in my apartment when I'm not there?' she would say when I accompanied her on tours and the apartment would be empty. She pondered how people posing as plumbers, electricians and decorators could have planted listening devices. She thought, 'If a stranger can get into the Queen's bedroom [as Michael Fagan did in 1982] then they can get into mine.' So the entire apartments were swept. I watched as the phones were taken apart and mouth pieces removed. I rolled up carpets and pulled up floorboards. I even removed a panel in the bathtub to look in the void behind, but we found nothing.

But Diana was convinced that someone was eavesdropping.

We took down every wall mirror in the palace, having been told that a beam from a satellite could be bounced from a mirror to listen to conversations in the room.

At times, it felt like I was living in a James Bond movie.

We have no proof that anyone hacked Princess Diana's phone but they may well have done. She was, at the time, arguably the most famous woman in the world and a person of significant interest to national and international newspapers. We can only speculate as we will never know the truth. She could also have been listened to by secret services. We will never know.

When I met with Prince William and Prince Harry in 2017, they vowed to get to the bottom of it all.

Prince Harry has pursued the matter in court. He has settled his phone hacking claims against Mirror Group Newspapers. The duke was awarded £140,600 in damages after winning fifteen claims against the Group in December 2023 and then the rest in February 2024 with the publisher paying his legal costs in addition to the damages. The settlement, relating to claims of unlawful intrusion on 115 stories, marks the end of a four-year battle between the prince and the publisher.

Prince Harry has perceived this to be his 'great crusade' and has even said that the Queen encouraged him to pursue legal action and would be 'very much up there saying "see this through to the end"'.

But I do not believe for a minute that the Queen would have condoned his actions. She hated confrontation herself so she would not counsel her grandchildren to go into battle. She always tried to avoid any kind of public controversy with her main aim always being to preserve the monarchy.

She would have been more likely to tell him, 'Let it go and the fire will go out because the more that you talk about it, the more you blow the embers and the flames will grow.'

There is no doubt that she was very fond of her grandson but she would not want any drama.

The Royals do not want to ruffle any feathers, particularly within the British media.

As far as they are concerned, the press are there to convey their message. They need their help in maintaining the popularity of the monarchy. You cannot go up against them. So by engaging in war with the press barons, Harry has railed against the system – and he's even managed to have a go at me in the process.

He has transformed the sanctuary of the courtroom to become his battleground where he can air his frustrations and personal vendettas. The Royal Family is appalled by this.

William took action in his own way in 2020 and received a substantial sum to settle a phone hacking claim with Rupert Murdoch's News UK, formally News International, the owner of the *News of the World*, but he did it quietly and out of court. This was only revealed to the world in the court documents submitted by Harry during his own legal battles.

It is not just the Royal Family who have had a hard time in the press. I can't say that I have had an easy ride with the media over the past thirty years. Some of the outrageous and inaccurate headlines that have been published have hurt me and my family enormously. In the past, I have been on the front page of the 'red tops' and some of the stories were unrecognisable from the truth and very different from what actually happened.

I always remember what a Fleet Street editor once told me: 'I don't know why you get so upset. We have never let the truth get in the way of a good story.'

There was once a time when nobody knew who I was and I

valued my anonymity but through a set of uncontrollable circumstances, I became known.

I was no longer invisible but I did not have the protection of the Royal Household and at times, it has felt like open season on Paul Burrell.

I suffered the indignity of wrongful public prosecution which was covered in great detail in newspapers and on television for months. Eventually all charges were dropped.

Sometimes I look back on press clippings and photographs and think, Was that me?

But I have survived, against all the odds.

The best way to describe it is as a double-edged sword. I have never asked for this public profile but I try to be pragmatic as there is much to appreciate about it too. I have had quite an extraordinary life and been presented with some amazing opportunities. I have also been given a public platform to raise awareness about important issues such as prostate cancer, which has been very humbling. And it led to me writing my book *A Royal Duty*. Now, twenty years later, you can judge my words in this book as the truth as witnessed by me.

16

Trials and Tribulations – How the Queen Saved the Day

All Saints' Day is 1 November and it is the day when all prayers are answered. Never more so than on 1 November 2002 when my pleas for help were heard and the Queen saved me as had she done many times before. But this time was powerful and meaningful. Her Majesty broke all protocols and procedures and became the first monarch in British history to intervene in a criminal court case. The poignancy was not lost on me. While I do not in any way claim to be a saint, I am not a thief.

As I left the Old Bailey on that cold autumn day, the weight of a potential custodial sentence was lifted from my shoulders and I was a free man. I was released from my nightmare by the best possible witness, the Queen herself. At the time the media joked about the case being Regina versus Paul Burrell but that was never the case; Regina was always on my side.

This period of my life was an ultimate low for me; I had been accused of stealing possessions from the estate of Diana, Princess of Wales by the Crown Prosecution Service, supported by the Spencer family and the then Prince of Wales.

I could see no way out of this horrific reality even though I knew I was innocent. Diana could have come to my defence and told the truth but she was dead. My next best hope was William and Harry but they were minors and the idea of having to put the future king in the dock as a witness filled me with dread. His mother would never have wanted that.

Prince Charles had no inclination to save me. After all, I was deemed an 'enemy of the state'. I was Diana's man and her colours were and still are nailed to my mast.

And then there was the Queen, for whom I had worked. She was possibly my best witness as she knew me well, but she was out of reach. As head of state and monarch she is the only person in the country who cannot be called to give evidence. Not since 1891 had a member of the Royal Family been called into a courtroom to give evidence.

But who could I turn to?

My small army of Diana's friends – Susie Kassem, Rosa Monckton, Debbie Frank and Lucia Flecha de Lima – were all on my side to testify as to how loyal and true I was.

Despite this and as the months passed, the toll of the severity of the impending trial and the embarrassment that surrounded it weighed heavily on me. I turned to drink. I lost all hope. I contemplated suicide. I went so far as to drive to a lay-by off the A41 in Cheshire with a bottle of paracetamol tablets. Thankfully I didn't go through with it, realising that if I died, my family would live with that guilt and stigma and I would have been considered guilty by my actions.

Maria encouraged me to keep going for my sons. I will always be grateful to her for that.

But I was living a nightmare.

My problems really started in 1997 on the death of Princess Diana. I had shared such an intensely private world with the princess in a situation that was so unique that no one who hadn't witnessed it could possibly understand. After all, I was merely a butler, doing my job and my duty, but perhaps people thought that I had got too close to the princess, had gone above my station and needed to be brought down a peg or two. As I was told at the Diana, Princess of Wales Memorial Fund, I had become 'too big for my boots'.

By December 1998, I had left the memorial fund after my job was made 'redundant'. So at forty-two, for the first time in my working life, I was without a job. I had been in constant employment since I'd left catering college in 1976. It was disconcerting but I put my royal knowledge to good use and published a book on social etiquette called *Entertaining with Style* (it was called *In the Royal Manner* in the US). This led to me moving onto the lecturing circuit to speak about how to be the perfect host with impeccable manners. I would sometimes lecture free of charge at charity events, always remembering Diana's motivation of trying to help others and applying it to my life. It was the income that I was earning from book royalties and lectures that would draw me to the attention of Scotland Yard.

Shortly before dawn on Thursday, 18 January 2001, I was awoken by my wife who had answered a knock at our front door in Farndon, Cheshire. It was dark outside and I was still in bed. She was mouthing, 'It's the police.'

Not just any police. It was Scotland Yard's 'Special Inquiry Team', a unit known as SO6. Two smartly dressed individuals, DCI Maxine de Brunner and DS Roger Milburn, arrived to question me in connection with an inquiry which had begun the previous year into the theft and sale of a jewel-encrusted model of an Arabian dhow worth £500,000, a wedding present to the Prince and Princess of Wales from the Emir of Bahrain. It had been offered for sale by Spink the jewellers in London. The police had been told a tall story that I had been involved in trying to sell it.

But it wasn't just the dhow they were interested in. They asked to see the manuscript for the memoir I was writing. More non-sense. It did not exist. I only began writing *A Royal Duty* in April 2003 – as a direct result of the police arriving at my door that morning and all that followed. It continued. They were looking for a mahogany box which belonged to Diana which was locked and contained important and sensitive papers.

Three more detectives had been waiting outside in a vehicle. They were instructed to conduct a robust search of my home.

My ex-wife, my children and I just had to stand open-mouthed as the police raided our home and turned our world upside down. It was so invasive and surreal: as if we were watching a burglary in reverse. Strangers rifling through our belongings. Floorboards were lifted, pictures taken down from walls and slit open, cup-boards, wardrobes and drawers were emptied. Every part of our home, our sanctuary, was invaded. Dozens of police polythene bags were filled with precious memories and keepsakes and la-belled 'evidence'.

Nobody in the police force knew the culture of 'gift giving' within royal households. All royal servants' homes are filled with memorabilia from their life of service.

The police did not find the gold dhow nor the box but instead what they deemed to be a treasure trove of royal memorabilia that they had decided no servant should have; items that Princess Diana and Prince Charles had given me, Maria and my boys over the years were taken away, including Diana's clothes, shoes and handbags that she had gifted to Maria rather than a charity shop and a writing bureau she had given to my son on which he could do his homework. Diana was generous. She knew I loved films so a whip given by Harrison Ford at the *Indiana Jones* premiere was given to me. I had also taken home many other items that had been intended to be thrown away and discarded but which seemed too precious for me to send to the rubbish tip. I even had a roll of carpet woven with the emblem of the fleur-de-lys used throughout the apartments at Kensington Palace as it was replaced after Diana's divorce. I had said to her, 'Would you mind if I kept a piece for old time's sake?'

'Of course not,' Diana had replied. I just wanted a reminder of those heady days we had shared in apartments 8 and 9.

Even the biblical text I had read to the princess during the vigil the night before her funeral was taken. Everything was assumed to be stolen. Private documents that Diana had asked me to look after for safekeeping were being passed around. They ripped through her most personal belongings. The search which had started at 7 a.m. lasted until 8 p.m. that evening. The world I had tried to protect was being exposed for all to see.

It was undoubtedly the lowest point of my life.

When I arrived at Runcorn police station, I found myself surrounded by paparazzi. They had clearly been tipped off as I should have been held at Chester police station. I kept thinking as I sat in the police cell that surely this was a mistake, and when the Royal Family heard what had happened it would all be sorted out.

Even now, nearly a quarter of a century later, it affects me to think of it and the impact it had on my family. Sometimes I awake from vivid dreams in a cold sweat thinking it is all about to happen again.

My boys still carry the trauma of that day. They had to see their father arrested and taken into custody. They were bullied in the playground, chased home from school, called names and shamed because the world had been led to believe that their father was a thief.

The months that followed were even harder.

In January 2001, one of Prince Charles's advisors had suggested that I write a letter explaining why the property was in my house as a 'step to sorting this out'.

I followed the suggestion but because of the constraints of my bail terms, I had to be careful as to how I expressed myself because anything I said could be used as evidence in court. My solicitor Andrew Shaw and I penned a letter saying how my intentions were honourable and that I had been entrusted by the princess to be the caretaker of sensitive items as well as there being many items which were given as gifts. I begged for a meeting to straighten out the confusion.

But Prince Charles did not hear my pleas. The letter was read by St James's Palace but not Charles himself.

In my opinion, this was a missed opportunity as the prosecution built their case on the fact that I had not told anyone of my intention to keep items from Kensington Palace for 'safekeeping', but this was incorrect.

Not only had I told Charles in that letter, I also wrote to William in April 2001 while he was on his gap year, telling him the same thing. I had first mentioned it to the Queen shortly after Diana's death in 1997.

But no one listened.

And I had become a social pariah. The calls for work dried up. I wasn't even wanted for free events. Only one company stuck by me – Cunard. The company who had offered me that job back in 1976 continued to employ me as a guest speaker on transatlantic crossings on board the *QE2*.

We were in dire straits financially. Maria started cleaning a friend's house, falling back on her skills learned in the Royal Household. She had to pawn her jewellery. We cashed in our life policies and the children's savings accounts all to help survive and make ends meet. They were desperate times.

I was grateful for the generosity of friends like the Wrights in Kentucky and Ginsbergs in New York who sent us money to help with mortgage payments. With the assistance of a legacy of £50,000 from the estate of Princess Diana, we eventually scraped enough together to rent a florist shop in the village of Holt. Using my floristry skills from the palace, it became my sanctuary – not just financially.

I was a broken man. I'd close the shop in the evening and collapse into tears. I was on a downward spiral and at this point I was not just a hopeless husband but also a terrible father. I could not function as this travesty hung over me. And all of this suffering was because I had tirelessly tried to preserve and protect the memory of and artefacts from Diana's world.

I don't often agree with Prince Harry, but when he speaks of royal aides who wield all the power, I understand. I have had my dealings with the 'grey suits' of the household who act in what they believe to be the best interests of the Royal Family. It is a discretion that gives some of them delusions of power.

One such incident was when Maria and I were invited to Prince Philip's eightieth birthday reception at Windsor Castle. Maria was thrilled that her old boss had thought to include her and I was buoyed up by the invitation too. With the imminent onset of my trial, I had begun to feel that everyone was against me. A few weeks later, a call came from the duke's private secretary, Brigadier Hunt-Davis, suggesting that it would not be in our best interests to go to the reception. When I said I was not ashamed and I would still be going, he interrupted and explained that our invitation had actually been rescinded. I know with certainty that that decision was made without consulting the Queen, and how happy she would have been to see me.

On 2 August 2002, I received word via Mark Bolland, the prince's deputy private secretary, that 'the eldest son would like to meet you' and an appointment was made for the following day.

It was to be a clandestine meeting. Both Scotland Yard and Fiona Shackleton, Prince Charles's divorce solicitor who had been advising on the trial, were kept in the dark.

I was on my way by car to the meeting with my brother Graham when we received a telephone call to say that the meeting had been called off as Prince Charles had had an accident playing polo.

That morning before the polo match, both DCI Maxine de Brunner and Commander John Yates of Scotland Yard had visited the Prince and William at Highgrove to provide a briefing on the case. In their evidence, they claimed that they had photographs of me wearing Diana's clothes at gay parties and that I had sold her possessions in America. Neither of these accusations were true and they were without any foundation whatsoever.

On 16 August 2001 I was charged with stealing 315 items from the estate of Diana, Princess of Wales, six items from Prince Charles and twenty-one items from Prince William. If I was found guilty, it was deemed such a breach of trust that I would serve up to five years in prison.

Despite knowing that I had done nothing wrong, I felt like a criminal.

At the end of August, Sir Michael Peat, who had been appointed as private secretary to Prince Charles, met with Scotland Yard and questioned the strength of the case. The problem was that the estate of Diana wasn't just the concern of the Royal Family but the Spencer family too. I had been told that the Spencers were 'sick to the back teeth of hearing how much that bloody butler was a rock to Diana' and that they were determined to have their day in court.

Thankfully I had a senior Royal write to me assuring me that they believed in my innocence. Having support from the House of Windsor comforted me. Another reminded me that the Queen had always believed that any individual is innocent until proven guilty.

It seemed that I was to have my day in court; the trial at the Old Bailey was set for Monday 14 October 2002.

The press descended in their droves with one journalist calling it 'the greatest show in town' as they hoped that they would be offered a glimpse inside the walls of the House of Windsor.

I sat in the dock on a seat previously occupied by the country's worst criminals – murderers, rapists, armed robbers – as Mrs Justice Rafferty started the trial.

I was a nervous wreck as I heard the charges read out. To each count I replied, 'Not guilty.'

During that time, I received so many heart-warming letters of support. They arrived by the bagful. Even now, after all these years have passed, I still feel gratitude for the hands of kindness extended to me – whether it was the Sisters of Assumption convent in Galway who had all their nuns praying for me or television presenter Richard Madeley and his wife Judy Finnigan whom I had met on their television programme *This Morning*.

Richard had experienced being on the wrong side of the law when he was charged with theft from a Tesco store during his time as presenter on the show. In the months before the trial, he and his wife wrote several letters of encouragement to me, sometimes even sending me a note on the back of one of his scripts. They supported and encouraged me in my darkest days. In one letter, he told me that it would seem as if I was in the eye of the storm and that everything was happening around me. He knew as he had been there. He advised me to let the legal process happen and remain close as a family and be strong just as he had done.

Over and over the Crown Prosecution Service argued that I had not told anyone that I was taking items for safekeeping; I wanted to scream, 'I had! I had!'

On day two of the trial, someone spotted a plain-clothes policeman enter the room, flash his warrant card and sit in the public seats. At one point he gestured to one of the female members of the jury and they nodded to each other.

It turned out that this detective inspector was acknowledging his wife on the jury. It was their wedding anniversary and he had planned to have lunch with her. He was not just any policeman; he had worked as a member of the Royal Protection Group between 1986 and 1989. He had been working with the Royal Diplomatic Section looking after foreign embassies and had carried out duties within Kensington Palace. He had also worked in Peckham in the 1990s serving alongside DCI Maxine de Brunner, the senior investigating officer on this case.

Of course the fairness of my trial was called into question so we had to start again with a fresh jury of five women and seven men.

When DCI de Brunner was on the stand, she talked about how she had briefed Charles and William about their investigation before I was charged, explaining that 'Mr Burrell's lifestyle and finances altered drastically after the death of Diana, Princess of Wales.'

It was presumed that my bank balance had increased by selling items belonging to the princess when it was actually income from my etiquette book and the subsequent lecturing circuit.

It was so incredibly frustrating to have to listen to falsehoods about me and also to know that they had been told to the Palace and Prince Charles too.

When Mrs Frances Shand Kydd, Diana's mother, took to the stand, she did not look at me once. Nor did she call me Paul. It was always 'Mr Burrell' or 'the defendant'.

It seemed strange that when she had spent some time with me in my home after her daughter's death, she had given me a cross on a chain for protection. She talked about how the princess was very careful with the gifts she gave to people. She also said that Diana referred to many people as 'her rock'.

But she did admit she had been destroying documents relating to the princess. It was the shredding of these letters and the destruction of history that led me to speak to the Queen in December 1997 and express my concerns.

On Friday, 25 October 2002, while the trial continued, the Queen, the Duke of Edinburgh and Prince Charles were en route to St Paul's Cathedral for a memorial service for the victims of the Bali bombing. A conversation happened that day that would change the course of the trial.

On Tuesday, 29 October, the trial was scheduled to start as usual. My legal team felt that we were gaining ground and I was due to take the witness stand the next day at the start of the defence.

Prior to the proceedings beginning, Mrs Justice Rafferty had been locked in her chambers with the prosecution. She returned to court to inform the jury that there had been a delay and that the trial had been adjourned for the day.

No one knew what was going on. I was starting to panic as it felt like something very serious was happening. My legal team and I wracked our brains as to whether there was anything else that could be brought up. But I had told them everything.

We were informed that the court would not be sitting for the next two days.

The waiting sent me into a paranoia and I couldn't sleep with the mental torture of it all.

I had started to hope that the case was going my way but the adjournment felt like I had been put on the back foot. I was extremely down.

The night before the trial restarted I had a meeting with my legal team. We talked about the letters to Charles and William and my meeting with the Queen.

They then asked if I had mentioned to the Queen my concerns about Diana's mother shredding letters.

'Yes,' I said.

Everyone looked in my direction in shock.

I am not sure that I realised the significance of that conversation. It seemed no different from what I had told Charles and William.

It merely felt like a useful piece of information for me to mention on the stand but never did any of us think that we were armed with the secret weapon to cause the trial to collapse.

But when we arrived at the Old Bailey on All Saints' Day, we were told that 'something was happening and it was big'.

I waited outside the court and my mobile phone rang. It was a journalist friend and his voice was shaking. 'Paul it's going to collapse. No one knows why but it's going to end.'

I didn't really know what his words meant. I couldn't take it in.

I entered court and the prosecution barrister William Boyce took to his feet to address the judge, saying, 'My lady, it has been an important part of the prosecution case that there was no evidence that Mr Burrell informed anyone that he was holding any property belonging to the executors of the estate of Diana, Princess of Wales. On Monday of this week, the prosecution was informed by the police that during a private meeting with the Queen in the weeks following the death of Diana, Princess of Wales, Mr Burrell mentioned ...'

I don't think I took in the rest of what he said but during the journey to the Bali bombing memorial service, the Duke of Edinburgh had mentioned to Charles that the Queen had been told by me that I had taken documents for safekeeping. Prince Charles informed his private secretary the next day who was able to confirm this account with the Queen. St James's Palace then reported this 'new evidence' to Scotland Yard.

William Boyce finished by saying, 'I invite the jury to find him not guilty.' The judge smiled and said, 'Mr Burrell, you are free to go.'

The Queen had come to my rescue again.

Trust is earned and not given freely in the Royal Household.

The Queen learned to trust me over the time I served her.

She encouraged Tall Paul to trust me too.

We had come a long way since 1976 when two fresh-faced eighteen-year-olds joined Her Majesty's service at Buckingham Palace ... and they were both called Paul.

For ten years, I was beside the Queen. Tall Paul was with her until the end of her life and was her longest-serving servant: forty-eight years in total.

Paul had always been careful not to ruffle any feathers with any of the household or the Royal Family. So following the Old Bailey court case and when I wrote *A Royal Duty*, he was naturally nervous and distanced himself from me.

Our friendship waned over those years. I understand that it was very difficult for him.

But the Queen helped Tall Paul to reignite the friendship a few years ago by suggesting that he stay with me and my husband Coop at our home in Cheshire to break up his long journey to Balmoral. She approved and gave her consent for our friendship to be rebuilt and it continues to this day.

He told me that she had said to him, 'This is silly. It shouldn't be like this. He's your lifelong friend and you're going to need him when I'm not here. You pass Paul's door on the way to Balmoral. Why not stay a night or two? You have been friends for so many years.'

She reminded him of our long bond in service. She knew it wasn't an easy life and that I was someone who understood what Paul had been through and how his life would change when she was no longer around.

He would stay the night and regale me with tales of his world and we would wallow in nostalgia for our golden years of service.

His visits added to their conversations at Balmoral when she would interrogate him for gossip about me.

In those heady days I would often appear on television programmes such as *I'm a Celebrity* ... and I would be mentioned in newspapers like the *Daily Mirror*, which serialised *A Royal Duty*.

Each morning the newspapers would be placed on the table for the Queen to read with her cup of Fortnum & Mason Earl Grey tea and a slice of wholemeal toast.

On occasion the Queen would point to an article and say to Tall Paul, 'Have you seen what he is doing now?' or 'Look at this! I wonder if it is true?'

That was an indication for him to ring me and find out the real story.

I corresponded with the Queen over the years to inform her of events in my life as a courtesy as I realised that she wanted to know the truth about me, especially from me.

I thanked her for saving me and for all the wisdom she imparted to me.

I always signed my letters, 'Your humble and obedient servant.'

I was confident in knowing that Her Majesty always knew what I knew and more importantly what I had never talked about in public.

Of course I have much to thank Paul for but mostly for orchestrating that fateful meeting with the Queen a few months after the death of Diana, which saved me from incarceration.

By December 1997 I was feeling alone and vulnerable with no idea of what the future would hold for me. I spent my days cataloguing and packing away every item in the princess's world. I wrote in my diary that I couldn't stand by and watch her legacy career out of control: 'I felt it my duty to do something about it'.

But I had a personal dilemma. 'Who could I turn to?' I wrote.

I knew that by the end of February my job would be complete. I worried that I would be unemployed and homeless.

The Spencers didn't understand. 'Charles didn't help his sister so why should he help me,' I wrote. Lady Sarah McCorquodale, Diana's sister, already had far too much on her plate. She was executor of Diana's will and trustee of the memorial fund. Lady Jane Fellowes, Diana's other sister, was married to Robert Fellowes, the Queen's private secretary. She had allegiances to the Spencer family and to the Royal Family. William and Harry were too young and had enough to worry about. I wouldn't wish to burden them. I couldn't turn to the Prince of Wales as it would feel like a betrayal of the Boss. Anyway, he wouldn't understand or even listen.

'Who would listen?' I wrote. Then I knew exactly who to turn to. Her Majesty the Queen. So I rang Tall Paul, and my diary tells me exactly what happened next.

'Do you think that the Queen would see me and spare me five minutes?' I asked.

'Leave it with me and I will let you know,' he said.

The answer came back the next day: 'The Queen will be delighted to see you at 2 p.m. on Friday 19 December.'

I was delighted. Much later, Paul told me that I was the topic of conversation as she dined alone that night. As Paul served her candle-lit dinner at Buckingham Palace, she told him, 'I am not surprised to hear from Paul. I feel very sorry for him.'

She had obviously given my dilemma some thought but I wondered how she would react face to face. Either way, I felt that she should be told the truth. The conversation that follows is part of a contemporaneous note of that meeting. It is a first-hand recollection of what the Queen said to me.

At approximately 1.30 p.m. on 19 December I walked down Buckingham Palace Road with mixed emotions as I was heading for my meeting. I had much to tell her since Diana's passing and it had been ten years since I had seen the Queen. I was excited and nervous at the same time. The Diana years had been divisive. I was now Diana's man and not the Queen's man and I had no idea how I would be received. Would she be the same Queen whom I had known in the past? With trepidation, I entered the side door police station at the tradesman's entrance.

Much had changed. Security was tighter. Where a policeman once sat at a desk there was now a double 'air lock' security door into which I stepped and was released through the other side. The policemen were friendly and chatty. They knew exactly who I was and when to expect me. 'You know your way,' they said, so I wandered alone through the giant service doors and into the cavernous basement. I passed two staff telephones housed in wooden boxes from where as a young footman I had phoned home so many times and the staff canteen where I had been fed by the royal kitchens. I could hear the usual clatter of pans and dishes as the place was alive with sounds and people as the court was in residence. I passed through several other doors, the still room, cellars and the laundry room and finally reached the flower room where Penny, the court florist, had taught me the basics of flower arranging before I joined the Waleses' household. This is where the two-man lift is located, a service elevator which ascends to the Queen's apartments on the first floor. There I reached a utility area with a linoleum floor like the one in Chapel Road where I was born. Then a very large mahogany door took me onto the plush red-carpeted floor of the Queen's corridor.

Some corgis greeted me but none that I knew – this was the next generation. I passed the dining room outside which on a sideboard stood a small silver coffee pot on a silver salver. I smiled to myself. Nothing had changed. Time had stood still. I found Paul in the pantry where I had spent many of my days on duty. 'Oh, you have found your way then!' he joked to which I replied, 'I could step back into this world tomorrow'. He laughed. 'But would you want to when you are the one who got away?' he said. 'She has just had coffee and will be through soon,' he continued. Like clockwork and true to form, the little red disc dropped into the box labelled 'Dining Room': the Queen's signal to say that she had finished lunch. We waited for a few minutes and another red disc dropped, this time into a box labelled 'Sitting Room'.

Paul escorted me into the Queen's sitting room and announced, 'Paul, Your Majesty.' We both bowed and I handed her a small hand-tied posy of blue hyacinths and white narcissi.

'How very kind,' she said, raising them to her nose. 'And they smell so good.' I knew that they were her favourites. She handed them to Paul. 'Would you put them in water?' It was his signal to leave us alone. He disappeared and closed the door behind him leaving the Queen and her former footman alone.

I have never recounted much of this conversation but I now feel that the time is right to illustrate how concerned Her Majesty was. It sheds a light on her character. I wanted to vent my concerns and frustrations to someone whom I could trust. I was angry that my voice had been silenced and that Diana's world was being destroyed and was concerned that the Queen had no idea what was happening inside Kensington Palace. Of course I was respectful and courteous. After all, this was our Queen and she had granted me this opportunity to tell my side of the story from which she would learn the truth. I had no idea at the time that this meeting would have such a direct impact on my life when it would be revealed at my trial at the Old Bailey that I had confided in Her Majesty and pledged to keep Diana's world safe.

The corgis settled down after their initial curiosity about this stranger in their midst. The room was familiar to me. The décor – a mix of grey and salmon pink – was exactly the same. Everything was in the same place. Her pile of *Telegraph* crosswords, her dog treats, her magazines. Nothing had changed. There she stood, a little older, a little greyer, wearing a blue dress, three rows of pearls and a huge heart-shaped diamond brooch, the Cullinan V brooch bequeathed to the Queen by Queen Mary with a central stone weighing an impressive 18.8 carats. She approached me, shook my hand and smiled. 'Hello, Paul. How good of you to come and see me.' She inspected me over her half-rimmed spectacles. I had changed too over the past ten years.

'It's a very strange business,' she said, opening the conversation.

'Can I just say, Your Majesty, what a privilege and honour it is to be stood here, and thank you for giving me the opportunity to speak with you. It means such a great deal to me. There is absolutely no one whom I can confide in. You are my only answer,' I replied.

'Well, Paul, you know that it has always been difficult for me. I have tried not to get too involved before. It inevitably leads to arguments between the conflicting parties. I have tried to help in the past but my gestures have either not been welcomed or simply misunderstood.'

'Unfortunately, Your Majesty, unless it was blatantly obvious and stood out in black and white, the princess may possibly have not seen those signs,' I responded. 'The princess lived in a world of colour, not black and white.'

The Queen nodded and agreed, adding, 'Communication was difficult at times. But tell me what is happening with the memorial fund and how many people are involved.'

I answered her the best I could. 'At the moment, Your Majesty, the fund is split into two camps, one situated at Mishcon de Reya and one at Kensington Palace under the control of Michael Gibbins.'

'Ah ... Julius,' the Queen said knowingly. Anthony Julius had been administering the fund from Mishcon de Reya's offices in Southampton Row.

'He is a very clever man,' she said. 'And how do you see it all moving forward?'

I told her that I would love to be involved in the memorial fund in some way if possible and in an ideal world, for us all to remain at Kensington Palace, keeping it close to where Diana had lived for most of her life.

'I wonder if that would be possible, Your Majesty?' I enquired. She looked puzzled but said, 'I will look into the possibility with the Crown Estate and talk to Charles over the Christmas holidays.

Then he can talk to Sarah [McCorquodale] and Frances [Shand Kydd] privately without solicitors. They should come to an agreement between them.'

The Queen then changed the subject: 'Has anyone been to see you at the apartment?'

'Oh, William and Harry have. They have been to see what they would like to furnish their new apartment at York House,' I told her. 'At the moment they are fighting over a giant stuffed hippo. The huge plasma television has been very popular with both boys. William was very practical in his choices, Your Majesty, and interested in furnishings.'

'Yes, he is very practical,' she said. 'I am pleased that he has addressed that. It's so unsettling for William and Harry and it will be good for them to be surrounded by familiar things. I remember when my grandmother [Queen Mary] died. I went across to Marlborough House to find stickers on everything. I was too late. Everyone had descended like vultures. That is the most awful part. All I got was her jewellery and the two old herons who looked after her! How have the family been with you Paul?'

I told the Queen that I had been very grateful to have been included in so many decisions but I had grave concerns.

'Oh,' she said. 'What would they be?'

There was so much that I wanted to tell her. 'Well, the family have been through all the princess's personal belongings and have taken away a great deal of her property, much of which I believe William and Harry should have. I was asked to bring down her monogrammed luggage which was filled with her clothes and Mrs Shand Kydd sits on the princess's settee sorting through papers and shredding personal correspondence including letters from you. That shredding machine is smoking, Your Majesty!'

The Queen laughed out loud.

I continued, 'So I have taken it upon myself to rescue documents which I think are important. I could not stand by and watch history be erased or the princess's world changed. She had fought so hard for the little privacy that she had and I have kept safe the personal items which she entrusted to me and were locked in my filing cabinet in my pantry.'

The Queen raised her eyebrows but said nothing.

'Frances has rung me on occasion,' she then said.

'May I say that you were very brave to be in, Your Majesty,' I replied.

The Queen chuckled. 'But I couldn't always understand what she was saying as she was so drunk.'

'Well she has worked her way through most of the princess's Montrachet,' I said.

The Queen wasn't finished yet.

'I have known that family for a very long time. They are quite extraordinary. I remember when Frances left Johnny and ran off to Australia, leaving the children behind. That was the first time that I had seen a family break apart. It was so sad and destructive but did you know that Sarah once saved my life?'

'No, I had no idea, Your Majesty.'

'I was out riding one day at Sandringham,' the Queen said, gesturing a gallop as if riding, 'and little did I know my girth had snapped. A young girl shouted, "I think you should get off your horse and walk." That girl turned out to be Sarah Spencer. If I hadn't taken notice I could have had a serious accident and could have been killed. So I have always had a soft spot for that girl.'

The Queen shook her head and pursed her lips; she was deep in thought. 'It's all such a dreadful business. Diana was such a complex and complicated person. What she did best of all is connect with people. She was at home with people less fortunate, people wanting. She had an affinity with people. She could talk to anyone and often told me that she enjoyed that.

'I remember walking with the dogs on the hillside at Balmoral when I was much fitter and I bumped into Charles walking alone.

He had tears in his eyes. "What on earth is wrong?" I asked him. He replied, "Oh, it's Diana. She is so impossible at times. I just don't understand her." So, Paul, even in those early days, life was difficult.'

I realised that I was listening to the confessions of a queen and that I was stepping into very personal territory. Our Queen was opening up to me like never before.

I needed to respond. 'Your Majesty, can I just tell you that the princess always had a place in her heart for the Prince of Wales. As I have been packing away her life at Kensington Palace, I have seen so many pictures of them all as a family and many of just the boys and their father. If she had been a bitter woman then she would have destroyed them or cut his face out of them.'

The Queen smiled and understood.

We talked of many things that afternoon. We talked of Paris and that dreadful day and what I witnessed before the arrival of the Prince of Wales and Diana's sisters.

'It must have been awful for you,' she said.

I talked of the many people with whom I had spoken and seen, at which point she offered me a stark warning: 'Do be careful. There are forces at work in my country of which even I have no knowledge.'

I realised that the meeting was coming to an end but I still had so much to say. The Queen had been incredibly warm, friendly and open. I was reminded of her tremendous compassion.

'These are changing times,' she said. 'Diana's work will continue through the memorial fund. Her name will live on in countries around the world. It's all very humbling, Paul, and I know that such work makes one a better person.'

She approached her desk and pushed the button on her bell. I could hear a faint buzz outside in the pantry and imagined that red disc dropping into the box marked 'Sitting Room'. I knew that my audience was over. Before Paul reappeared as if by magic, the

Queen said, 'Happy Christmas to you and Maria and please keep in touch.'

Her two Pauls, Tall Paul and Small Paul, bowed, turned and left her sitting room. That was the last time I saw her but it wasn't the last time I would hear from her. As we entered the pantry, Paul said to me, 'I thought you were never coming out. I thought you had both nodded off!'

Looking back on this now, I cannot believe how honest, frank and open the Queen was with me. And funny too.

I had no idea at the time that this meeting arranged by Tall Paul would save me from a cruel fate.

So the artefacts which were entrusted to me by the Princess for safekeeping and those papers which I had kept safe were eventually passed to William and Harry and those which the police had wrongfully taken from me were returned to me.

Later Paul confided in me that they often joked about my letters arriving – my familiar green-edged Smythson stationery from my home in Cheshire.

'Look what I've had today,' she would say to him, waving my envelopes.

'I've had one too,' he would reply and they would swap notes.

Tall Paul was with the Queen for a lifetime. He has now officially retired and was awarded the Commander of the Royal Victorian Order at the end of his service. No other servant has been awarded such a high honour.

I am so grateful that I met him back in those early days of service and our friendship continues to this day; I am very happy to be the Small Paul to his Tall Paul.

17

The C Word for Both the King and Me

When the Queen passed away in September 2022, it left a huge chasm in the nation. For many of us she had been a constant guiding force throughout our lives. It sounds silly but many felt she was invincible and that there would never be a time when she wasn't there. Her death at the age of ninety-six still took many people by surprise. We expected her to have longevity like her mother and live to be at least one hundred years of age.

It was a time for mourning and reflection. Many considered the loved ones that they had lost and reflected on their own mortality.

I was no different. In October 2022, I was diagnosed with prostate cancer. I was once again reminded of how short and fleeting this lifetime is. 'Cancer' is a frightening word and once mentioned, death is probably everyone's next thought.

I have lived with death, grieving and mourning over the years. I am sixty-seven years old and have already lived longer than my mother, who died at the age of fifty-nine.

I have lived through and mourned the deaths of Diana, Princess of Wales, and Her Majesty the Queen, both unique and inspirational women in their own right.

But now I was wondering whether it was my turn.

Thoughts inevitably turn to the lives we have lived and the impressions we have made along the way. My greatest achievement in life is my two sons, Alexander and Nicholas.

I have always felt that I have had someone watching over me, but especially when I decided to take part in *I'm a Celebrity... Get Me Out of Here! South Africa* in the summer of 2022. I will never forget where I was when I heard the news of my illness. Standing in the middle of Old Compton Street in London's West End, I received a mobile call from the doctor I had just seen at Harley Street only hours earlier to check my vitals ahead of taking part in the show.

I was concerned that he was contacting me so soon.

'Is everything all right?' I enquired.

One of the results from a blood test he ran showed that I had a surprisingly high PSA test result. My PSA test had come back as a nine on the scale when anything below a four is acceptable. The test is fallible but it can be an early warning that something is wrong.

There wasn't time to undertake further tests before my journey to South Africa but the doctor assured me that it was safe to compete in the show and that I should see my GP as soon as I got home.

Once I was back at home, an MRI scan was arranged. This would be a sure way of detecting the presence of cancer in the prostate. I will be honest: I never expected the results to come back with negative news. I truly hoped that it was just a blip which would have worked itself out while I was away. After all, I had had no symptoms – well, none that I would have recognised. Men usually go to the bathroom during the night, which could be a symptom, and some men might fail in the bedroom department now and then, another symptom. And as men get older, we may not be able to hit the back of the urinal, another symptom.

There is no doubt that early detection of any cancer is imperative for its treatment and elimination. I had no idea that I had prostate cancer and that I was one of the one in eight men in Britain who would develop it.

Why me? I thought. It seems to be a lottery.

When my consultant at Leighton Hospital in Crewe had reviewed my MRI scan, he was certain that the shadow he saw was suspicious enough to warrant further investigation.

I underwent an uncomfortable biopsy which confirmed that I did indeed have cancer as he suspected.

It was a life-changing moment. In fact, his first words confirming cancer seemed not to sink in. I asked him to repeat what he had said.

'You have prostate cancer, Mr Burrell.'

Then the reassuring – 'We will do what we can to treat it' – came. Although for me it wasn't as reassuring as it should have been as I was still reeling from the word 'cancer'.

I was frightened. None of my relatives had been diagnosed with cancer before. This was new territory for me. I hadn't been seriously ill in my life. Now this! I squeezed Coop's hand.

'We are going to get through this together,' he said.

Cancer doesn't only affect you but also the ones you love. It changes the path of your life. At that moment, I had no idea as to how much.

My sadness spilled into Christmas. I remember wrapping presents and crying, thinking, Is this the last time I will ever do this?

It really is an unbearable thought that you might leave this world and those you love behind prematurely.

I thought, I'm not even a grandad yet. I'm not ready to go.

Maria and I both wept over a Zoom call as I told her the bad news.

'I can't imagine life without you, darling,' she said through her tears.

I made her promise not to tell our sons as I wanted to speak to them face to face, just as I had done several years earlier when I came out to them.

I went to America over the Christmas break to see my boys. I asked them if they could both pick Coop and me up at Orlando International Airport. They thought it strange but they agreed. They knew something was wrong when I suggested we stop for a coffee.

We sat outside the coffee shop in the warm Florida evening sun and I grabbed their hands across the table and started to cry. What a Christmas welcome that was.

'I have cancer,' I blurted out. 'Don't worry, I will beat this. I just want one of you to make me a grandfather before I'm done.'

There was much to discuss and hundreds of questions and as we left the coffee shop, Alex turned to me and said, 'Dad, promise me that we will spend more time with you.'

It gave me the fight I needed but it was the start of a roller-coaster ride.

I was admitted to the Christie hospital in Manchester in February 2023, where I underwent a procedure called brachyther-apy. Under general anaesthetic, seeds of radium were planted into the affected area in my prostate which killed the cancer cells but also destroyed the prostate.

I had opted not to have my prostate removed as it is so close to the urinary tract and there was a risk of incontinence on removal. I didn't want to take the chance of that happening, particularly when I understood that brachytherapy and a prostatectomy have a similar outcome as far as the cancer is concerned.

There then followed a course of radiotherapy over fifteen days where my prostate would be blasted just to make sure that the cancer had been eliminated. This procedure was exhausting and I often fell asleep in the afternoon after the treatment.

I was very proud to ring the bell at the Christie hospital on the last day of my treatment to mark its completion. It was an emo-tional day.

I was then placed on a hormone therapy regime for two years. Testosterone had to be reduced in my system as it acts as a fertiliser for cancer in men, so I now receive an injection of Zoladex every three months to keep my testosterone levels low.

There are side effects of course: weight gain around the waist and chest, tiredness, no sex drive, hot sweats and mood swings. My beard doesn't grow the way it should and I also have hot flushes and become very emotional for no reason.

Throughout this rollercoaster ride, Coop has been by my side. Despite recently having had a knee replacement, he is always there for me.

The journey I have been on will be familiar to many men. I was lucky to survive due to an early diagnosis. I would encourage all men over fifty years of age to request a PSA test, particularly if prostate cancer is prevalent in the family.

There is no national screening programme at this time for this killer disease as the PSA test is not sufficiently accurate. Often there are no visible signs to indicate the presence of prostate cancer. A simple examination by a doctor cannot identify when cancer is present but a positive PSA test may lead to further investigation which can result in an early diagnosis.

One in eight men will develop prostate cancer (and one in four black men), and early diagnosis is vital if there is a chance of it being cured.

No one likes talking about it, but with the help of Lorraine Kelly and her producer Samuel Courtney, I was able to tell my story and raise awareness of this invisible killer on her morning television show, *Lorraine*.

I had been on television so many times to offer commentary on the Royal Family, but appearing on the sofa that day was so out of my comfort zone. Nevertheless, I am passionate about helping others and the opportunity to raise awareness gave me the confidence to do it.

Again my life took an unexpected turn when I was asked to take part in another television programme, *The Real Full Monty: Jingle Balls*, for which I had to learn the steps to a dance routine which ultimately involved stripping off and being totally naked in front of a live audience. I wasn't alone as I performed the routine with an incredible cast, including Pete Wicks, Gemma Collins and Coleen Nolan, each of whose lives have been touched by cancer in some way. It was all done in the best possible taste, again to raise awareness about cancer. Sometimes I would love to go back and tell that shy teenage boy who used to stare out over the fields in Grassmoor that someday he would be getting naked in front of millions of people!

It was by no means easy and I had my wobbles (both metaphorically and physically) when I stood watching the other stars pick up the steps in the routine choreographed by Ashley Banjo from Diversity with no problems. Even though I attended every training session, I struggled to learn the routine but I got there in the end.

Taking my clothes off on national television was a walk in the park after my rollercoaster ride through cancer.

My cancer treatment is progressing well and the results from my PSA tests are low which is good news. The procedures that I have gone through seem to have worked but everyone is different and responds in different ways.

I am grateful that early diagnosis appears to have prevented the cancer from spreading and I am on the way to recovery. There are side effects but none of them are life-threatening and I can live with them.

I don't think that men are particularly good at going to the doctor so I hope that my story encourages them to get checked. I'm not sure that I would have known about the cancer at such an early stage if I had not gone into the jungle. There are not many who can claim that a television show such as *I'm a Celebrity . . . Get Me Out of Here!* saved their life, but I can.

We all face trials and tribulations in life. This was my personal battle but it's one that I share with so many survivors.

Cancer is indiscriminate and just as I was on my road to recovery, King Charles was diagnosed with cancer in February 2024 and began his treatment shortly afterwards. He later said he was 'shocked' to get the news, which I can really relate to.

He has never revealed the type of cancer he has but it was discovered during treatment for an enlarged prostate. Like me, he had the difficult job of telling his two sons the devastating news and whereas I had to go to America to tell my boys, Harry jetted over to see his father immediately on hearing the news. Cancer is destructive but it does tend to bring families together and reminds you of how fragile life can be.

It really has brought me closer to my sons. We speak almost every day now. We went through periods where we didn't speak as regularly as they are in America and I'm in the UK but now we make time to speak to each other. I do hope that this has started to mend the rift between Prince Harry and his father.

Unlike Diana, who kept all of her medical issues private, it was quite a new approach from the Royal Family to be so open about Charles's condition.

I suspect that Camilla would have been responsible for the King's decision to go public with his diagnosis. There is no doubt that she has been a steady hand for her husband during turbulent times and she has taught him a lot in recent years. She is a stabilising force for the monarchy. It is commendable that Charles has been open about his condition because after he spoke out, searches about the disease on the NHS website shot up by fifty-one per cent. He has also become the patron of Cancer Research UK and intends to help raise awareness around the importance of early detection.

While his return to good health appears promising, his funeral plans are already in place, just as they were for his mother before him. While the plans in place for the Queen were known as Operation London Bridge, those for Charles are known as Operation Menai Bridge. The protocols have already been rehearsed and practised.

Charles will be a caretaker king. He was seventy-four when he ascended to the throne so his reign will be much shorter than that of Queen Elizabeth II.

He will be the bridge between his mother's Elizabethan court and the court of the next monarch William V. It is unlikely that the Carolean court will last longer than ten years, after which the Gulielmian court will succeed. The name of each court is of Latin derivation. The term 'Carolean' comes from the word Carolus which is Latin for Charles. If William chooses to be known as William V when he is king, the Latinised version of his name would make his court the Gulielmian court.

Other European monarchs are choosing to abdicate in favour of their heirs so that they may see their children succeed. As Charles has such a short time to be king, I doubt that this will happen here, but time will tell. There is no precedent other than that of King Edward VIII, the Queen's uncle, but he abdicated in December 1936 under pressure from the government, as a result of his affair with an American divorcee, Wallis Simpson. No British king has abdicated voluntarily in favour of his son.

Charles may or may not wish to see his son on the throne in his lifetime, but he is certainly mindful that the future of the monarchy is in William's hands.

William has experienced some pressure since he became Prince of Wales. Not only has he had to deal with his father's illness and the ongoing issues with his brother but also his wife's battle with cancer.

Following abdominal surgery in 2024, surgeons removed some

tissue from Catherine's abdomen which was tested and found to be malignant. The Palace announced in March that she was undergoing treatment but again, the type of cancer has not been revealed. She finished her treatment in September 2024 admitting that the previous nine months had been incredibly tough for her and her focus now is staying 'cancer free'.

Charles knows that being monarch is not easy and his duty as king overrides his private life. With Catherine still in recovery and William cherishing being a husband and a father watching his children grow, Charles is letting William have the space and time before he has to take on the huge responsibility of monarchy. There was a school of thought that Charles might pass over the opportunity of becoming king in favour of his son William but logically, Charles has done the right thing.

Because of my personal connections, my allegiances are different. I have seen this family at close quarters and my loyalty is skewed. I was never in favour of Camilla becoming queen but I am stoic and realistic. We have to cross the bridge with King Charles and Queen Camilla in order to reach King William and Queen Catherine. Diana would say, 'Paul, my son will be king one day.' And that's the end goal. When William ascends to the throne, whenever that is, I hope that I am there to see it and we will have come full circle with Diana's son as king and Diana's ring in its rightful place on the hand of a queen, where it was always intended to be.

18

The Future

Monarchies around the world are changing and adapting to the times. We have witnessed the second Elizabethan court. Elizabeth II will be known as the last of the great monarchs.

The pageantry and processions of her seventy-year reign will be distant memories archived on grainy footage for future generations. Our grandchildren will be in awe of the spectacle of these times.

The Carolean court and all that King Charles III holds dear will change significantly in the reign of King William V and Queen Catherine. William will have to be a very different monarch.

The Victorian and Edwardian protocols will be erased and the Royal Family will become relevant to this century and not the last one.

The majority of the pomp and theatre will be shelved. William will strip away much of the formality and become the 'people's king', taking inspiration from his mother. He is already educating his family and his people to accept his informal and relaxed approach.

Curtsying and bowing has, in the past, been a form of respect when greeting members of the Royal Family – but in this day and age is it really necessary to bow or curtsy to Prince Andrew or Princesses Beatrice and Eugenie?

Who knows how to do it, when to do it or to whom?

It will be a slimmed-down monarchy – something William's father is striving to achieve – for William, just himself, his queen and his children. He already has fewer servants than other Royals, and in private he prefers the more normal life that he has experienced with his in-laws, the Middletons.

All he needs at the moment is a valet to take care of his clothes and keep his uniforms in order, a lady's maid to maintain Catherine's wardrobe, a housekeeper and a nanny to help out with their three children. They are a modern family who usually cook for themselves unless entertaining. If need be, their staff can be supplemented by the King's staff. Their household is very small compared to that of his father and grandmother.

Carriage drives with horse and carriage will be less frequent and become echoes of the past. They will still be part of the spectacle of state visits, Royal Ascot and, of course, William's coronation. A plethora of titles have recently been handed out to members of the Royal Family but I suspect that this will happen less frequently in the future.

The Royal Family are there because people want them to be there. I am a monarchist; I always have been. My family has supported the monarchy for generations. Our king or queen is part of the fabric of our country and has been for a thousand years. The monarch is the beating heart of our nation in good times and bad, carries the torch for philanthropic causes and lights the way. I believe that the system should continue but it cannot remain in the past and must adapt to be more relevant to modern life.

The alternative would be a president as head of state and for me, that would change the face of the United Kingdom and not for the better. The Queen's adage of 'if it is not broken, why fix it?' rings true for me in this instance.

I hope and believe that William, as the people's king, will be a force for good.

He will never return to the formalities of the courts of either his grandmother or his father but William will always remember the principles and standards that his grandmother taught him during those Sunday afternoon teas when he walked up the hill from Eton to visit her. Interestingly, she never gave these lessons to her own son.

William is educating George, his son and heir, in the same way, and teaching him about what his future will hold.

Of course there is no rule book for this. The Queen barely faltered in her reign. One of the few times that she stumbled was over the death of Princess Diana, but there was no precedent for that. She always looked at things logically and at that time she probably thought, Diana is divorced from the Royal Family. She is a Spencer so it is up to her family as to what to do.

But she did not realise that the public still saw Diana as royal and she got caught in the crossfire between looking after her grandchildren and keeping her family secure at Balmoral and the country needing their Queen.

William will have learned from these past experiences. He is a game changer. He has chosen not to send George to Eton and instead George is currently at Lambrook School with his siblings. William regularly takes George to see Aston Villa play football at Villa Park in Birmingham, an unlikely sporting venue for a Royal. It is also quite a different sporting event from the polo matches that his father, grandfather and great-grandfather enjoyed at Smith's Lawn in Windsor Great Park.

There is a possibility that Charles could delegate some of his powers to his son over time and create a regency, especially if his illness continues. This would allow a gradual transition between father and son, something that wasn't possible between mother and son.

William and Catherine's time spent at RAF Valley in Anglesey, when William was flying Wessex helicopters, was idyllic for them.

Their early years out of the spotlight gave them a grounding in married life, much the same as the time Princess Elizabeth and Prince Philip spent in Malta before she assumed the responsibilities of being queen.

Inspired by Prince Philip, the Royal Family has always embraced the development of technology. While the public did not start sending emails in any volume until the late 1990s, the Queen sent her first email in 1976 after it was developed as a way for academics to send messages between universities. She also sent Tweets and used Instagram to share a photograph of a letter from computer pioneer Charles Babbage sent to her great-great-grandfather in 1843 . . . but she never carried a mobile phone. Her birth coincided with the development of television and she used this form of mass communication to give her Christmas Day address in every year of her reign to reach her people. She was also one of the first people to ride through the Channel Tunnel, the undersea railway linking Britain to the rest of Europe. I imagine her grandson William will be no different and as king will embrace technologies which have not yet been invented.

Perhaps the biggest change in recent years is the way that social media has shaped the royal world. Back in the 1980s, we didn't have social media. We didn't have mobile phones. We had to buy newspapers to get the news rather than having it at the touch of a button.

We live in a very different world now. News is immediate. People are always there with a mobile phone, something which is obvious to William. The Queen would have stepped out at a garden party at Buckingham Palace in the past and no one would have taken a photograph but now when William and Catherine are present everyone has their mobile phone out to take a picture.

Instead of shaking hands with the Royals, people are now filming them. The world continues to change at an increasing rate and

William will have to adapt and respond to this change to ensure that the monarchy modernises and stays relevant.

I am sure that some things will remain the same. The Order of The Garter, which was founded by Edward III in 1348, continues to be given as the personal gift of the monarch in recognition of national contribution or service. It is an integral part of the fabric of monarchy as are the crown jewels, the symbols of monarchy and state housed in the Tower of London.

Another tradition that I am sure will survive is the service held at the cenotaph on Remembrance Sunday when the country pays its respects to those who paid the ultimate sacrifice and gave their lives for their country. The Royal Family invariably attend to lead the nation in memory and bow their heads in respect alongside ordinary people.

I have seen the Queen stand in torrential rain soaked to the skin on this occasion but she was determined to play her part in the nation's act of remembrance.

In her seventy-year reign she only missed the service seven times due to ill health, being abroad on Royal tours or while she was pregnant; I know that this day was one of the most important in her calendar.

As for the future, I just hope that I am here to cheer, 'Long live King William V!'

Epilogue

Life is short, only thirty-six years for Diana. There is an inevitability that we will all die but I hope that when I do, we will all meet up again in another place. The thought that what happens here doesn't define eternity keeps me going. Many people do not have time to take stock of their lives or atone for their actions but I do and am grateful that I can.

I am an ordinary man from a humble background but I have had an extraordinary life. I have survived despite the many ups and downs. I am a survivor. I consider myself lucky to have stood beside two iconic women of our times: Her Majesty Queen Elizabeth II and Diana, Princess of Wales.

Women have shaped most of my life. My mother, whom I adored, sent me on my life journey. The Queen taught me much about life in my formative adult years. Princess Diana embraced me and trusted me with her dreams. And not forgetting my ex-wife Maria whom I still love and who gave me my greatest gifts in life, my sons Alexander and Nicholas. Now, in the autumn of my life, men are at the helm of my ship to guide me through the waters that lie ahead.

My boys wrote to me recently and said: 'Dad, did you ever wonder what this did to us growing up? Were you ever aware that we were bullied and chased down streets with people calling your name? Did you ever wonder how hurt we were? And how much we loved you?'

I am guilty and saddened when I admit that I didn't.

I was too consumed by my royal duty. I have to atone for that. I look back and wonder if I would have changed anything but I am not sure that I would. I have learned not to think of 'what ifs', 'should haves', 'could haves' or regrets. I have thought a lot about death since my cancer diagnosis. I hope and pray that I have time to try to correct my mistakes, especially with the people I love, before I leave this world.

I have always been driven by a sense of duty, particularly when it comes to the Royal Family. For twenty-one years I was in a privileged position and shared the daily lives of the Queen and Princess Diana. Now that neither of these two wonderful women are here, that duty continues for me in the need to help to protect their legacy. I am aware that there are generations now learning about the history of the Royal Family that were not alive during Diana's lifetime. I do not want her story to be whitewashed. I have always defended her memory and will continue to do so. I was there. I heard it. I saw it. I feel a pressure from a historical perspective as someone who witnessed these monumental events to preserve the truth for the next generation and beyond. I remember my mother's words: 'The truth always remains the truth'.

This book is part of the process. I know people will criticise it but I have been true to myself and that is not always easy.

You may be dealing with similar issues. Whether it is dealing with the loss of someone you love – a mother, a friend or a lover – being accused of something you did not do, struggling with your sexuality or battling with cancer.

I certainly haven't got it all figured out but I hope that my words will be of some help and comfort. Stay close to those you love, stay true to yourself and be honest.

As the princess used to say to me, if you could make a positive difference to one person's life each day, think of what a difference you would make over a lifetime. She set out to do exactly that. I still feel the energy to try and do the same each and every day.

I will enjoy the years I have left, live and laugh with those I love and forever be grateful to have been on this incredible royal journey.

Acknowledgements

This is what happened to a coal-miner's son who found himself on an incredible journey from a two-up two-down to a palace and beyond.

I was privileged to witness history at first hand. It would be impossible to write this book without acknowledging those who have made it possible.

My mother, whom I adored and who left our lives too soon. Thank you is inadequate for bringing me into the world and for instilling in me the core values of family life, hard work and self- sufficiency. She chose my path and sent me to Buckingham Palace.

Our dear late Queen, who taught me much about the world. She trusted me for ten years and showed me the true meaning of duty, loyalty and respect – and she filled my life with history.

Prince Charles, now King Charles III, who opened a door for me with the words 'I would like to welcome you to Highgrove . . . this is the future, Paul'. And I thank him.

Diana, Princess of Wales, whom I met in a dark corridor at Balmoral. She was eighteen and I was twenty-one. She would invite me into her household and take me from the State Opening of Parliament to the minefields of Angola.

My ex-wife Maria, who loved me unconditionally. Our marriage gave us two wonderful sons. I will always love you.

My sons Alex and Nick, of whom I am very proud. Thank you for standing by me – no matter what.

My adorable grandson Lucca, who lights up my life.

Thank you to Leighton Hospital in Crewe and the Christie Hospitals in Manchester and Macclesfield. This is where I saw the NHS at its best. You saved my life. Thank you.

Thank you to Kelly Allen, my ghost writer, who gave me the framework for this book and her invaluable assistance.

My agents Tom Gribby and Leisa Maloney, for their constant support and encouragement.

My publishers at Little, Brown: Kelly Ellis, Sophie Ellis, Louise Harvey, Henry Lord, Nithya Rae and Linda Silverman. You all had faith in this book.

My friends and neighbours in England and America who encouraged me along the way, especially my 'Best Judy' Chuck.

My friends from the 'Golden Days' at Buck House, especially my life-long friend Tall Paul, who I met when we were both eighteen.

And lastly, but by no means least, my husband, Coop. Our very own 'brief encounter' was a 'sliding doors' moment in my life. Thank you for accepting this particular challenge, for keeping me safe and for your love, understanding and patience for over twenty years.

I will never forget our wedding day and the joy it brought to so many people.

It truly was an 'enchanted evening'.